212581

YOUR CHILD
IN SCHOOL

Also by Tom and Harriet Sobol

Your Child in School:
*Kindergarten Through
Second Grade*

Tom and Harriet Sobol

YOUR CHILD
IN SCHOOL

The Intermediate Years, Grades 3–5

Arbor House ● **New York**

Manufactured in the United States of America

10 9 8 7 6 5 4 3 2 1

Library of Congress Cataloging in Publication Data
(Revised for vol. 2)

Sobol, Tom.
  Your child in school.

  Contents: [1]. Kindergarten through second grade—
[2]. The intermediate years: grades 3–5.
  1. School children—United States. 2. Education,
Elementary—United States. 3. Home and school.
I. Sobol, Harriet Langsam.
LB1555.S665 1987 372'.21 86-20652
ISBN: 0-87795-924-2

This book is for Rose,
who taught Harriet to read,
And for Morris,
who taught Harriet to think,
And for Joe,
who taught Tom about work,
And for Margaret,
who taught Tom about the senses,
And for Aunt March,
who taught Tom about the mind

And for all parents and loving aunts and uncles
of all children everywhere

Contents

Acknowledgments

The idea for this book was originated by Edward A. Shergalis, Jr. Without him we would not have undertaken this project.

Many teachers and parents generously shared their time and knowledge with us. We thank them all, but most especially Hal Baron, Rochelle Blatt, Vin Dempsey, Sandra Eckstein, Adele Fiderer, Cora Five, Ernie Machnits, Joan McCann, Jane Moriarty, Gay Reetz, Shirley Schechter, Fran Slote, Ann Spindel, Dick Sprague, Paula Sternberg, Refna Wilkin, Grace Zuckerman, the staff of the Scarsdale Public Library, and all our patient friends and animals.

The Authors

Preface

This is a book for parents of school-age children. It is written by two parents and teachers who have spent their lives in the schools. Its aim is to help you understand what happens to your child in school, so that you will be able to help make his or her experience more successful and productive.

We all know how important it is for our children to achieve well in school. We want them to acquire the skills and knowledge they will need, and we understand how important it is that they find a secure place for themselves in the social world of their agemates. And so for most of the working days of the year, month after month, year after year, we entrust our children to the care of the people who work behind the schoolhouse door.

But who are these people? What do they *do* with your child at school, all day long, day after day? How do you, as a parent, particularly if your own schedule is a busy one, know how well things are going? How do you know if the teachers are doing the right things, and how do you know if your child is making normal progress? And if your child is not making normal progress, when should you worry, and what should you do about it?

This book takes you behind the doors to describe the curriculum and learning activities of typical American elementary schools. It gives you some sense of what your child *should* be doing, so that you can compare your own child's experience with the norm. And it makes suggestions about ways in which you can enhance your child's growth and cope with any problems that may arise.

We feel comfortable writing about these matters. Between us, we have taught children in elementary school, adolescents in junior high school and senior high school, young adults in college and graduate school, and older people in adult-education classes. We have talked with our students' parents and friends, and we have supervised teachers at all levels. We have attended and worked in schools in the favored suburbs and in the inner cities. And as superintendent of schools, one of us has spent years listening to parents and trying to help them deal with their anxieties about their children.

What's more, we like schools and school people. We know how dull and commonplace things can be sometimes, but by and large we think that the people who staff America's schools are good people, genuinely committed to helping young people grow and ready to do their honest best given an ounce of support and encouragement. We hope that they will like what they read in these pages.

Finally, a word about you—the parent. As the authors know full well (having between us raised six children), being a parent is not always easy. Nevertheless, we envy you. Our children are grown up now, and although their young adulthood brings new rewards (and challenges), we treasure the memory of the years when they were younger. The time you have with your children now in these later-childhood years, while it may seem long in prospect, will seem short indeed when you look back upon it a few years from now. These are wonderful years. Be alive to them, and savor the time.

How to Use This Book

This book has five parts: "The Intermediate Child as a Learner, "Third Grade," "Fourth Grade," "Fifth Grade," and "The Intermediate Years." The first part discusses the way in which children develop mentally and talks about the tasks of schooling at this age. The three middle parts describe, grade level by grade level, the teaching and learning of those subjects that are more sequential in nature—mathematics and reading. The part "The Intermediate Years" deals with less sequential subjects and with other matters, like tests and learning problems, which are not specific to a given grade level.

Some readers may wish to read straight through from beginning to end. That, after all, is how your child will do it—from September of the third grade through June of the fifth grade. If you read the book in this fashion, you will gain a sense of what your child's experience in school will be, in both its continuing freshness and its regularity and repetition. Be alert for surprises, but do not expect each year to be fundamentally different from the last.

Others may wish to refer to those grade levels or topics of particular importance to them. For that reason we have included relevant information on certain topics at each grade level, even at the risk of repetition. The teaching of reading, for example, is not fundamentally different in the fifth grade from that in the fourth. Teachers build on what children have already learned, but because children learn at different rates, most of what is taught in fourth-grade classrooms appears in fifth-grade classrooms as well. Rather than refer the reader to the "Fourth Grade" section, we have restated the fourth-grade material in somewhat altered form in the "Fifth Grade" section. We hope the reader will pardon the redundancy, which mirrors the experience your child will have in school.

If you do use this book as a resource on specific topics or a specific grade level, we urge you always to read a little before and a little after the section you have chosen. Life in schools is not as neatly compartmentalized as a table of contents suggests.

Finally a word about the "he/she" problem. The English language has not yet made up its mind about the niceties of nonsexist locution. When we began writing, we said "he or she" until we could stand the awkwardness no longer. Then we varied pronouns—sometimes "he," sometimes "she"—until we couldn't remember which sex we were using. Eventually we gave up and said "he" for the child and "she" for the teacher, the latter on the factual grounds that more elementary teachers are female than male. Needless to say, we mean all children and all teachers, regardless of gender.

THE
INTERMEDIATE
CHILD AS A
LEARNER

There was a child went forth every day,
And the first object he looked upon, that object he became,
And that object became part of him for the day or a certain
  part of the day,
Or for many years or stretching cycles of years. . . .

Walt Whitman reminds us how fresh the world is to the
growing child, how keen his senses are, and how impression-
able his mind is. The child from age seven to age ten, like the
primary-school child before him, is still propelled by a genetic
drive to learn. Throughout the intermediate elementary school
years the child's thirst for experience continues undiminished.
He needs to exercise his developing capacities and to understand
the meaning of the world around him. As his powers of body
and mind develop, he ventures more and more fully into the
world outside the home and family. And out in that world—on
the street, in the playground, and above all, in the schoolhouse—the experiences he has become a part of him, shaping
what he will become.

   As a parent, you are concerned with the quality of your
child's experience. You want body, mind, and spirit to grow in
healthy ways, ways that lead to personal fulfillment for your

child and to happiness in the family. For that reason, you provide a loving, secure, stimulating home. Remember, too, that during these years your child will spend the bulk of his waking hours in school. There he will learn the ways of other children and other adults; there he will be steeped in the values that the school reflects; there he will (or will not) acquire the skills and knowledge he will need to succeed in later life; there, in trying out his powers and interacting with others, he will begin to discover his own unique identity.

Do not leave the quality of this experience to chance. Education proceeds best when home and school work together on the child's behalf. As a parent, you have the right and the responsibility to remain involved in your child's education. Along with the teacher and other school personnel, it is up to you to see that the experience your child has is productive and appropriate for him. You need not, and probably should not, become his teacher. But a knowledgeable, active interest in his school experience will motivate your child and will prepare you to deal effectively with the problems that may arise.

This book will help you to be an effective partner in your child's education. The more you know about the school that will claim so much of your child's life, the more you will be able to steer things wisely.

And so we begin where all parents and all good schools begin—with the nature of the child himself.

The Child From Seven to Ten: An Overview

Most children enter the third grade at age seven or eight and leave the fifth grade at age ten or eleven. These are the golden years of childhood, the years of Cub Scouts and Brownies, of Little League, of music lessons, of growing friendships and family trips. During these years, the child becomes independent enough to have a mind and dreams and activities of his own, but he is still young enough to relish family life. Behind and all but forgotten are the gropings of infancy and the fears of early childhood; ahead lie the stirrings of puberty and the turbulence of adolescence. For the time being, in this seemingly long and stable period, the child can enjoy being himself, secure at home but exploring new worlds outside it, trying out new relationships, acquiring new skills and knowledge, gaining ever-increasing control of his body, his mind, and his imagination.

We tend to think of these later childhood years as a relatively calm and settled period, a time for consolidating the incredible growth of infancy and early childhood. And in some ways this description is appropriate. Although the child continues to grow, his bodily changes are much less dramatic than those in the first few years of life. Although his powers of written and oral language continue to increase, there is no parallel in these years to the miraculous development of speech

5

and the first success in reading and writing. Although the child remains keenly aware of sex differences, his sexual feelings are relatively dormant; indeed, psychiatrists speak of these years as the period of latency. For the most part, your child is more apt to seem the same to you from day to day throughout these years than when he was younger and developing so rapidly or when he is older and puberty triggers the mechanisms of new growth.

But beneath this seemingly placid surface, growth and change of profound importance are occurring. Impelled by the relentless ticking of his biological clock and guided by the incredibly intricate patterns of his genetic inheritance, the child becomes more and more his own person each day, growing in body and mind and spirit. And as he interacts with the culture around him, he is both shaped by it and shapes it to his own needs and perceptions. In the most general way, he is doing both what his nature requires him to do and what we want him to do. He is becoming human.

Only human beings, who must learn so much to become truly adult, require such a long childhood. Our biological cousin the chimpanzee, for example, is fully mature by the age of five. Human beings, with their more complex neurological organization, require a longer period in which to mature biologically and learn the patterns of their culture. For humans, these prolonged childhood years play an important part in the process of development. They give the child time to acquire the skills and knowledge he will need in adulthood before the urgencies of sexual life affect his behavior. As Herman and Anne Roiphe say in their 1985 book *Your Child's Mind,*

> From the ages of six to nine, sexual feelings mostly rest, as when a flower goes into the dormant season, as when bears hibernate. In this, biology is working with society, or society is in total harmony with biology, because the lowered sexual thermometer permits the spring season of

civilization, knowledge, and reason to take root and establish itself.

The child just entering the third grade is still tied closely to home and family. He may have regular playmates, but his circle of friends is apt to be small and his voluntary participation in organized group activity is likely to be brief and fragmentary. His sense of time and distance is still limited; he measures events by their impact on himself and family members. He is beginning to understand adult behavior and relationships, but he rarely tries to enter into them as an equal. When you talk to him, you know you are dealing with a child.

During the intermediate years, and as the body grows and as the child continues to experience the world around him, so grows what we call the mind. Not only does the child's store of knowledge increase, but also his capacity to understand and act upon the world. The path of development is not always straight and even; there may be bumps and detours, spurts of growth and apparent regressions, periods of equilibrium and disequilibrium. But as child psychologists Gesell, Ilg, and Ames say, "The ultimate and over-all trend is toward a higher level of maturity. Development is like a stream: it carves the best possible channel; it flows onward; it reaches a goal."

By the time the child is ready to leave the fifth grade, he has become a much more well-defined person. Children of ten or eleven exhibit many of the traits they will continue to have as adults—Sally speaks rapidly and laughs a lot, Billy is quiet and intense. The ten-year-old's understanding of social relationships has deepened; he begins to see adults, including his parents, as individuals, and he has one or more well-developed friendships with others of his age and sex. He is more aware of his own feelings and the feelings of others. His perception of time and space becomes more like that of adults. His attention span has lengthened, and he may spend hours building model airplanes, playing with a doll house, tending a collection, or working at some other hobby. His fears and anxieties, although they may persist, are more closely related to the real world—he is more likely to fear robbers or muggers than ghosts. He still needs the family, but he is beginning to see himself as an independent person outside of it. As he leaves the fifth grade, he has completed an important stage of his development. If things have progressed normally, he is ready for the onset of puberty and the sexual transformation that must occur before he can become a full-fledged adult human being.

Learning and Mental Development

In general, the child's learning and mental development throughout these later childhood years are the result of his maturing neurological capacity and his interaction with people and the world around him. But much can be done to stimulate and nurture this growth. Parents and teachers want the child to develop his capacities to the fullest, and they are concerned about the quality of the child's learning experience in these formative years. In order to be truly helpful, we must know more about the nature of the child and his development. How do children actually learn? How do they develop mentally? What research or insight can serve as a useful guide for those who influence the child at home and at school?

JEAN PIAGET

The world's most influential writer about young children as learners is the Swiss psychologist Jean Piaget. Piaget and his followers studied children's mental growth closely from infancy throughout childhood and proposed a theory of development based upon their observations. According to Piaget, all children proceed more or less uniformly through a series of fixed stages of increasing complexity. They begin by observing and manipulating material objects and then move in these fixed stages to greater and greater abstraction, toward abstract formal systems whose relationships are matters of logic rather than observation.

From birth to one and a half or two years, the child is in the *sensory–motor* stage. At this stage, the child's intelligence develops through physical manipulation of his immediate environment. His focus is on the mastery of objects—toys, blocks, pots and pans, rocks, and so on. Gradually, the child develops a sense of *object constancy* (that people and things exist even when he can't see them), a primitive sense of cause and effect, and a rough sense of time.

From about two to seven years of age, the child is in the *pre-operational* stage. At this stage, children increasingly learn to substitute language and mental images for the direct physical gropings of infancy. Through play and make-believe, they imitate the ways of the adults in their lives, and in their minds they create pictures of the world beyond their immediate senses, although the pictures may often be inaccurate from an adult's point of view. (For example, a child may believe that the moon rises only for him and that it follows him down the street.)

From about seven to eleven or twelve years of age, the child is in the stage of *concrete operations*. At this stage, children can think about objects and actions without perceiving or performing them. They understand numbers and relationships. They can project things into the past or future and imagine things in new combinations. They can also communicate more easily as their power of language continues to grow. However, their thought remains closely tied to their actual concrete experience. They are not yet ready to think about abstractions that transcend physical reality as they have known it.

At about eleven or twelve years of age, the child enters the stage of *formal operations*. At this stage, normally the time of early adolescence, children can think about abstract ideas as well as about things. They can entertain hypotheses, construct mental models, discover general laws that underlie discrete phenomena. Their intellectual functioning, although not necessarily their knowledge or their wisdom, is fully mature.

CRITICS OF PIAGET

Many educators in the United States espouse Piaget's theory, and those who do not are heavily influenced by it. In recent years, however, a new generation of psychologists has begun to question certain aspects of this theory. New studies have shown that while Piaget's broad outline may be accurate, the actual progress of children's mental development is more continuous and gradual than his stages suggest. Children do not suddenly leap to a whole new level of mental functioning—they arrive more gradually. For example, a child may first be able to understand the conservation of numbers with some materials and not with others. And a child may be able to accomplish tasks involving concrete operations in the pre-operational years if the adult working with him makes adjustments in the problem.

Some critics maintain that Piaget overemphasizes the role of the child's developing innate abilities and slights the role of the environment in development. Others point out that Piaget does not account for the development of originality or creativity. Still others believe that while Piaget's theory may help us understand the development of one kind of intelligence, there are other important forms of intelligence for which it does not account. (We return to this problem in the next chapter.) Despite these valid criticisms, Piaget's work remains central to understanding how children learn to think. It was Piaget who first focused our attention upon the child's actions with physical objects, who emphasized the importance of mathematical ideas like number, who traced the child's gradual progress from outward physical action to inner symbolic thinking. The child psychologists who have followed him acknowledge that they are standing on the shoulders of a giant.

IMPLICATIONS OF PIAGET'S WORK

Of what importance is the work of Piaget and his followers for you and your child?

- *Respect your child's mind.* Children in the stage of concrete operations are not ready for some kinds of abstract thought, but they may be highly intelligent nonetheless. Don't talk down to them or become impatient if they do not yet see problems the way you do. Talk to them directly at their level of understanding; by asking questions and providing guidance you can help them see more clearly.
- *Let your child learn by doing.* During these intermediate years, as in early childhood, children need to base as much of their learning as possible on concrete, physical objects and experience. Good teachers know that telling is not teaching. They get children involved in working with a wide variety of materials in a wide variety of mediums and help them make sense out of their experience. As Piaget says, knowledge is a construction from within.
- *Remember that growth requires play as well as work.* A fifth-grade classroom looks very different from a kindergarten room, and intermediate-age children become able to concentrate upon their work for longer and longer periods. However, learning at this age requires unstructured time as well, even if it looks

to an adult like play or daydreaming. Children rework their experience and make sense of it at such times. Give your child time to be a child; it is an important part of his mental and emotional development.

- *Allow time for growth.* Remember that your child is following his own biological clock, one that you yourself helped create. Don't try to force things—you will only frustrate yourself and upset your child. It is the quality of your child's mental activity that counts, not his speed of development.

- *Remember that the chief goal of learning is to help your child develop his mind.* Children are not passive recipients of knowledge poured into them by adults. They are active young human beings genetically programmed to learn about their environment. The specific facts and skills they learn are important, but more important is their development as learners. As your child goes through the intermediate school years, remember that the chief goal is not to master a fixed body of knowledge but to cultivate curiosity, keenness of thought, the art of asking good questions, and the ability to make fresh and surprising connections.

The Concept of Intelligence

The main task of the child in the intermediate years is to grow in body and in mind. We all know what we mean by *body*. But what do we mean by *mind?*

In the common-sense, everyday world we have no difficulty in determining who has "a good mind" and who does not. *A* is "intelligent"; *B* is "dull"; *C* may be "truly gifted"; *D* is "rather ordinary"; and so on. We prize the quality of intelligence, and all other things being equal, we tend to respect people who have more of "it" than others.

But even in everyday life the matter is not so simple. *A* may be very good at taking tests and writing papers, but he has no business sense and his affairs are in a mess. *B* was an average student in secondary school and college, but is remarkably perceptive of other people's moods and feelings and is wonderfully skilled in organizing group activity. *C* creates elegant computer programs, but his thinking is consistently linear and he cannot visualize the three-dimensional designs his own programs generate. *D* seems limited in conversation, but she invented a device that saved her employer thousands of dollars in a manufacturing process. As soon as we look at people more closely, we realize that they can be intelligent in one way and not in another. Either there is more than one kind of intelligence or general intelligence can be used (or not used) in many ways.

Another problem that educators encounter in attempting to define *mind* or *intelligence* is that there is no such thing—that is, there is no identifiable physical object that one can point to or measure or weigh. (Even the brain will not do, because the brain alone cannot function independently of the billions of nerve cells strung throughout the body.) Intelligence is a quality that can only be inferred from action. A person does *X*, and we say the action shows intelligence. A person does *Y*, and we say the action lacks intelligence. But what we see (and measure) in each case is not intelligence but a person doing *X* or *Y*. Intelligence is a verbal construct, not a physical thing.

Small wonder, then, that there has been so much confusion and controversy about measuring intelligence in the schools. It exists in many forms; we do not always agree on what it is; a person can have it in some ways and not in others; and it is very difficult to measure. Nevertheless, for much of the twentieth century the idea that each child has a certain amount of innate intelligence that can be satisfactorily measured has pervaded school practice. Psychologists, including the Frenchmen Alfred Binet and Theodore Simon, developed intelligence tests involving language, arithmetic, and abstract thought and used them to identify mentally retarded children and to classify other children according to their ability. The intelligence quotient (IQ) derived from these tests seemed as fixed and immutable as the color of a child's eyes, and for many years it was widely used in schools to place children in appropriate classes and to gauge what could be expected of them. (For more about IQ tests, see the chapter "Tests in the Intermediate Years" in the last part of the book.)

We know that children who do well on the tasks contained in IQ tests do tend to do well on the typical tasks in school. The IQ tests does serve as a reasonably reliable predictor of later success in school. In recent years, however, the limitations of IQ tests and the oversimplified definition of intelligence they reflect have become increasingly obvious.

To begin with, we have become much more aware of the inherent limitations of the tests themselves. A child spends an hour or less with a psychologist (or sits in a group of twenty to thirty children and marks down answers to multiple-choice questions in a test booklet) and answers questions that assess the following:

- His vocabulary:
  Example   *Insult* means (a) ask, (b) injure, (c) inform, (d) offend, (e) wrap.
- His fund of information:
  Example   *Tomato* is to *plant* as blueberry is to (a) tree, (b) pie, (c) bush, (d) vine, (e) flower. (The child must not only know the meaning of the words, he must know that blueberries grow on bushes.)
- His ability to reason arithmetically:
  Example   Which number should come next in this series? 4, 5, 7, 10, 14 —? (a) 11, (b) 17, (c) 18, (d) 19, (e) 20.
- His ability to see patterns:
  Example   The shapes in the boxes go together to make a series:

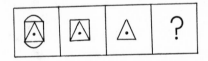

Which shape belongs in the box with the question mark (?)?

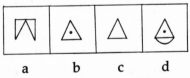

a   b   c   d

- His ability to solve problems posed in language:
  Example   Ann, Sue, and Sally were all born in the same year. Ann is older than Sue. Sue is younger than Sally. Sally

is one month older than Ann. Whose birthday will come first next year? (a) Ann's, (b) Sue's, (c) Sally's.

The child's score is compared with the scores of other children of the same age, and an IQ is derived—supposedly the fixed sum of the child's intelligence. But even if the child's score were to be the same each time he took the test—which it would not be—no such test can measure all of the child's mental capacities. The tests measure only those abilities that lend themselves to a classroom testing format. They do not, for example, measure the child's ability to get from one side of town to another in a strange city or his skill in translating a three-dimensional design into a computer language—surely abilities that indicate intelligence.

Even more important than the limits of the tests themselves is the limited view of intelligence that they reflect. When one considers the wide range of ways in which people exhibit intelligence in life—consider the corporate executive, the successful attorney, the effective psychiatrist, the investment banker, the undersea explorer, the computer scientist, the musical composer, the wilderness survivor, and so much more—a definition of intelligence that has to do with marking answers to short multiple-choice questions seems trivial in the extreme. There is more to intelligence than doing well on tests in school. If that were not the case, how could we account for those who did not do especially well in school but whose intellect has helped shape our civilization—people like Winston Churchill and Albert Einstein, for example?

One contemporary psychologist whose work has been very helpful in expanding our thinking is Howard Gardner, a professor at the Harvard Graduate School of Education. In the field of intelligence testing there has been a long-standing debate between those who believe in the existence of "g," a general factor of intelligence that is measured by every question on an intelligence test, and those who believe that intelligence is a cluster of relatively discrete mental abilities. Gardner is one of the leading adherents of the latter group. Drawing upon such varied sources as the psychology of learning, anthropological studies, and research into the functioning of various parts of the brain, he has advanced the theory of multiple intelligences, according to which there are separate mental capacities (or "intelligences") that are relatively independent of one another, and individuals may possess each to varying degrees. In general, if not always exactly, these intelligences result from the development and operation of the various parts of the human brain. (We know, for example, that the part of the brain that controls the semantic aspect of language is a specific region called Broca's orca. When this region is damaged, otherwise normal persons continue to retain some language functions, such as the ability to distinguish sounds and to understand the meaning of separate words, but lose their syntactic powers.) In Gardner's formulation, there are seven human intelligences:

1. *Linguistic intelligence*—the ability to use and respond to patterns of words that convey thought, information, imagination, and feeling.
2. *Musical intelligence*—the ability to generate and respond to patterns of tones, rhythms, and musical structures (related in evolutionary history to the development of intricate, meaningful patterns in the songs of birds).
3. *Logical-mathematical intelligence*—the ability to proceed logically, in Gardner's words, from "objects to statements, from actions to the relations among actions, from the realm of the sensori-motor to the realm of pure abstraction—ultimately, to the heights of logic and science."
4. *Spatial intelligence*—the ability to perceive physical objects and relationships fully and accurately, to visualize transfortation in these objects and relationships, and to re-create visual experience accurately even without cues.
5. *Bodily-kinesthetic intelligence*—the ability to use one's body

effectively in a variety of ways and to skillfully handle physical objects.

6. *Personal intelligences*—the ability to have access to one's own feelings and to draw upon them as a guide to understanding and behavior, and the ability to make distinctions among other people and to notice their moods and feelings.

Whether or not future research supports Gardner's theory in whole or in part, his work has important implications for teachers and parents. First, however, let us examine the final, and perhaps the most serious, problem with the outdated notion of equating intelligence with IQ, namely that the IQ is not immutable. It can change. With proper stimulation and support, children can raise their IQ scores appreciably. Almost twenty years ago the psychologist Robert Rosenthal conducted a classic study of this phenomenon. A group of evenly matched primary-school children was given a made-up "intelligence test" that they and their teachers thought was real. The experimenters told the teachers that a number of the children, chosen at random, were "late bloomers" who had great potential and should be given special attention. And sure enough, this group did indeed begin to bloom, so much so that their supposedly fixed IQ scores rose significantly. The study confirmed the powerful effect of the teacher's level of expectation of the child's performance—in effect, the teacher got what she was looking for or what she herself created (hence the title of Rosenthal's study: *Pygmalion in the Classroom*).

We observe the same phenomenon today in the remarkable success enjoyed by many Japanese students who attend American schools. According to one important study, the reason for this success is not, considering the population as a whole, superior intelligence. It arises from the contrast between Japanese and American parents' assumptions about learning and their expectations of their children. American parents tend to think that intelligence is innate and that it varies from one individual to another. Thus if the child does not do well, it is probably because of his limitations (or some failure on the part of the school). Japanese parents tend to think that all children are capable of doing well in school provided they work hard enough; Japanese parents *expect* their children to work hard and do well. And once again, the expectation conditions the result.

The matter revives the controversy of nature versus nurture. For years scientists have argued about the extent to which our mental capacities are inherited and the extent to which they are shaped by our environment. Some argue that as much as 80 percent of our intelligence is due to heredity. Others, citing studies that show tremendous mental growth under favorable conditions, argue that the proportion is much smaller, perhaps 20 percent. Most estimates fall in the middle range. As Gardner says, "There is considerable agreement that physical traits are most straightforwardly genetic, that aspects of temperament are also largely genetic; but that when one comes to aspects of cognitive style or personality, the case for high heritability is far less convincing."

The most current theories—espoused by such people as Gardner and the psychologist Kurt Fischer—hold that children's mental abilities develop from a combination of unfolding genetic potential and interaction with the environment, particularly children's social environment. And it is abundantly clear that, whatever their genetic capacity, children develop more fully and attain more skill and knowledge when they receive proper stimulation and support. From the moment your child is conceived, you can do nothing to change his genetic potential, but there is much that you and his teachers can do, for years and years to come, to help him develop that potential to the fullest.

IMPLICATIONS FOR PARENTS AND TEACHERS

It may be many years before we fully understand how human intelligence has evolved, how it develops in children, or even all the forms in which it may be expressed or the heights to which it can be extended. But as a practical matter we know enough to be effective in helping our children make the most of their abilities. As your child progresses through the intermediate grades, remember the following:

- Expect your child to do well. Treat him as a capable person with strong mental abilities. As Benjamin Bloom, the famous educator and child psychologist, has taught us, all normal children can master the school curriculum, given adequate support and time. Never suggest—in the absence of a specifically diagnosed learning problem—that your child is anything but capable.
- Don't label your child, and don't let the school label him either. Remember that intelligence comes in many forms and that it is not fully represented by an IQ test (or any other of the standardized tests commonly given in schools). Remember also that most people never fully develop their mental capacities and that some people with less genetic endowment consistently perform better than those with more. Given appropriate instruction and support, your child can do well, no matter what!
- Stimulate your child in many ways. All of your child's mental abilities—linguistic, musical, logical-mathematical, spatial, kinesthetic, and personal—need lively interaction with the environment to develop properly. Immerse your child in books, conversation, games, puzzles, music, dance, and travel, and look for natural interests that you can nurture and reinforce.
- Encourage your child's teacher to teach in many modalities—

to use a wide variety of teaching materials, devices, and activities. All children don't learn in the same way. But given enough variety in instruction, all children can learn!

- Support and encourage your child. Expect much and be positive about what your child does well. Don't be critical or discouraged if your child progresses slowly. People tend to do what they feel good about doing. Help your child feel good about his ability to use his mind!

The Importance of School in the Intermediate Years

Throughout the years of later childhood, school is likely to be the most important experience in your child's life outside the family. In school he will learn the traditions, symbols, and skills that the adults in his culture think it is important to teach him. There he will also learn what he can do well and what he cannot, how his family compares to other families, and how he fits in with his agemates and with his teachers. He will make his friends there, have disputes there, and attune his life to the rhythms of the school calendar, with its emotional beginnings and endings and its long stretches of tedium punctuated by bursts of excitement. In large part, school will be his life.

What are the goals of this experience? What does society seek of its children through the schools it provides, and what does the child seek from his experience in school?

THE GOALS OF SCHOOLING

Our country does not have a nationally controlled system of schools. The U.S. Constitution leaves education to the states. Although the role of the federal government in requiring certain programs and providing funding for certain purposes has grown in recent decades, typically it is the fifty states, and the local school districts that the states have authorized, that set the goals for the schools.

Despite this apparent diversity, there is a consensus of agreement among the thousands of school districts in our country about the goals of education. As part of his superb *A Study of Schooling* (1984), perhaps the most comprehensive study of American schools ever published, John Goodlad and his associates analyzed a vast array of written documents and interviewed hundreds of parents and teachers in order to determine what the goals of school should be. Throughout all strata of society they found consensus that schools should have the following four broad goals for children:

1. Academic, including all the fundamental intellectual skills and all the major areas of knowledge.
2. Vocational, in the general sense of providing the skills and habits children will need to be constructive workers in society.
3. Social and civic, including an understanding of our complex society and preparation to participate effectively in it.
4. Personal, involving the development of individual talents and a sense of responsibility for one's actions.

Schools and individuals vary in the emphasis they place upon each of these goals, as well as in the means by which they pursue them. We shall discuss these differences below. But here, at the outset, the breadth of these goals and wide base of support they enjoy seem worth noting. Parents want their children to acquire the basics of a solid academic education, of course. Schools that fail pupils in this regard fail—period. But parents want much more as well. They want their children to be prepared to enter confidently and productively into the adult world of work and social relationships. They want them to develop all of their personal abilities—mental, emotional, physical, artistic. And they want them to be good citizens, people who feel good about themselves and who respect the rights of others. Much of what makes a good school good is a nurturing climate that helps children progress toward these broader goals. "Back to basics" and an emphasis on academics alone is not enough. In this book we shall focus on the school's role in helping children develop their mental capacities. But always in the background is our sense that mental growth cannot be separated from the totality of a child's education, either in the child himself or in the school.

UNSTATED GOALS—THE IMPORTANT SIDE EFFECTS OF SCHOOLING

In addition to their stated goals, schools perform other functions in our society as well. Our system of schooling is so well established, and in a sense is taken so much for granted, that we are often unaware of these important side effects. But simply by virtue of their existence and form of organization, schools perform important functions that have little direct relationship with their stated educational purposes. In thinking about your child's educational experience, you should be aware of the school's role as custodial care-giver, as transmitter of values, and as accrediting agent.

The School as Custodial Care-Giver

Throughout the United States compulsory attendance laws require school-age children to be in school for about six hours a day on about one of every two days in the year, including most traditional workdays. Families know that for at least those hours on school days they can count on the school to provide a safe, wholesome environment for their children. (In those unfortunate circumstances where the school environment may not be safe or wholesome, families are understandably distressed.)

In a society in which over one-half of all mothers of school-age children are in the work force and in which 60 percent of today's two-year-olds will live in a single-parent household by age eighteen, this is a fact of enormous economic and social importance. Occasionally some "expert" will predict that in the future children will be able to master their reading and math skills at home, working at a computer. Perhaps they could—but only if someone were there to watch them.

Children will still need to "be" someplace and be supervised someplace each day, and it will probably be in school, not in the home. Nor is the importance of the school's custodial function confined to urban or low-income areas. In the authors' affluent suburb, in the past on days of heavy snow elementary-school children would be sent home at lunchtime and told not to come back in the afternoon. No longer. Nowadays there are too many locked and empty houses, and the school must continue to provide care regardless of the weather.

Because the school performs this *in loco parentis* role, parents should get to know the teachers and other school personnel who will be dealing with their children. (We say more about this matter in the chapter "School Resource People" in the last part of the book.)

The School as Transmitter of Values

Most working days the schools in our society bring most of the children in each neighborhood together in one place. There the children are segregated by age and assigned to classes that have lessons together, study together, play at recess together, eat lunch together, and provide a context for forming friendships and alliances. In the process, the school creates a peer culture that becomes increasingly important as children become more independent of their families. Together with the organization of the school and the messages that the adults in the school transmit, this peer culture comes to play an important role in shaping children's values.

All schools transmit values, whether they intend to or not. The way the school is organized and run itself reflects a value system—some people have more authority than others, some behavior is rewarded and other behavior is discouraged. The adults in the school transmit their own personal values simply by acting like the kind of people they are and by communicating their own standards of behavior. And the peer culture acts as a rich medium for the exchange of values, as children are exposed to ways of thinking and feeling about things that may differ from those of their parents. In this general sense, no school is value-neutral.

Most schools do not think very much about the values they transmit. They make the common-sense assumption that virtually everyone in our society agrees on a core of values common to our culture—values like honesty, respect for others, respect for property—and they go about the business of teaching the academic curriculum in ways consistent with these values, without ever raising the question of what values should be taught. Where the values of a community are thoroughly consistent with the values of its schools, this arrangement works well.

Sometimes, however, conflicts can arise. What if some families think the school should do more to instill discipline, while others think children should be free to express themselves? What if some families believe that the schools should do more to inculcate the values of a particular religion, while others believe in the absolute separation of church and state? What if some families believe that the schools should teach children about human sexuality, while others regard this topic as the province of the home? In a pluralistic society such as ours, such conflicts are all but unavoidable. How they get resolved depends on how the political structure of the school is organized and who is able to influence it most. And the answers will have a significant effect on the kind of school your child will attend.

The most practical advice the authors can give parents about these matters is to choose, if you can, a school in a community where most of the children and most of the families are likely to have values and aspirations similar to your own. (This approach is not inconsistent with public education's ideal of the "common school." Many of us want our children to experience ethnic and socioeconomic diversity as part of the educational experience, but the diverse population of the school should share the same general goals and value system.) If you are not in a position to choose a school for your child, spend some time ascertaining what the climate of your child's school is and then work constructively in partnership with others to effect desirable changes. (See the chapter "How to Improve Your School" in the last part of the book.)

The School as Accrediting Agent

A third important function that schools perform in our society is that of accrediting agent. Our economy and our system of higher education require some means of sorting out those who are presumably qualified for employment or admission and those who are not. This function is performed largely by the school. Schools certify those who have been graduated and those who have taken certain courses; they assess students' abilities and channel some students in one direction and some in another. Employees and others rely on the judgments made by school personnel about a candidate's character and ability. This accrediting function becomes more important as children progress through the grades into high school, but even in these intermediate years parents should begin to be aware of the records children are making and of any classifying labels the school has assigned to them.

THE CHILD'S GOALS FOR SCHOOL

All of the foregoing goals and functions are, of course, very distant from what your child has on his mind. The child aged seven to ten is not concerned with the school's implicit values or with its accrediting function. He is more apt to be concerned with the fairness of his teacher or the length of the bus ride. But since school looms so large in his experience, it seems important to know what your child wants from school and to view it occasionally through his eyes.

Surprisingly, relatively little research has been done on what children look for in their school experience. Perhaps the words "look for" are inappropriate in this context. Most children don't seek out a school because they want to go there—they go because they have to. They go because their parents and teachers tell them they must and because all the other children their age go there, too. It is simply the normal thing to do.

Once there, however, children do come to have goals, and we have come to know a little about them. More than anything else, children want to be accepted by their teachers as competent members of their class and they want to be accepted by their friends as peers who "belong." When the climate of the school is such that these two drives—to become academically competent and to be accepted socially—reinforce each other, everything tends to go well. When they are in conflict (as they can be in a situation where showing off to gain the approval of one's friends involves behavior offensive to the teacher), trouble occurs. Fortunately, most children attend elementary schools in which they can acquire competence and make friends at the same time.

Children have other standards by which they judge their schools as well. They want their teachers to be "fair" and not "mean"; they want to be known and accepted for who they are; they enjoy variety in their activity so that things are not so "boring" every day. But all such standards are subordinate to the two chief goals of becoming competent and being accepted by peers. The wise parent and teacher will understand these drives and find ways to help the child experience success.

SCHOOLS ARE NOT THE ONLY TEACHERS

Your child's experience in school is of course a crucial part of his total education. Indeed, the rest of this book is devoted to explaining what happens in school and to suggesting ways in which you can improve the school. But before we conclude this discussion, it seems important to note that schools are not your child's only teachers.

By far the most influential people in your child's total education are you, the parents. Not only do you give your child your genes, but what you say and do from infancy through adolescence and who you are help shape his thoughts, his beliefs, his values, his attitudes toward himself, and his habitual ways of relating to people and events. Indeed, for the rest of his days, from now until long after you have gone, your child will never be far from the sound of your voice.

Beyond you there is the extended family and perhaps a small circle of adult friends. These people, too, impart their knowledge and their values, especially when the child is young.

If your child belongs to a church or a temple, these institutions also play an important part. So, too, in a smaller way, do such organizations as the Boy Scouts or Girl Scouts. And we have already discussed the influence of the child's peer culture, particularly as he progresses into adolescence.

However, the most powerful educational forces in our society, apart from home, school, and religion are the news and entertainment media—especially television. By the time children enter kindergarten, they may have spent up to 5,000 hours watching television. The average intermediate-age child spends more hours watching television every week than he spends in school. The effect of this experience on children's knowledge, habits, thoughts, and relationship to the adult world can scarcely be overemphasized.

Because of their exposure to television, children nowadays come to school knowing more than the children of earlier generations. The camera has taken them to places all around the globe and into outer space. Today's children have seen the devastation and suffering wreaked by natural and manmade violence; they are in touch with "what's happening," real or fanciful, wherever the action is each day. Through comedies, game shows, commercials, and the news, they are exposed to the adult values of society, to what is sold, to what is made to seem valuable. They watch how other people live, or are made to seem to live. And they know that they are part of a larger world not bounded by the experience and values of their family, their neighborhood, their school.

Television watching has an impact of its own, separate from the content of its programs. Many children have developed mental habits appropriate to a television culture rather than a book culture. In order to read, a child must master the skills of written language. But to watch television, no skill is required and no gratification must be postponed. When the set is turned on, there is instant reward. The images are quick and fleeting; they communciate through immediate sensory impact, not through sequential thought and imagination. If the program is dull, a quick turn of the dial produces another program. (Many experienced teachers talk of their increasing difficulty in getting today's children to pay sustained attention to a task or project.)

Furthermore, the world of commercial television is open to all viewers, adults and children alike. No longer can parents and the school limit the child's knowledge to what seems appropriate by carefully selecting the films he can watch. Violence, greed, and folly are not confined to a few "bad" programs—they are everywhere, even in commercials. On the surface, at least, the innocence of childhood is becoming a thing of the past.

It is difficult to say whether the job of the school has been made harder or easier by television's pervasive influence. On the one hand, it is helpful that today's children come to school better informed about the world than the children of earlier generations. It saves time and it gives the school a broader base of knowledge to build upon. On the other hand, it does not help that the school must often compete with a style of entertainment and a set of values that clash with the school's menu of discipline, hard work, and delayed gratification. To many children, particularly to those who do not feel successful in our schools, the world reflected in television appears much more attractive than the world of the classroom.

Perhaps in time our society will become more conscious of television's role in our children's education and will find ways consistent with our democratic traditions to make it more constructive. In the meantime, the schools and the media will continue to coexist. Wise parents will be aware of both the good and the harm that television can do, will limit their children's viewing time, and will be vigilant about the kinds of programs their children are permitted to watch.

SAMENESSES AND DIFFERENCES AMONG SCHOOLS

A visitor from another country, touring America's elementary schools, might first be struck by their diversity. The nation's elementary schools vary in size, shape, wealth, resources, and the social and ethnic backgrounds of the children who attend them. Gray fortresses in the inner cities contrast with red-brick Georgian structures in the older towns and with sprawling, one-story buildings on spacious lawns in the suburbs. In some schools, all or nearly all the pupils and teachers are white and English-speaking; in others, such pupils and teachers are in the minority. In some, the doors are always locked and children climb the stairs at lunchtime to play on fenced-in asphalt rooftops; in others, the doors to each classroom open freely as children and their parents come and go. Our visitor, knowing that we have no national system of schools, might wonder what holds such teeming diversity together.

A closer look, however, reveals that beneath this variety lies a surprising uniformity of instructional practice. Almost all of our elementary schools are organized into classes of about twenty to thirty-five children of the same age. The teacher's first preoccupation, if she is to achieve anything at all, is the maintenance of order. The teacher dominates the activity and tone of the class. Children work within a group setting but are judged according to individual performance, not the performance of the group as a team. They spend much time listening to the teacher, answering questions, filling out worksheets, giving reports, and taking tests and quizzes. As John Goodlad says in his 1984 book *A Place Called School*, "*Schools* differ; *schooling* is everywhere very much the same."

The heart of the elementary school curriculum is also much the same from one region of the country to another. Dominating the curriculum are reading, writing, and arithmetic, with an emphasis on basic facts and skills. Programs in these subjects are remarkably the same from school to school, whether because of tradition or because of the influence exerted by the major national textbook publishers. (A third-grade child can move from the Midwest to California and feel at home in reading or math activities.) Next in importance (and in the time devoted to them) are social studies and science. Here there is much less agreement about what the curriculum should be; there is considerable similarity in the *style* of instruction, but much less similarity of *content*. Rounding out the curriculum are art, music, health, education, and physical education. Almost all schools provide some sort of experience in these areas, but the kind of experience and its extent vary widely.

Still, despite the differences, American schools are more similar with respect to curriculum and instructional practice than they are different. The chapters that follow will serve as a useful guide no matter where you live. Where schools *truly* differ is in their prevailing climate, or ethos—and that is something only people close to the scene are able to sense.

The sociologist Seymour Sarason has stated that each school has a distinctive culture of its own—distinctive ways of doing things, distinctive interpersonal relationships, distinctive attitudes toward learning, children, parents, teachers, and others. (Often people bent upon reforming some aspect of schooling fail because they do not take this total culture into account.) The culture creates a pervading climate that an uninformed observer may not sense but that is strongly experienced by those closely connected with the school. As John Goodlad says in *A Place Called School,*

> Schools are more different, it seems, in the somewhat elusive qualities making up their ambiance—the ways students and teachers relate to one another, the school's orientation to academic concerns, the degree to which students are caught up in peer-group interests other than academic, the

way principals and teachers regard one another, the degree of autonomy possessed by principals and teachers in conducting their work, the nature of the relationship between the school and its parent clientele; and so on.

The differences in school climate are of great importance to you and your child. But precisely because such differences are specific to individual schools in individual communities, they are beyond the scope of this book. The picture to hold in your mind as you read these pages is one of surface diversity undergirded by remarkable consistency of curriculum and instruction, with local variations in the ethos or tone of individual schools.

TASKS OF THE CHILD, THE SCHOOL, AND THE PARENT

Your child enters the third grade still closely tied to home and family. Three years later he will leave the fifth grade on the brink of adolescence, with much of his identity already formed and a growing life of his own. What, in general, are the crucial tasks of these intermediate elementary schools years?

- The task of the child is to develop his body and his mind; to learn the basic skills, symbols, and traditions of the culture; and to develop an independent identity through interaction with children and adults outside the family.
- The task of the school is to help the child develop and learn in a stimulating, nurturing, safe environment.
- The task of the parent is to support the child in his developmental process—to praise success, to cushion failure, to maintain interest, and gradually to begin to let go as the child who goes forth becomes more and more himself.

THIRD GRADE

The Third-Grade
Child as a Learner

The typical third-grade child is eight years old. He is developing rapidly and, in his self-confidence and secure knowledge of his place at home and in school, is very different from the more tentative child he was two or three years before. Although he is still tied closely to home and family, his friends are increasingly more important to him, and he looks forward to the time he spends with them at school. He is active and energetic, and eagerly seeks out new experiences, whether through reading or television or family travel or through trying things out with his hands.

Most third-grade children have progressed to Piaget's stage of concrete operations. They increasingly understand numbers and relationships, they communicate more easily, and they have better perceptions of the concepts of past and future. During the third-grade year, most children will master the basic decoding skills of reading and will begin to read for comprehension and enjoyment. They will establish a solid foundation of arithmetic skills, especially in addition and subtraction, and will learn to solve mathematical problems appropriate to their level. Their writing, although more self-conscious now than it was a year or more ago, will continue to improve.

In short, the third-grade child is a self-confident, enthusiastic learner who is gradually making a unique place for himself both outside the home and within it. He is ready to master the basic mechanics of reading and mathematics so that he can embark on the more challenging and rewarding work that lies ahead.

The Elementary School Day

In the secondary schools, where each subject is taught by a different teacher in a different room, the school day is divided into fixed periods of instruction, typically one period per day per subject. In the elementary grades, where the prevailing form of organization is a "self-contained" classroom consisting of one teacher and a class of twenty to thirty-five children, the daily schedule is more flexible. Ideally, this flexibility permits teachers to adjust the amount of time they spend on given activities to reflect the nature of the activity, to promote interdisciplinary learning, to take advantage of children's interest, and to provide for individual differences among children within the class. To some degree, teachers do make such adjustments. In many situations, however, other realities of school life affect the way in which teachers and children must schedule their time. Children are required to be in the cafeteria for lunch at a certain time each day and in the playground for recess at a certain time each day. Lessons with teachers of *special* subjects, like music, art, and physical education, are scheduled for specific times. Individual children with out-of-class obligations (instrumental music practice, sessions with a remedial reading teacher) are pulled out of class at stated times. As a result, the ideal flexibility is reduced, and the elementary school day, particularly in the intermediate years, takes on a more structured character.

There are two chief issues regarding the scheduling and use of school time—quantity and quality. With respect to quantity, recent studies have confirmed the common-sense belief that the more time you study a subject, the better you are apt to learn it. These time-on-task studies have spawned a series of comparisons of how schools use time—American schools compared with those abroad and American schools compared with one another. Most elementary-school children in the United States attend school for about 180 days per year. For most, the school day is about five hours long excluding lunch. (In some foreign countries, like Japan, the school year and school day are longer.)

The amount of time devoted to each subject within the day (or week) and the amount of time spent directly on instructional matters (as opposed to, for example, housekeeping routines and discipline) vary from school to school. In *A Place Called School*, Goodlad displays a sample of intermediate elementary teachers' reports of the average number of hours of instruction per week per subject as follows:

English/language arts	7.41
Mathematics	5.12
Social studies	3.83
Science	2.93
Art	1.29
Music	1.35
Drama	0.07
Dance	0.17
Physical education	2.26

Of course, the pattern of time in a given class could vary.

Similarly, Goodlad reports the following average pattern of use of time in average intermediate classrooms:

Instruction	72.89 percent
Routines	20.71 percent
Behavior	4.39 percent
Social	2.01 percent

Again, class-to-class and school-to-school variations were substantial, with the amount of time spent in instruction ranging from 64 to 84 percent of the total time. Not every minute of your child's day can be spent in alert, engaged attention to an instructional task. But a teacher's lax or sloppy management can handicap your child's learning. You have a right to know how your child spends his time, and if his weekly schedule is significantly below these averages, you should talk to his teacher and, if necessary, the principal.

To help you deal with these hours and percentages, as well as to get a clear perspective of your child's day and week, we have provided a sample schedule on page 44. Please remember that this schedule is not an ideal one but a prototype that should be modified to meet the needs of your child and his classmates in their specific situation.

As we noted above, given effective instruction, the more time spent on a task, the more and better the learning. But the quality of this time is also critical. Dull, lifeless, and inappropriate instruction does not improve with repetition. In the pages that follow, we hope you will get some sense of what school can be like for your child given a well-designed program taught by capable teachers.

A SAMPLE WEEKDAY SCHEDULE

	Monday	Tuesday	Wednesday	Thursday	Friday
8:45	Attendance, lunch count, daily planning, etc.				
9:00 9:15 9:30	Math	Math	Math	Math	Math
9:45 10:00	Music	Physical Education	Health	Music	Physical Education
10:15			Recess		
10:30	Recess	Recess	Social Studies	Recess	Recess
10:45 11:00	Reading	Reading		Reading	Reading
11:15 11:30			Writing		
11:45	Spelling	Spelling		Spelling	Spelling
12:00 12:15 12:30 12:45	Lunch	Lunch	Lunch	Lunch	Lunch
1:00 1:15 1:30 1:45	Writing	Writing	Reading	Writing	Writing
2:00 2:15 2:30 2:45 3:00	Science	Social Studies	Art	Science	Social Studies

Reading in the Third Grade

THE IMPORTANCE OF READING

Nothing is more important to your child's success in school and adult life than his ability to read. Even in this increasingly audiovisual and computer-oriented society, reading is the key that unlocks the doors to mankind's accumulated knowledge and wisdom. The child who learns to read well has the skill he needs to master much of what he will be asked to learn in school and will want to continue learning throughout his lifetime. The child who struggles with reading is deprived of a basic foothold in our culture; in time he may learn to compensate, but he will do so at a price.

Most parents are aware that this is so. What they want to know is, How do children learn to read? What do good teachers do to help them learn to read? How does one know if one's child is making normal progress? This chapter (and others in this series) may help you answer these and similar questions.

LEARNING TO READ

The process of learning to read has been likened to a journey. There is no single step that enables a person to read. Rather, there are many related steps that must be taken before progress becomes visible. Nor is there a fixed and final destination. The ultimate goal—that of being a fluent, accomplished reader—is something to continue to develop.

Children progress through three broad stages in their development as readers: (1) *readiness/early reading,* (2) *basic skill development,* and (3) *reading to learn.* For most children, the first stage occurs at age four to six, ending in kindergarten or the first grade. At this stage, children become accustomed to the sight and use of written language, acquire a *sight vocabulary* of familiar words, and begin to read very simple material. (You may want to read our description of this process in the first book of this series: *Your Child in School: Kindergarten Through Second Grade.*) The second stage—basic skill development—normally occurs at between six and nine years of age, in grades 1 through 3. At this stage, children acquire the skills that enable them to *decode* unfamiliar words and to understand written material appropriate to their age and experience. They also enlarge their reading vocabulary and begin to develop effective study skills. The third stage—reading to learn—begins about the time that children enter grade 4. At this stage, children begin to apply their ability to read to the content areas—social studies, science, literature, mathematics, and so on. As they do so, they both acquire new knowledge of these subjects and develop their skills as thoughtful, critical readers.

If your child is making normal progress, the third grade is probably the last in which he will be involved in a reading program focused chiefly on basic skill development. Therefore, it is important that he acquire the necessary skills by the end of this year.

Word Recognition Skills

By the time they enter the third grade, most children should be able to

- Recognize, pronounce, and understand a sight vocabulary of about 500 words.
- Pronounce the appropriate sounds of single consonants, consonant blends and digraphs, vowels, and diphthongs.
- Blend letter sounds into words.
- Separate words into syllables.
- Separate roots from prefixes and suffixes.
- Use phonics clues, structural analysis clues, and context clues to identify unknown words.

Comprehension Skills

Given reading material on the second-grade level, your child by the end of the year should be able to

- Understand the meaning of sentences and paragraphs.
- Understand the main idea of a paragraph or short passage.
- Find significant details within a paragraph or passage.
- Recognize time intervals.
- Recognize cause and effect.
- Predict outcomes based on what is known.
- Follow simple directions.
- Solve simple problems.
- Distinguish fact from fiction.

Most third-grade teachers spend some time at the beginning of the year assessing each child's general reading level and particular skills needs. If you are concerned about your child's reading progress, we suggest that you confer with your child's teacher early in the fall in order to find out how the teacher plans to help your child overcome any deficits before the end of the year.

THE THIRD-GRADE READING CURRICULUM

The basic skills taught in most third-grade reading programs are of three kinds: (1) *word recognition skills*, (2) *comprehension skills*, and (3) *study skills*.

Word Recognition Skills

Word recognition skills consist of *sight word* skills and *word attack* skills. Sight word skills enable a reader to recognize a word correctly on sight, as the reader of this passage no doubt is doing. Most adult readers apply sight word skills to most of the reading that we do; we do not need to decode words that are instantly familiar to us. Word attack skills enable readers to decode unfamiliar words—to relate printed symbols to sounds and gain meaning from the page. Adult readers use word attack skills on unfamiliar words, but such skills are chiefly used by beginning readers in the stage of basic skills development. The sight vocabulary of beginning readers increases rapidly with practice in reading. When children first begin to read, they can speak many more words than they recognize in print. Indeed, the task in reading is to match the words children see in print with the words they already know in speech. (For this reason, good teachers devote considerable time to activities that increase the child's speaking and listening vocabulary.) In time, as children develop skill and practice in reading, the balance shifts. The child gradually comes to recognize in print all the words he knows in speech and then to acquire a *reading vocabulary* of words recognized on sight that he rarely, if at all, uses in speech. Recognition of individual words does not guarantee comprehension of a passage (as any of us who have struggled with an income tax form or an insurance policy can attest), but without a large sight vocabulary an adult reader is sorely handicapped.

The word attack skills of developing readers consist chiefly of phonic analysis, contextual analysis, and structural analysis. Phonics involves the relationship of letters to sounds. Children are taught to identify letters and groups of letters, to associate an appropriate sound with each letter or letter group, and to *blend* the separate sounds together so as to pronounce the word. Once the child has grasped the principle of letter-sound relationships and a fund of appropriate letter sounds, he has the key that enables him to decode a limitless number of unfamiliar printed words.

Phonics programs vary in their scope, design, and thoroughness. Almost all, however, begin by teaching the sounds of initial consonants (*c*at, *d*og, *m*an) and proceed in one order or another with the following:

- Consonants occurring in the word (bo*x*, bu*tt*er).
- Consonants that have two sounds (*c*ar, *c*ity).
- Consonant blends and digraphs (*str*ing, *ch*air).
- Short and long vowel sounds (c*a*t, g*a*te).
- Vowel diphthongs and digraphs (b*oy*, m*ea*t).
- Silent letters (*k*nit, lam*b*).

When the skills of phonetic analysis are taught well—thoroughly, but as an aid to understanding, not as an end in themselves—they are a powerful reading tool, as well as an aid to correct spelling. Most schools and teachers today understand the importance of a solid grounding in phonic analysis. However, a reading curriculum that overemphasizes phonics to the neglect of other important word recognition and comprehension skills would shortchange your child. Many competent readers have never studied phonics, and many who have studied phonics do not read well. Probably the most sensible advice on the matter has been given by *Becoming a Nation of Readers,* the 1985 report of the Commission on Reading: "The right maxims for phonics are: Do it early. Keep it simple. Except in cases of diagnosed individual need, phonics instruction should have been completed by the end of the second grade."

The word attack skill of contextual analysis enables a reader to infer the meaning of a word from its placement among words that are already known. For example, the child may not recognize the printed word *hungry* but can identify it correctly in the sentence, "The monkey ate six bananas because it was hungry." Experienced readers continue to use the skills of contextual analysis throughout their lifetime, especially when reading material on unfamiliar topics.

The word attack skill of structural analysis enables readers to determine the meaning of words by separating their component parts—syllables, roots, prefixes, suffixes, and so on. Thus, a child who might otherwise be thrown by the unfamiliar (to him) word *nonconformist* is helped if he knows the prefix *non-* and the suffix *-ist*, and even better helped if he understands the meaning of *con-* in the word *conform*.

There is no single list of word recognition skills that is (or should be) followed by all schools and teachers, nor is there a single sequence in which the skills should be learned by all children. What *is* important, however, is that your child's school have a consistent plan that enables the teacher to guide and monitor your child's progress. You have a right to know what the plan is. If you have concerns, ask your child's teacher or, if necessary, principal.

Comprehension Skills

The point of learning to read is to be able to understand what others have written. Necessary as they are, all the word recognition skills in the world will not suffice if a text remains a collection of unrelated words. Good teachers do not teach word recognition skills in isolation; from the very beginning of reading instruction, they help children understand the meaning of what they are reading. Reading involves more than the ability to pronounce unfamiliar words and attach meaning to them separate from the context—it involves comprehending the sense of the entire passage, following the story, understanding the point, noting the important details, and bringing to bear one's own imagination and thinking. Good teachers help children acquire comprehension skills by discussing and analyzing the content of the stories and passages they read.

We shall have more to say about comprehension skills in the sections on grades 4 and 5, when the reading curriculum moves to a higher plane. But even throughout the primary grades and in grade 3 children should read for understanding. They should be helped to understand the meaning of each sentence, to grasp the main idea of a passage, to find important details, to follow sequences of time or action, to note cause-effect relationships, to predict outcomes, to make inferences, and to interpret feelings. In this way, their powers of comprehension increase at the same time that they master technical skills, and they are motivated to read more.

Study Skills

As children progress in their ability to read, they increasingly branch out beyond the basic reading books. They read a wide assortment of fiction and nonfiction works for information and enjoyment, and they may begin to read textbooks about history, geography, science, and other subjects. In doing so, they need to learn the study skills that will enable them to make the most of these materials. A good third-grade reading program pays attention to the development of these skills. Children at this level are taught to

- Alphabetize—arrange letters in sequence, fill in gaps in alphabetical sequences (for example, *h—j*), arrange words in alphabetical order (first by the initial letter, then by two or more).
- Use a dictionary—find words, understand explanations of a word's structure and meaning(s).
- Use maps, charts, and globes—usually taught as part of social studies.
- Understand the organization of a book—recognize and use title pages, tables of contents, chapter headings, indexes.
- Follow written directions—to find locations, create time lines, perform experiments, and so on.
- Read for a purpose—to get the main idea, to find important details, to answer a specific question, and so forth.

TEACHING THE THIRD-GRADE READING CURRICULUM

Basal Reading Programs

The most common form of reading instruction in America's schools is the basal reading program. Estimates show that basal programs are used by about 90 percent of all primary school (grades K–2) teachers and about 75 percent of all intermediate (grades 3–6) teachers. These programs (and the relatively few publishing companies that produce and market them) exert a strong influence on the way America's children are taught to read.

Basal reading programs are complete packages of materials for learning to read. They can be used alone, as the entire reading curriculum, or in combination with other teaching approaches. Typically, they consist of a *scope and sequence chart*, which lists in order the skills to be learned; a graded set of books, or *readers*, for children to read; sets of practice exercises for children, in the form of workbooks and worksheets; teachers' manuals, which describe in great detail the steps the teacher is to follow; and a variety of supplemental materials, such as tests, charts, word cards, sentence cards, audiotapes, filmstrips, and supplementary reading books. A complete basal reading program for grades K–6 would fill at least two large cardboard boxes.

The programs organize their materials into reading levels that roughly correspond to the grade structure of American schools. A typical arrangement is as follows:

Level 1—Readiness
Level 2—Preprimer
Level 3—Primer
Level 4—First Reader
Level 5—First half of second grade
Level 6—Second half of second grade
Level 7—First half of third grade
Level 8—Second half of third grade
Level 9—Fourth grade
Level 10—Fifth grade
Level 11—Sixth grade

The programs follow certain basic principles. They arrange their reading materials in a progression of gradually increasing difficulty, teaching all the reading skills in sequential fashion.

The vocabulary used in the readers is limited to words that are thought to be within the children's listening and speaking vocabularies. The number of new words in each reading selection is carefully controlled, and familiar words are repeated for reinforcement. The number of words in each sentence is kept small. Most of the selections are in story form and are based on experiences presumably familiar to the child. (Traditionally, the standard story was about a middle-class suburban family in which there is a father who goes to work, a mother who keeps house, two children who never fight, and a variety of pets who jump and run. In recent years, some series have introduced characters who live in cities in different family circumstances. However, much of the middle-class stereotype remains in the readers used in many American classrooms.) Finally, the basal programs are written to be a total reading program, complete in themselves. And for many teachers, particularly beginning teachers or those without access to other resources, they constitute most or all of the formal reading program.

The typical basal reader lesson consists of five steps:

1. The teacher prepares the children by motivating them to read the story, by discussing new words that appear in the story, by reminding them of skills already learned (such as certain phonic skills or the use of particular punctuation marks), and by discussing concepts on which the story may be based.
2. The children are given a purpose for reading and asked to read the story silently.
3. The children read all or part of the story and discuss it with the teacher. In the lower grades, the children usually read aloud. In the third grade, they more commonly read silently.
4. The teacher assigns follow-up activities according to the children's individual needs. Some children may practice a skill just taught in the lesson; others may practice an old skill; and still others may apply the new skill on a more sophisticated level.

5. The teacher introduces a variety of activities to reinforce and extend the skill just taught. Children may read another story on a related theme, or they may make a picture or write stories of their own

Obviously, these steps can be combined or given differen-temphasis, but most basal reading lessons follow a somewhat similar pattern.

Grouping for Reading Instruction

The typical third-grade class contains children with a wide range of reading abilities. It is not uncommon to find a span from those who are still at the primer level to some who are reading at the fourth- or fifth-grade level. In order to deal effectively with these differences, most teachers form small groups of children for the purpose of reading instruction.

The most common basis for grouping is reading ability. In a class of, say, twenty-six children, the teacher may have three reading groups—for example one reading at level 5, one at level 7, and one at level 8. The teacher works with one group, while the children in the other groups engage in other quiet activities. (These activities, sometimes called *seatwork*, run the gamut from filling in the blanks on relatively mindless skills worksheets to creative, challenging reading and writing assignments.) In this way the teacher can instruct children at an appropriate level of difficulty and involve them more directly in the teaching-learning process.

The potential problems with grouping, of course, is that the poorer, or more slowly developing, readers lose the benefit of interacting with children who are more advanced, and they may become stigmatized and feel like failures. (Few of us are enthusiastic about undertaking activities in which we don't do well.) Meanwhile, the more advanced readers are deprived of

the chance to learn from interacting with some of their classmates, and they may develop attitudes of superiority that are
not fully warranted. For these reasons, good teachers vary the
composition of the groups they form. They *do* group by ability
for certain purposes: There is no point in trying to instruct a
child on level 8 along with a child on level 2. But they also group
from time to time according to special needs (regardless of
reading level) or according to interests. Thus, a group may be
formed so that the teacher can provide instruction about a
specific skill, or a group may be formed so that children of
different instructional levels can collaborate on a project of
mutual interest.

Whatever the form of grouping, instruction in basal reading
programs is usually provided to individual smaller groups of
pupils rather than to the class as a whole. The teacher makes
additional attempts to individualize instruction by giving extra
help to children who are having difficulty and by providing
more challenging library books or supplementary readers on a
higher level to those who are more advanced.

Enriching the Basal Reading Program

Basal reading programs serve a very useful purpose. They
provide a comprehensive and systematic approach to teaching
reading for the many teachers who are relatively inexperienced
and for the many more who would lack the skill and resources
to create their own programs. However, competent, experienced
teachers build upon a basal program to offer their children even
more. They do so in a variety of ways.

Teachers often use books and other materials from more
than one basal program in the same class. In this way, a
third-grade child who is still reading at the second-grade level
can be given fresh reading material, not the same readers he
used (and probably struggled with) the previous year. Teachers

encourage children to read a wide variety of books from the classroom and school library, above and beyond the basal readers themselves. In this way, they spur interest and give children ample opportunity to practice their developing skill. Teachers use a wide variety of instructional materials to supplement the basal program: phonics workbooks, picture books, filmstrips, audiotapes—anything that diversifies the materials of instruction and therefore makes it more likely that each child's individual learning style will be engaged.

One third-grade teacher we know uses the basal program four days a week. On the fifth day she groups the children according to interest in different types of literature, such as myths, fables, fairy tales, and animal stories. She assembles a collection of books in each category and helps each child choose books appropriate to his level of ability. When a child has finished a book, he tells the rest of his group about it, and together the children compile a written record of what they have read. Another teacher occasionally takes time out of the basal program to group children according to themes in children's literature. Again, each child is guided to books on his level of ability. When he has finished reading a book, he has an individual conference with the teacher, who notes his progress and problems, if any, and guides the child to his next book. In ways like these the structure and continuity of the basal program are essentially preserved, but the teacher's creativity and resourcefulness are tapped and the child is exposed to a richer lode of reading material.

Individualized Reading Programs

A more thoroughgoing alternative to the basal reading program is the individualized reading program. In such a program the books that the child reads are selected by the child himself with guidance by the teacher. The child chooses books that interest him and that are of an appropriate level of reading difficulty. The teacher ensures that the selected books are at the right level of skills development, monitors the child's progress through frequent individual conferences, and develops appropriate independent study activities for him.

Such a program, while it may seem to be dictated by the child's interests (indeed, the child may actually experience it that way), in fact requires much knowledge and planning on the part of the teacher. The teacher must determine each child's reading skills needs so that she can help children choose books appropriate for their instructional level. She must come to know and remember each child's reading interests. She must know in what setting and with what materials each child works best. She must know and make available a wide range of books and instructional materials. She must make time for frequent individual conferences. And she must keep full and careful records of each child's experience and progress.

The advantages of an individualized program are that each child is reading books at his own level of difficulty; he is not held back or pulled ahead by other children in the group; and he learns skills in a relevant situation as he needs them. Because the child chooses the books, his level of motivation is presumably higher, and because the potential range of reading material is broader than in a basal series, there are more opportunities to read books of literary worth.

Needless to say, such a program, while desirable, is difficult to teach. Because of this, as well as from a concern that all children have the same experience, relatively few classroom teachers organize their reading programs in this manner. (More typically, one sees teachers using an individualized approach with the top readers in a class.) In the authors' view, the parent whose child is already involved in an individualized program is truly lucky. However, be sure that your child's teacher is experienced and energetic enough to manage it well before suggesting that she undertake such a program.

WHAT TO LOOK FOR IN A GOOD THIRD-GRADE READING PROGRAM

There is no single best way to teach reading. Studies have shown that good teaching can occur with many methods. Unhappily, poor teaching can occur with many methods as well. From the parents' point of view, the method that works best is one that is working with your child.

Fortunately, you don't need to be a trained reading teacher to know whether your child is receiving effective instruction or not. If the answers to most of the following questions are yes, chances are your child is participating in an effective reading program. If many of the answers are no, you should talk to your child's teacher and, perhaps, the principal to see what changes can be made.

- Does the teacher have a plan for reading instruction? Can she describe clearly and specifically how her program is organized? Can she list the word recognition and comprehension skills she is trying to teach?
- Does the teacher know your child's instructional level? Can she tell you not only what book he is in, but exactly what skills he is working on?
- Does the teacher provide time for reading instruction each day? Is there time for both reading for pleasure and working on skills?
- Does the teacher frequently read aloud to the children, to share her enthusiasm and to motivate the children to read?
- Are books, magazines, and other reading materials abundantly available in the classrooms?
- Do the children make frequent use of the school and/or community library?
- Does your child like to read at home?

- Does your child score at least on grade level on standardized reading tests?

HOW TO HELP YOUR CHILD AT HOME

Most parents should not try to teach their children to read. Teaching reading requires special skill and knowledge, and even when a parent is a trained reading teacher, he or she may do more harm than good by creating tension with the child or by conflicting with the teacher's methods. However, there are things that you can do at home in order to create an atmosphere that will encourage your child to read.

Do's

- Praise and encourage your child's successful efforts to read.
- Continue to read to your child, every day if possible, but frequently no matter what. Don't think that your child is too old to be read to now that he can read by himself—most children this age still love the time they spend with their parents this way.
- Encourage your child to read to you when he feels comfortable doing so.
- When your child is reading to you, pronounce for him the words he cannot pronounce himself. Let your reading together be fun—don't make it into a test.
- Buy your child books as presents. Make them special.
- Visit the library with your child and help him choose books that he may like.
- Limit the amount of television your child is allowed to watch. Research has shown that viewing television for about ten

hours per week may actually aid reading achievement. Beyond this amount, achievement tends to decline.

- Make constructive use of the television your child does watch. Be selective about the programs he sees; talk with him about the content of the programs; find reading material related to matters that interest him on television.
- Talk often with your child to help him enlarge his vocabulary and to use language to think and to express himself.
- Confer periodically with your child's teacher to learn about his progress at school.

Don'ts

- Don't pressure your child into reading if he seems reluctant or uncomfortable.
- Don't make your child demonstrate what he is learning. For example, don't ask him to sound out words with which he is having trouble. Again, reading with you should be a pleasure, not a test.

THE SIGNS OF PROGRESS

No single test can measure accurately your child's annual progress in reading, and surely no single set of questions can do so. However, the following subtest, taken from the Scott Foresman Company's grade 3 reader *Step Right Up!* may give you some idea of the kind of passage your child should be able to read and the kinds of questions he should be able to answer by the end of the third grade.

Subtest 4
Read the story and answer the questions.

At nine o'clock Saturday morning, Bob and Al decided to ride to the park. Before they left, Al put a new horn on his bike. As Al was doing that, Bob rode to the store. He got some peanuts to feed the squirrels. At ten o'clock they rode off. Fifteen minutes later, a pedal came off Bob's bike.

11. When did Al put on the horn?

a. before Bob went to the store
b. while Bob went to the store
c. after Bob came back

12. How long did it take the boys to get ready?

a. one hour   b. two hours   c. fifteen minutes

13. When did they start to the park?

a. at nine o'clock
b. at ten o'clock
c. at fifteen minutes after ten

14. Which happened last?

a. Bob got some peanuts.
b. A pedal came off Bob's bike.
c. Al put a horn on his bike.

Literature in the
Third Grade

James James
Morrison Morrison
Weatherby George Dupree
Took great
Care of his Mother
Though he was only three. . . .

*   *   *

The friendly cow all red and white,
  I love with all my heart:
She gives me cream with all her might,
  To eat with apple-tart. . . .

And blown by all the winds that pass
  And wet with all the showers,
She walks among the meadow grass
  And eats the meadow flowers.

The rhymes and poems of childhood resonate in memory, recalling happy times, tuning the pitch of the language, and, like the smooth, round stone saved from the ocean's edge so many years ago, holding truth constant throughout the changes of time and season. Like Stevenson's cow, the authors feel "blown by all the winds that pass" and "wet with all the showers," but what in part sustains them is the power of language to shape sensibility and to forge human connections across space and time.

Your child is heir to a rich tradition. The English language is a remarkably subtle instrument for the expression of thought and feeling, and the literature of our language is a living treasury of human experience. Much of your child's education should be devoted to exploring this tradition.

In the third grade, when most children are still learning to read, much of the initiative still comes from the teacher. Good teachers spend much time reading aloud to their children (for a certain portion of each day in some classes), finding appealing books of appropriate difficulty for children to read, talking about stories and poems, and sharing their pleasure and enthusiasm with the class.

There is no end to the variety and number of things to be read. Children should read or listen to folktales, fairy tales, fables, myths, legends. They should explore stories of all kinds—adventure stories, fantasy stories, realistic stories, animal stories, stories about science, stories about the past, stories about other people in other lands, stories and biographies about famous men and women. They should read and hear poetry of all kinds—story poems, nonsense poems, nursery rhymes, song lyrics, poems about nature and animals and space travel and people and children like themselves.

Some of this literature should be old—the children's classics of our tradition. Children should not grow up in our society without experiencing the great works that have entertained and instructed generations, works like those of the Brothers Grimm and Hans Christian Andersen, the stories and poems of A. A. Milne, contemporary classics by Dr. Seuss and Ludwig Bemelmans. But some of the literature should be new, with a more contemporary ring and feel. Most third-grade children enjoy such works as *Where the Wild Things Are* by Maurice Sendak,

Crow Boy by Taro Yashima, *Stone Soup* by Marcia Brown, and *Annie and the Old One* by Miska Miles.

Good teachers employ many techniques to introduce their children to such literature and to motivate them to read it. They read aloud to the class, making the story hour a warm and special time. They bring new books to the class, show them to the children, talk about them. They create displays of books and book jackets on counters, bulletin boards, doorframes. They arrange *reading corners* in their classrooms—snug nooks with a rug for lying on, a special lamp, and dozens of new books, waiting to be tried. They distribute book lists to children and parents. They call attention to films and movies based on books and make the books available to their classes. They organize book clubs. They take their children to the library often, and they bring books from the library into class. They make every effort to create an environment in which reading is made fun and important and easy to do.

Obviously, when children read literary works and discuss them with their teachers or classmates, they are improving their reading skills. Indeed, we have seen that in some reading programs, such works constitute the bulk of the reading that children do. In an individualized reading program, for example, trade books are the vehicle for teaching fundamental skills. In any program, however, good teachers never forget that the basic reason for reading literature is to enjoy it. Whatever other benefits may be derived—reading skill, human understanding, enlarged vocabulary, ability to write—they are secondary to the sheer pleasure that comes from reading a well-written piece that has something to say.

The literature program is one part of the school curriculum in which parents *can* play an important role. Because the purpose at this level is not so much to teach children about literature as to immerse them in it, parents can be very helpful simply by encouraging children to read, finding books for them to read, and reading to them at home. Establish your own story hour—even once or twice a week, if you are busy—and make it special and important. Balance the familiar works that your child wants to hear again and again with works that are new to him (and you). Talk with your child about what you have read. And, since in the end it is your behavior and not the teacher's that your child is more likely to emulate, spend time reading for enjoyment yourself.

Writing in the Third Grade

Writing is central to much of the language arts curriculum in the third grade and becomes more important as children go through the middle grades. Children do some content writing (simple reports) in the third grade, in addition to their personal writing.

In past years, writing was often assigned and corrected by the teacher, with little teaching going on between the assignment and correction. Some elementary school teachers still teach writing this way. Recently, in many school districts, teachers have adopted a process approach, working closely with the children from the beginning of their writing—when they choose a topic—and on through the drafting, conferencing, revising, editing, and publishing stages.

THE WRITING PROCESS

Writing cannot and must not be disassociated from other expressions of language—speaking, thinking, and reading. It is a process that must begin with thinking.

Before pencil is put to paper, the writer thinks about ideas and often discusses them with others. Some scholars of the writing process call this thinking or talking step *rehearsal,* or *pre-writing;* others call it *brainstorming.* Although no actual writing, except possibly a list-making of topics, takes place during this part of the process, this is a vital part of the writing process.

After the writer has chosen and narrowed down a topic, he makes a rough first attempt. This step is usually called *drafting.* Content is primary during this part of the process. Little attention is paid to handwriting, spelling, and punctuation. This is the composing step. The writer calls his product a *rough draft.*

At this point, some writers continue to work alone. Others look to a friendly audience for help. The audience may be an editor, a friend, or a relative. This step is sometimes called *conferencing* or *critiquing.* A helpful audience listens carefully and asks good questions. An audience needs to learn to ask good questions, to be supportive but critical in a helpful way.

After the writer has listened to his audience's questions and comments, he has a new perspective on his writing. He evaluates the comments, reflects on them, and *revises* his work. When he is sure that his work says what he wishes it to say, he adds the final touches by *editing.* He checks his spelling and punctuation, recopies the work, and types it or asks someone else to type it.

For the most part, writers follow this process. Since writing is very personal, there is clearly variation in method. However, there is enough general agreement about the broad steps of the writing process to help teachers teach writing better.

THE THIRD-GRADE WRITER

The third-grade writer is aware that he is growing up and is more self-conscious about his writing than he was the year before. Some of the freedom of expression of the primary grades wanes as children become more concerned with truth, detail, and correctness. As a response to this growing awareness of audience, the good teacher provides a supportive environment that encourages risk taking in writing.

Third-grade writers have difficulty limiting their topics. They tend to choose broad topics, like a vacation, and tell the story from packing the suitcase the day before vacation to unpacking the suitcase the day after. With interested and focused questions, the teacher can help children select one small event from the vacation to write about. "What was the thing you had the most fun doing? Did you meet any new, interesting people? Did you have a particularly adventurous day? Was there a day when everything went wrong?" might be some questions the teacher may ask to help the child set some limits for his piece.

This selection or focusing process is best done during the *rehearsing,* or "talking about it" step. Once material is written down, it's more difficult for a child not to use it.

Sometimes selecting a topic is the hardest part of the writing process. "I have nothing to write about" is an often heard refrain.

It is important for children to understand that their personal experiences have value. Personal experience is where a child should begin his writing. Since he is an expert on his own experiences, he is able to write with authority about them.

Children can be taught to help one another when they have to choose a writing topic. In one classroom one third grader said to another who was having a problem selecting a topic, "Do you have a brother? Did anything scary ever happen to him?" Her classmate responded with a story about her brother walking into a door and having to go to the emergency room. After the conversation, the questioning classmate said, "I think you should write about that."

Most third graders write their narratives chronologically, giving equal time to all events. Staying very close to the truth or what really happened is important to them. Therefore, their writing is rambling and overloaded with facts and details.

Third-grade revision tends to be limited to changing words or correcting usage. Once written, it's hard for the third grader to see his writing re-created in a new form. If encouraged by his peers or teachers, he is sometimes willing to experiment with new leads and endings.

Conferencing with other children and/or the teacher allows children to think critically about their classmates' writing, as well as to listen to suggestions about their own.

Many third-grade classrooms have bulletin boards devoted to writing. One third-grade bulletin board displayed children's stories with the following titles, revealing important events and people in the children's lives:

> *My Pesty Brother*
> *My Camping Trip*
> *A Pet*
> *My Helpful Sister*
> *A Terrible Day*
> *A Sleepless Night*
> *I Lost My Tooth*
> *A Rainy Day*
> *At the Hospital*
> *A Scary Experience*
> *A Day with My Grandparents*
> *When I Moved*
> *Burglars*
> *A Nightmare*

Teachers adapt their method of teaching writing to their own particular style. Some teachers encourage children to keep daily journals as a source for topics. One third-grade writing bulletin board had these suggestions about journal writing:

Some Ideas for Journal Writing

Things that happened
Thoughts, feelings, ideas
A place I like to go
When I was little
A time I was really proud
If I had three wishes
Things I like to do
Things I don't like to do
What makes me feel happy

Dramatic expression is a teaching technique used by some teachers to help children make their writing lively. At the beginning of a writing lesson, one third-grade teacher wrote on the bulletin board: "The teacher is angry." Then she walked out of the room and closed the door. She reentered, slammed the door, threw her books on the desk, and stood in front of the class with her arms folded. She asked the class to read the sentence on the blackboard and then asked, "What did you notice about what the teacher just did?"

As they dictated, she wrote on the blackboard:

The teacher walked very fast.
She threw her books on the desk.

She asked, "If you couldn't see me throw the books on the desk, would you have heard anything? Give me a sentence about the sound."

"There was a big slam," said one child.

"What was my face doing?" asked the teacher. "Give me a sentence that tells me."

"The teacher frowned," said a boy in back.

The class talked about the difference between the sentence "The teacher is angry" and the sentences that illustrated that the teacher was angry. The children saw that the sentences that *showed* the teacher was angry were more powerful than the sentence that simply *told* that the teacher was angry. Teachers will often discriminate between writing that tells and writing that shows. The teacher and the children talked about words that showed anger, like *marched, flung,* and *slammed*. Finally, the teacher read passages that illustrated good writing about anger from Beverly Cleary's *Ramona the Brave* and Judy Blume's *Tales of a Fourth Grade Nothing*.

The following day the teacher reminded the class of the "angry lesson" and asked the students to talk about a time each of them had felt angry. After some discussion, the children were given time to draft a piece either about a time they felt angry or about any other personal experience.

WORD PROCESSING

By the time children reach third grade, many are familiar with computers. Some children have computers at home, and many elementary schools have them in classrooms or computer rooms. Third grade is not too early for children to begin to draft their writing on a computer. Simple word-processing programs like *Bank Street Writer* can be particularly helpful to a child who has bad handwriting or whose coordination makes writing a problem. (Without the aid of good keyboarding skills, one of the authors has been drafting her personal essays, first on a typewriter—and now on a word processor—since college. If a word processor had been available to that author in the elementary years, life would have been much simpler for her.)

Once a piece of writing is on the computer, the child is free to insert and delete information. There is no recopying. Spelling errors can be eliminated because most word-processing programs have a spell-check that identifies misspelled words and typographical errors.

SPELLING AND HANDWRITING IN THE THIRD GRADE

Most third-grade teachers use a commercial spelling program. Good teachers enrich the list with words selected from current events, everyday class activities, and other areas of the curriculum. Spelling activities usually follow a weekly routine with pretesting, discussion of words, use of words in sentences, study, and testing. Often, spelling activities are assigned as homework. Teachers may make personal spelling lists from misspelled words from their own writing.

Many children are first introduced to cursive writing in the third grade; as a result, often children's minds may be focused on the mechanical component of handwriting rather than on the composing aspect. Some children adapt to cursive writing quickly and have a lovely hand the rest of their lives. Others find it difficult and a terrible chore. Fortunately, typewriters and word processors exist for those who will always find writing by hand an onerous task.

If you notice that your child is having particular difficulty with his handwriting and/or spelling, speak to the teacher and see what you can do to help. He may be showing signs of learning disabilities. The chapter "The Child With Learning Problems" in the last part of the book may be helpful to you should the problem be severe.

A GOOD WRITING PROGRAM

A good writing program is one that

- Values children's experience and their perception of it.
- Helps children to be good observers, to listen to sounds and conversation, to notice smells, to see detail.

- Helps children translate details they observe into spoken and written words.
- Helps children to focus on important details and not to merely catalog all detail.
- Provides time for the entire writing process—and time for children to listen to and read their classmates' writing. Some classrooms have libraries of "books" by classroom authors. Some schools have parent volunteer programs with parents editing and typing books by children.
- Teaches children how to be good editors, to ask the right questions, to be specific, to be positive and encouraging yet helpful, to be committed to helping others create a better place.
- Recognizes the difference between handwriting and writing, helping children whose handwriting is an overwhelming task by allowing them occasionally to dictate stories or use a word processor.
- Values literature, encourages children to read, and provides time for reading aloud to them.
- Recognizes that writing, like speaking, is a trial-and-error skill and needs encouragement and nurturing.
- Displays children's writing prominently and attractively.
- Stresses the specifics of what is good about some writing samples.
- Shows interest in every child's writing.
- Uses illustration of particular techniques from literature.

What I Would like to Be
by Jessica Kronstadt

I would like to be an author. I really think I well enjoy writing.

I like to write what I feel. Also the characters can do anything I want them to. It would be nice to finally let my imagination run away with me.

I am glad we have freedom to the press. I am glad because I plan to write depressing stories. I already am about to blow up whith my ideas. I even have started to write a movie.

I would be able to also have another job. I really would like to be an author more than anything

Mathematics in the Third Grade

The ancient Egyptian farmer driving stakes into the ground to reclaim his land in the springtime mud of the Nile delta, the mission control officer tracking the spaceship's orbit through space, the young child counting her change to see if she has enough money for an ice cream cone—all of these people are using mathematics to understand and control the world around them. No area of mental activity better displays the power of the human mind. With mathematics, we can quantify experience, relate space to number, understand and express relationships of matter, energy, space, and time. Without mathematics, we would have no commerce, no engineering, no architecture, no computer technology, no science as we know it. Mathematics clearly deserves its fundamental place in the school curriculum.

Much of your child's success in school and in his working life will depend upon his ability to use mathematics effectively. Fortunately, most children can master the mathematics taught in the intermediate grades of our elementary schools and thereby acquire a level of mastery beyond that of most of the population not so many generations ago. Most schools will do a good job of teaching your child the math he needs at this level. But if your child begins to experience problems, it is your job to step in and talk to the school about it. Don't let your child—boy or girl—develop a math phobia. Attitudes set now may well last a lifetime. This book will help you know what to look for and what to do if action becomes necessary.

By the time your child enters the third grade, he should already have a solid foundation in mathematical thinking and ability. He should be able to count, read, and write the cardinal numbers from 1 to 1,000 and to relate these numbers to material objects and sets of objects. He should understand the meaning of each digit in three-digit numbers (hundreds, tens, ones) and the meaning of zero in the place-value system. He should know addition and subtraction facts through 18 and be able to add and subtract two-digit numbers requiring regrouping (also called *borrowing* or *carrying*). He should be able to solve simple word problems, to make simple estimates to see if his answers make sense, and to create simple charts and graphs to record measurements and other data. Above all, he should have developed a positive feeling about his ability to use his mind mathematically—to think, reason, and solve problems involving quantities and mathematical relationships.

Most third-grade teachers spend some time at the beginning of the year reviewing second-grade material. Unless such review is unusually prolonged, do not regard it as a waste of time. Children tend to become rusty at skills they have not practiced during the summer, and a period of sharpening up may be in order. Furthermore, some mathematical skills require extensive practice time before they become automatic, and thus the repetition involved in review may be useful. Also, your child's teacher may want to find out who in the class knows what before she introduces new material.

If your child's foundation in mathematics is shaky as he enters the third grade or if you have just moved to a new school district and are unfamiliar with the curriculum, a conference with your child's teacher may be useful. Find out exactly what the curriculum in your child's school calls for and ask the teacher how you and she can work together to help your child achieve success. Given proper attention, at this level a child can still regain without great difficulty whatever ground he may have lost. But gaps not filled now may become a severe problem two or three years hence.

THINKING IS THE BASIC SKILL

The teaching of mathematics in our elementary schools has changed markedly within the lifetime of today's young parents. In the 1940s and the 1950s, the schools emphasized the basic facts and operations of arithmetic—addition, subtraction, multiplication, and division. Most of the teaching was done by drill and practice, and most of the learning was by rote. It did not seem to matter whether a child understood what 9×7 *meant*, provided his response (63) was quick and accurate. The premise was that the child should learn his number facts first, so that he could apply them to real or hypothetical problems later.

Unfortunately, mathematical applications were not always made, or made successfully. When Sputnik was launched in 1957, many felt that the nation's children were not as well grounded in mathematics as society needed them to be. Educators realized that the old curriculum was outdated. With the new math they created a curriculum that included other forms of mathematics, such as geometry, statistics, probability, functions, and graphing, and that emphasized thinking and understanding rather than learning by rote. In these respects, the new math, which dominated the curriculum throughout the 1960s, was a valuable advance in education.

Unfortunately, the new approach proved to be excessively formalistic and preoccupied with the precise use of abstract language that often made little sense to children. For example, belaboring the distinction between a *number* and a *numeral* was a confusing waste of time for many children. Inevitably, there was a reaction against such excesses. During the 1970s, as test scores declined and the mood of the country changed, the back-to-basics movement demanded a return to an emphasis on computation and to a teaching style characterized by drill and practice.

Today, in the late 1980s, good schools and good teachers have learned to follow a sensible middle course. They know that a mathematics curriculum consisting solely of addition, subtraction, multiplication, and division is not enough. They also know that in an age of readily available calculators and computers, preoccupation with the skills of computation, to the neglect of other mathematical studies, is unwise. Children should still learn their number facts, but they should spend more time developing the ability to solve problems through the use of mathematics. As Stephen Willoughby has written for the Council for Basic Education in his monograph *Teaching Mathematics: What Is Basic?*,

> Computation was *never* basic to mathematics; and the wide availability of calculators and computers makes it less basic today than ever. The important, human parts of mathematics are the original abstraction of relevant features from a situation, the decision of what mathematics to apply to this material, and the interpretation of the results. . . . Thinking is the basic skill to be taught in school mathematics.

THE THIRD-GRADE MATHEMATICS CURRICULUM

Schools define mathematics curricula in various ways. In some cases, a textbook or series of textbooks is adopted for use in a given school, community, or state, and the teacher is required to follow the text or series as the basis of the curriculum. (The typical children's textbook contains brief explanations of new material, practice exercises, word problems, and tests; it is simply written, lavishly illustrated, relatively expensive, and intended for use by several children over a period of years. The accompanying teacher's manual contains suggestions for teaching the lessons, answers to test questions, and optional enrichment activities.) In other cases, a course of study, or *scope and sequence,* is outlined by the school system or the state, and the teacher is free to choose from a variety of books and other instructional materials. Whatever their origin, third-grade mathematics curricula are much more similar to one another throughout the United States than they are different.

Typically, the third-grade mathematics curriculum comprises five parts, or *strands:*

> Numbers and numeration
> Operations with whole numbers
> Operations with fractions
> Probability and statistics
> Geometry and measurement

Some curricula include a sixth part—problem solving. In the authors' view, however, problem solving is the goal of all mathematics and should be incorporated into the teaching and learning of each part of the curriculum.

The five main parts of the mathematics curriculum are taught throughout the elementary grades. Skills and topics are often repeated from grade to grade: Material may be introduced at one grade level, taught and practiced extensively at the next, and reviewed and "mastered" at the third. Such overlapping is not inefficient; it is a deliberate teaching strategy to ensure that the child gain a solid foundation in the subject. For this reason, you may wish to look at the chapter on Mathematics in the Fourth Grade in this book and the one on Mathematics in the Second Grade in *Your Child in School: Kindergarten Through Second Grade.*

In the third grade, the skills and knowledge on which children typically concentrate are discussed below.

Numbers and Numeration

- Counting—cardinal numbers: Learn to use cardinal numbers 1–10,000. Count forward and backward by all numbers from 1 through 10 on a number line.
- Counting—ordinal numbers: Learn to use ordinal numbers through 500th (or beyond).
- Numerals: Read and write numerals from 0 to 10,000. Recognize money notation to $10,000. Understand the meaning of the places to the right of the decimal point in money notation: *Example* $4.25 = 4 dollars and 25 cents. Read and write notation for fractions, including mixed numbers. Read and write Roman numerals from I to XII (1 to 12).
- Place value: Understand the concept of place value and know the meaning of each digit in five-digit numbers: *Example* 12,325 = 1 ten thousand, 2 thousands, 3 hundreds, 2 tens, and 5 ones.
- Even, odd: Consider the sum, difference, or product of whole numbers as even or odd.
- Estimation: Estimate quantities, length, width, height, distance, duration, and so forth. Round numbers to the nearest 10.
- Positive and negative: Understand the meaning of positive and negative numbers in familiar situations—numbers such as temperatures above and below zero and balanced and overdrawn bank accounts.

Operations with Whole Numbers

- Addition and subtraction: Learn addition and subtraction facts through 24. Add and subtract four-digit numbers, with or without regrouping (carrying or borrowing):

Examples

	4985	6384
	+5720	−2917
	10705	3467

Use addition and subtraction as inverse operations to check accuracy:

Examples

	5421	4698
	−723	+723
	4698	5421

Use rounding to estimate sums and differences. Solve inequalities in number sentences using addition and subtraction: *Example* From the set (1, 2, 3, 4, 5, 6, 7, 8, 9), choose the greatest number that will make the inequality $3 + \square < 8$ a true statement. Learn that the sum of any number added to *zero* is the number:

Examples $9 + 0 = 9$
$\square + 0 = \square$

• Multiplication and division: Use arrays and number lines to understand multiplication as repeated addition:

Example □□□□□
□□□□□ $5 \times 3 = 15$
□□□□□

Learn commutative property of multiplication:

Examples $9 \times 3 = 27$
$3 \times 9 = 27$

Learn multiplication facts through 10×10: Use arrays and number lines to understand division as repeated subtraction and as a process for finding the number of equivalent subsets of a given set:

Example  $15 \div 3 = 5$

Understand division as the inverse operation of multiplication:

Examples $\quad 32 \times 6 = 192$
$192 \div 6 = \;\; 32$

Learn division facts through $100 \div 10$. Understand that multiplication has the commutative property and that division does not:

Examples $\quad 12 \times 6 = 6 \times 12 \quad$ YES
$12 \div 6 = 6 \div 12 \quad$ NO

Learn to multiply two-digit and three-digit numbers by a one-digit number, with or without regrouping. Learn intermediate algorithms (procedures) first, then standard algorithms:

Examples $\quad$ INTERMEDIATE ALGORITHM

$$
\begin{array}{r}
723 \\
\times 7 \\
\hline
21 \\
140 \\
4900 \\
\hline
5061
\end{array}
$$

STANDARD ALGORITHM

$$
\begin{array}{r}
723 \\
\times 7 \\
\hline
5061
\end{array}
$$

Learn that the product of any number multiplied by 1 or the quotient of any number divided by 1 is the number:

$$\text{Examples} \quad 6 \times 1 = 6$$
$$\square \times 1 = \square$$
$$6 \div 1 = 6$$
$$\square \div 1 = \square$$

Learn that the product of any number multiplied by *zero* or the quotient of any number divided by *zero* is *zero:*

$$\text{Examples} \quad 5 \times 0 = 0$$
$$\square \times 0 = 0$$
$$5 \div 0 = 0$$
$$\square \div 0 = 0$$

Learn common division terminology and symbols:

Examples $4\overline{)24}$ $24 \div 4 = \square$ $\frac{24}{4} = \square$
"What does 24 divided by 4 equal?"
"How many times does 4 go into 24?"

Learn to divide two- and three-digit numbers by a one-digit number, with or without regrouping. Learn intermediate algorithms (procedures) first, then standard algorithms:

Examples   INTERMEDIATE ALGORITHMS

```
      6
     70              76
   6)456           6)456
    420              42
    ----            ----
     36              36
     36              36
    ----            ----
      0
```

STANDARD ALGORITHM

$$\begin{array}{r} 76 \\ 6\overline{)456} \end{array}$$

Solve inequalities in number sentences using multiplication and division:

Example   Identify five whole numbers that can be put into the frame in the inequality $\square \times 50 < 260$.

Word problems: Use addition, subtraction, multiplication, and division to solve word problems:

Example   Sally has twelve chickens. Each chicken laid four eggs. How many eggs were laid?

Operations with Fractions

- Practical uses: Identify the use of fractions in daily life: a half-hour TV program, an eighth note in music, a quarter pound of butter.
- Equal parts of a whole: Divide whole objects into equal parts and relate part to whole ($\frac{1}{2}\frac{1}{3}\frac{1}{4}\frac{1}{5}\frac{1}{6}\frac{1}{7}\frac{1}{8} \cdots \frac{1}{100}$).
- Equal parts of a set: Divide sets of objects into equal parts and relate parts to whole ($\frac{1}{2}\frac{1}{3}\frac{1}{4}\frac{1}{5}\frac{1}{6}\frac{1}{7}\frac{1}{8} \cdots \frac{1}{100}$).
- Notation: Understand the meaning of such fractions as $\frac{2}{3}$ and $\frac{3}{4}$, for both wholes and collections of things. Learn the terms *numerator* and *denominator*.
- Order, inequality: Compare and order halves, thirds, fourths, fifths, sixths, etc., using terms such as *greater than*, *less than*, and *between*.
- Relationship to division: Understand the relationship between fractions and division:

Example $9 \div 4$ may be written $\frac{9}{4}$

$$\frac{9}{4} = \frac{8}{4} + \frac{1}{4} = 2 + \frac{1}{4} = 2\frac{1}{4}$$
$$9 \div 4 = 2\frac{1}{4}$$

$\overbrace{\begin{pmatrix} X\ X \\ X\ X \end{pmatrix}}$ $\begin{pmatrix} X\ X \\ X\ X \end{pmatrix}$ X

- Addition and subtraction: Add and subtract fractions with like denominators.
- Measurement: Take measurements to nearest tenth of a meter and nearest eighth of an inch. Read halves, fourths, and eighths on a twelve-inch ruler and tenths of centimeters on a meter stick.
- Decimals: Add and subtract decimal fractions to tenths.

Probability and Statistics

- Data gathering and graphing: Collect, organize, and record information using two or more categories at a time. Arrange data in tables and graphs.
- Tallying: Tally the information obtained by data gathering and graphing. Compare the amounts in each category in terms of equality and inequality.
- Arrangements: Find orderly ways to count the number of possible arrangements within a set.

Examples   (1) Arrange three colored chips in a line in as many different ways as possible (R = red, W = white, B = black):

RWB   RBW   BRW   BWR   WBR   WRB

(2) How many different outcomes are possible if a coin is tossed three times? (*Answer:* 8)

• Predicting outcomes: Predict (estimate) outcomes of events:

Example   A laundry bag contains eight black socks and two white socks. If Carol picks one sock without looking, what are her chances of picking a white sock?

Geometry and Measurement

• Estimating: Continue concrete activities involving comparisons of size, distance, weight, capacity, temperature, and time. Make estimating an integral part of all measurement activity.
• Equivalence: Identify equivalent measures within a system of measurement.

> *Examples*   2 m = 200 cm
> 3 kg = 3000 g
> 5 L = 50 DL
> 1 yd = 36 in
> $6.00 = 600 cents

• Plane shapes: Construct two-dimensional geometric shapes (circles, quadrilaterals, pentagons) and explore their properties. Find lines of symmetry in plane figures. Discover figures with more than one line of symmetry:

Examples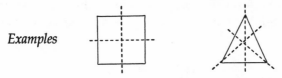

• Solids: Construct three-dimensional shapes (spheres, cubes, pyramids) and explore their properties.
Example   How many edges, faces, and vertices are there on a cereal box?

• Coordinates: Locate positions on a grid using coordinates: *Example*   Locate point (4, 3) on a grid. Place an X four steps to the right of zero and three steps up:

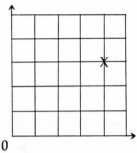

0

Problem Solving

The goal of the mathematics curriculum is to enable children to use mathematical thinking to solve real problems. Problem solving is not an enrichment activity to be scheduled if there is time at the end of a unit of instruction; it is of the essence. Children should be trying to pose and solve problems even as they are practicing skills they have not yet fully mastered. Good teachers continually challenge children to think—to use what they are learning to solve problems. They also teach the skills of problem solving straightforwardly and directly.

A *problem*, as the word is used here, should be distinguished from an *exercise*. An exercise is a task that the child already knows how to perform. For example, the teacher may assign exercises in multiplication in order to provide practice in computation. Exercises like

$$\begin{array}{ccc} 22 & 431 & 312 \\ \times 8 & \times 27 & \times 84 \end{array}$$

serve this useful function. They require the child to practice computational skills, but they do not require him to think. In a true problem situation, the child has to determine what information is relevant, what mathematical logic to use, and what operation to perform, and he must have some way of assessing the reasonableness of his answer and checking its accuracy.

Most problem-solving methods involve four steps:

1. *Understanding the problem.* The child should repeat the problem in his own words, identify the key questions, and select and, if necessary, write down the relevant facts. He should estimate a reasonable answer before trying to find the exact answer.
2. *Making a plan.* Different problems require different plans. The child should draw upon his skills and knowledge to devise a plan that may work. He may sort and classify, make tables or graphs and look for patterns and relationships, use diagrams or models to visualize the problems, and manipulate objects. He may need to use measurement or computational skills. The trick is to make use of what he knows and not to jump to an easy answer or to give up because the problem seems hard.
3. *Carrying out the plan.* Once the plan is made, it must be carried out. Often this is the step that requires measurement or written computations.
4. *Checking the answer.* Children should acquire the habit of first checking the *reasonableness* of the answer. (If the problem is to determine how many shoes there are in the classroom if the room contains 25 children and 1 teacher, 26 (25 + 1) is not a reasonable answer.) Then they should check the *accuracy* of their answer.

Many good teachers teach about this four-step problem-solving method with their children and give them practice in following it.

TEACHING THE THIRD-GRADE MATHEMATICS CURRICULUM

Teaching mathematics to an individual child is one thing; teaching the subject to a group of twenty to thirty or more children at once is another. Teachers must not only know the material well and be able to explain it clearly, they must be skillful in organizing the class and in planning the use of time and instructional materials so that each child is actively engaged in learning.

Most elementary schools schedule time each day for the study of math. The lessons are often taught in the morning, when the children are the most alert. Most commonly, the third-grade teacher works with the class as a whole. The lesson may begin with a review of what the class did the previous day, or the teacher may help the class go over a seatwork or homework assignment from the day before. Then the teacher will introduce the new knowledge or skill for the day, often using individual children and manipulative materials (blocks, counters, chips, buttons, and rods), as well as the blackboard, to illustrate and explain. The bulk of the lesson is spent in discussing this new concept or skill, with the teacher asking questions, helping the children make observations and see relationships, and providing encouragement and explanation where needed. Toward the end of the lesson, the teacher may assign some related exercises or other work to be done in class (*seatwork*) or at home (*homework*).

The advantages of working with the whole class are that it is easier to organize, that it requires less preparation time on the part of the teacher, and that it makes it easier for the teacher to keep track of what has been taught (and, presumably, learned). The major disadvantage, of course, is that since children vary in their levels of ability and rates of development, some children may already know the material being taught and be bored (perhaps no disaster in itself, but surely a waste of time), and some may be behind and not be able to follow the lesson.

Teachers cope with this problem in various ways. Many provide enrichment activities for the more mathematically able children, to be done in school or at home when they have finished the regular work. (At their best, these activities genuinely stretch children's minds—they are not just more of the same or a peek at the next day's lesson.) Teachers also work with small groups of less able children at other times of the day, going over the morning lesson, helping with the seatwork, or providing remedial instruction.

In some classes, teachers group children for mathematics instruction just as in the earlier grades children are grouped for reading instruction. For example, in a class of twenty-five children, there may be a group of eight doing more advanced work, a group of ten doing grade-level work, and a group of seven working at more basic material. The teacher will assign seatwork (or projects in another subject) to two groups while working individually with the third group.

In other classes, such grouping may not be permanent, but the teacher may occasionally form small groups for specific purposes. For example, a teacher whose review of children's seatwork assignments shows that six children need help in understanding the concept of place value may call these six together for special help while the rest of the class is busy with other assignments.

Teachers also work with individual children, of course. But few programs are so organized as to make individual instruction the main form of activity, and in most schools, the amount of time available for individual instruction is limited.

PRINCIPLES OF EFFECTIVE MATHEMATICS TEACHING

However their classes may be organized, effective mathematics teachers follow certain fundamental principles.

Children Must Develop Understanding as Well as Skill

The point of learning mathematics is to be able to solve problems requiring mathematical thought. Basic skills are required to solve problems, but if the child does not understand the problem, or cannot extract the relevant information from the problem situation, or cannot choose the right mathematical skill or principle to apply, then the basic skills alone will be of little use. For this reason, good teachers make sure that children understand the concepts underlying basic facts and skills.

Consider the child who knows his addition facts but makes this error:

$$\begin{array}{r} 23 \\ +4 \\ \hline 67 \end{array}$$

The child has obviously added $3 + 4$ and $2 + 4$ in order to arrive at the incorrect result. One could say that the child simply does not know the addition algorithm (procedure) well—that you only add the numbers in the right-hand column once. More to the point, any normal child who writes $23 + 4 = 67$ is simply not thinking. Few third-grade children would make such a mistake if they were looking at a number line such as this:

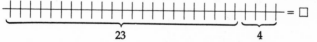

What the child who wrote

$$
\begin{array}{r}
23 \\
+4 \\
\hline
67
\end{array}
$$

lacks is an adequate understanding of the concept of place value in our base ten number system. Good teachers will have developed such an understanding by involving the child in many experiences with concrete objects involving counting and sorting the objects into groups of ten, then regrouping (borrowing or carrying) as made necessary by addition. (The reader may wish to refer to the lesson described in the chapter "Mathematics in the Second Grade" in the first book of our series *Your Child in School*.) In general, the concept is developed first, usually through actions performed on physical objects, then the notation associated with the concept (in this case, the vertical arrangement of the numerals, the "+" sign, the line ———— indicating addition), then the skill itself. Both understanding and skill are necessary, with understanding preceding skill.

Learning Proceeds From the Concrete to the Representational to the Abstract

In order to learn mathematical concepts thoroughly, children should experience the concept first in concrete physical form and then in representational or pictorial form before finally progressing to the use of abstract notation or doing mental arithmetic. Good teachers have children manipulate a wide variety of objects—blocks, chips, buttons, beans, Cuisenaire rods, balance beams—in order to have them observe firsthand the mathematical effect of their actions (thus the use of the jargon word *manipulatives* in school math programs). Consider the following example.

The class has been learning the multiplication table; today's lesson is on the multiplication fact 6 × 6. The class had already learned to multiply 1, 2, 3, 4, and 5 through 10 and had found 6 × 1, 6 × 2, 6 × 3, 6 × 4, and 6 × 5 easy to learn because "they already knew them." (What the children already knew is the commutative property of multiplication—$A \times B = B \times A$.) Now they were to learn 6 × 6. The teacher asks six children to come to the front of the room. She gives each child six pencils to hold. She then asks another child to come to the front of the room to count the pencils. The child does so and arrives at the figure 36. The teacher then asks the six children to put the pencils down and each to hold up six fingers and count off. The children count in turn, from 1 to 36. The teacher asks the class if there is an easier way to count the fingers.

A child says, "Count the sixes."

"Right," says the teacher. "Multiply the sixes." The teacher then asks a child to come to the blackboard and draw a .picture of 6 × 6. A child draws this figure:

111111   111111   111111   111111   111111   111111

"Good," says the teacher. "Now write a number sentence for us." The child writes, "6 × 6 = 36."

"Good," says the teacher again. She then asks the class, "What other numbers do we know when you multiply them by the same number?"

A child says, "5 × 5 = 25" . . . and the lesson continues.

This progression from the concrete to the representational to the abstract is standard in most good classrooms.

Skills and Knowledge Are First Introduced, Then Developed, Then Mastered

Most people regard the study of mathematics as sequential, with each successive step building on the one before it. In general, this view is accurate, as we shall see below. However, in a good mathematics program, skills and knowledge are not taught only once. Children are first introduced to a topic, then they are given extensive practice in developing it and applying it to problem situations, and finally they are expected to master it.

Most mathematics curriculum guides, or *scope and sequence* charts, reflect this approach. Topics like place value or multiplication by one-digit numbers are apt to appear in the guides for grades 2, 3, and 4. Good teachers do not assume that because something has been taught, it has been learned; nor do they assume that once something has been grasped, it will be retained, unless the child is given frequent practice in using the pertinent skill or knowledge.

Skills and Knowledge Are Taught Sequentially

Although repeated practice is usually necessary for true mastery, mathematics curricula still follow a logical progression from more simple to more complex skills and knowledge. In learning subtraction, for example, the child may follow a progression such as the following:

$$\begin{array}{r} 9 \\ -4 \\ \hline 5 \end{array}$$ Subtraction of single-digit numbers from single-digit numbers.

$$\begin{array}{r} 12 \\ -3 \\ \hline 9 \end{array}$$ Subtraction of single-digit numbers from double-digit numbers less than 12.

$$\begin{array}{r} 16 \\ -4 \\ \hline 12 \end{array}$$ Subtraction of single-digit numbers from double-digit numbers greater than 12, without regrouping (borrowing or carrying).

32	Subtraction of single-
−7	digit numbers from
25	double-digit numbers, with regrouping.

43	Subtraction of double-
−17	digit numbers from
26	double-digit numbers, with or without regrouping.

2543	Subtraction of up to
−316	four-digit numbers
2227	from up to four-digit numbers, with or without regrouping.

In good programs, such a progression is not pursued in isolation from other topics. Children do not first learn all there is to know about addition, then all there is to know about subtraction, then multiplication, then division. Rather, these operations are taught together as they reinforce and relate to one another. (Addition and subtraction are seen as inverse operations; division may be regarded as repeated subtraction; and so on.) But within each operation, the level of difficulty is carefully controlled until the child acquires mastery.

Skills and Knowledge Are Applied Constantly

In many mathematics programs (and in many mathematics textbooks), children are first taught a concept or skill, then given extensive practice in it, then led to apply it. The disadvantage of this approach is that when children reach the application stage—often the word problems at the end of the chapter—they may encounter difficulty because they have had no practice in the use of that skill or concept. (Also, the problems may be too artificial to hold their interest.)

Good teachers circumvent this potential problem by constantly having children use what they are learning in ways that seem natural and fun. They use classroom situations (the arithmetic involved in planning the class trip), classroom studies (the geometry involved in building a stockade for social studies), the news and weather (charts, graphs, and computations of temperature and rainfall), games, and puzzles—any activity that requires children to think and to apply what they are learning. For children so instructed, mathematics is not something to be learned for its own sake—its natural and inevitable use is problem solving.

The Teacher Helps Each Child Learn

Especially in the elementary school, the teacher's job is not simply to present material and the devil take the hindmost. The teacher's job—with appropriate help from the child, the parent, and the school's support staff—is to see that each child acquires the skills and knowledge considered important. Good teachers know what each child is learning and where each may be having difficulty, and they adapt their teaching accordingly and provide such help as may be needed.

In one small but telling example, we watched a teacher working with a child who had difficulty reading six-digit numbers. Quietly, she worked with the child while the rest of the class was busy. On the board she wrote the number 617,243. Then she covered the first three digits with her hand and asked the child to read the last three. "Two hundred forty-three," he said. Then she covered only the first two digits. "Seven thousand two hundred forty-three," he said. Then she covered only one digit, and at last none, until the child read, "Six hundred seventeen thousand two hundred forty-three."

"I knew you could do it!" said the teacher with a smile. The child beamed.

THE USE OF CALCULATORS

Inexpensive pocket calculators are in widespread use throughout our society. People use them at home, in the office, in stores—whenever an aid to quick and accurate computation is useful. Their presence in school raises important questions about the nature of instruction in mathematics.

Calculators enable children to solve accurately and quickly computational problems that might otherwise pose great difficulty. Some people therefore suggest that the schools should spend less time on drill and practice in computation and more time on problem solving, estimation, and the checking and interpretation of results. Others, however, voice concern that reliance on calculators will keep children from learning necessary lifelong computational skills. They urge schools to forbid their use until the basic skills have been mastered.

In the authors' view, the content and emphasis of the mathematics curriculum will change greatly in the age of calculators and computers—and no doubt the change will involve a shift away from some forms of computation (like multiplication or division of numbers with three or more digits) toward other mathematical pursuits (like problem solving and estimation). At present, however, since the math curriculum in most schools has not yet been changed by calculators, the authors suggest that children learn to use them as an aid to mastering fundamental computational skills.

Good teachers have children use calculators to

- Assist in learning number facts. The child enters a problem like 12 × 7. He gives the answer aloud, then presses the equals sign to obtain the correct answer and check his own response.
- Check accuracy. The child solves a problem or completes an exercise without using the calculator. He then repeats it on the calculator to check his own work.
- Serve as a motivating device to teach number facts. Many games requiring the child to use his knowledge of number facts may be played upon the calculator.

Children should also learn the limitations of the calculator. They should understand that its answers are only as accurate as the child's input. They should check the calculator for the reasonableness of its answers and not accept every response as correct. Perhaps the wrong number was entered or the number was entered in the wrong order or the wrong function key was pressed. Children should estimate the answer to a problem and use their common sense if a computer's response seems wide of the mark.

WHAT TO LOOK FOR IN A GOOD THIRD-GRADE MATHEMATICS PROGRAM

Like younger children, most third graders enjoy learning mathematics. If the program is one that stimulates their thinking without overtaxing their abilities, they respond readily to the challenge. If the answers to most or all of the following questions are yes, chances are your child is participating in an effective program. If many of the answers are no, you may want to inquire further by talking with your child's teacher and, possibly, the principal.

What to Look for in the Classroom

When you visit your child's classroom, do you see

- Number lines displayed on the walls or on the floor?
- Various graphs on various subjects, reflecting work that the teachers and the class have done?
- Chips, counters, Cuisenaire rods, and similar objects used for counting and sorting?
- Rulers, scales, thermometers, and other measuring devices?
- Pictures of two-dimensional shapes and three-dimensional objects used for exploring geometric properties?
- Worksheets showing good work done by children?

What to Look for From the Teacher

Does your child's third-grade teacher

- Describe clearly what the class has been doing in mathematics and what she plans for it to do?
- Provide time each day, or at least most days, for mathematical activity?
- Provide a program that follows the principles of effective mathematics teaching described above?
- Know your child's individual abilities and feelings about mathematics?
- Show enthusiasm about teaching mathematics?

What to Look for From Your Child

When you talk to your child during the third-grade year, does he

- Seem interested in using his mind for numbers, quantities, and mathematical relationships?

- Show a sense of excitement and confidence in using his mind for math?
- Describe math activities he has done in class?
- Bring home papers or worksheets reflecting work that he has done?
- Seem able to do the kind of work listed in the section "The Signs of Progress" (p. 103).

HOW TO HELP YOUR CHILD AT HOME

By the time your child is in third grade, he is no longer at the beginning of his formal study of mathematics. He has already spent two or three years in a planned program, with its own terminology, procedures, and expectations. For this reason, unless you are sure of your ground, you should be wary about confusing your child by trying to teach him yourself. However, after consulting with the teacher, there are things you can do at home to reinforce what your child is learning at school.

Do's

- Talk to your child's teacher to find out about your child's math program and to ask what you can do at home.
- Praise and encourage your child's efforts to use mathematics—to count, to estimate, to measure, to use numbers.
- Continue to estimate and measure with your child—estimate the contents of the cereal box, the ketchup bottle. If you build a tree house with him, have him help you draw up the plans, measure the boards, and determine how much lumber you will need.
- Get your child to use mathematics in everyday situations. Have him figure out the bill (and perhaps the tip) at the

restaurant; have him calculate how much farther you have to drive on your trip and how many more gallons of gasoline you are likely to need.

- Play math games with your child. Games can be fun, and they sharpen the child's ability to think quantitatively and spatially. Traditional card games, like go fish, old maid, and gin rummy, are fun and involve practice in matching numbers and simple computation. Checkers and chess require the perception of spatial patterns and the ability to think ahead. Many games that use dice are good for computational practice and for developing a feel for probability.
- Ask the teacher what kinds of mistakes your child makes in arithmetic. Find old workbooks that contain similar problems, and help your child with them. Do easy problems first, to build confidence.
- Help your child solve word problems (see the section "Problem Solving" earlier in this chapter). Be sure that your child understands the problem; have him state it in his own words. Be sure to estimate the answer beforehand and check it afterward.
- Help your child use a pocket calculator to assist in learning number facts and to check accuracy in computation.

Don'ts

- Don't be impatient. Your time with your child should be loving and supportive, not tense and anxiety-provoking.
- Don't persist with an activity if your child becomes frustrated or inattentive.
- Don't confuse your child or shake his confidence by criticizing the teacher's methods. Talk to the teacher if necessary, but work together, not at odds.
- Don't say that you (or some people) are "no good at math."

Almost everyone can learn third-grade mathematics. Don't promote a defeatist attitude.
- Don't suggest that girls aren't as good in math as boys.

THE SIGNS OF PROGRESS

By the end of third grade, children who are making normal progress in mathematics should have mastered most of the curriculum described above. At minimum, your child should be able to do the following:

Numbers and Numeration

- Count, read, and write the cardinal numbers from 1 to 10,000. Count forward and backward by all numbers from 1 through 10 on a number line.
- Read and write notations for fractions, including mixed numbers ($1\frac{1}{4}$, $16\frac{7}{8}$).
- Read and write money notations, including the decimal point ($3,145.72).
- Understand the meaning of each digit in five-digit numbers (17,819).
- Understand the meaning of zero in the place-value system.
- Understand the meaning of positive and negative numbers in familiar situations (-6 degrees Fahrenheit).

Operations With Whole Numbers

- Master addition and subtraction facts through 24.
- Add and subtract four-digit numbers, with or without regrouping (carrying or borrowing):

$$\begin{array}{r} Example \quad 6384 \\ -2917 \\ \hline 3467 \end{array}$$

- Use addition and subtraction as inverse operations to check accuracy.
- Understand multiplication as repeated addition.
- Practice multiplication facts through 10 × 10.
- Understand division as the inverse operation of multiplication.
- Practice division facts through 100 ÷ 10.
- Multiply two- and three-digit numbers by a one-digit number, with or without regrouping:

$$\begin{array}{r} Example \quad 723 \\ \times 7 \\ \hline 5061 \end{array}$$

- Use arithmetic knowledge and skill to solve simple word problems: *Examples*   (1) Betty picked 12 peaches. John picked 7. They ate 6 peaches and saved the rest. How many peaches did they save? (2) A grocer emptied 28 oranges from one box and 20 from another box. He placed all of the oranges in 8 rows. How many oranges were in each row?

Operations With Fractions

- Divide whole object into equal parts and relate parts to whole $(\frac{1}{2} \frac{1}{3} \frac{1}{4} \frac{1}{5} \frac{1}{6} \frac{1}{8} \cdots \frac{1}{100})$.

- Divide set of objects into equal parts and relate parts to whole $(\frac{1}{2}\ \frac{1}{3}\ \frac{1}{4}\ \frac{1}{5}\ \frac{1}{6}\ \frac{1}{8}\ \cdots\ \frac{1}{100})$.
- Understand the relationship between fractions and division:

  Example $9 \div 4$ may be written $\frac{9}{4}$.
- Subtract fractions with like denominators:

  Example $\frac{6}{8} - \frac{3}{8} = \frac{3}{8}$.

Probability and Statistics

- Collect, organize, and record information using two or more categories at a time. Arrange data in tables and graphs.
- Tally the information obtained by data gathering and graphing. Compare the amounts in each category in terms of number, equality, and inequality.
- Predict (estimate) outcomes of events.

Geometry and Measurement

- Identify equivalent measures within a system of measurement:

  Examples   2 m = 200 cm

  1 yd = 36 in

- Recognize and draw familiar two-dimensional geometric shapes (circles, quadrilaterals, pentagons).
- Construct three-dimensional shapes (spheres, cubes, pyramids) and explore their properties.
- Locate positions on a grid using coordinates.
- Read both the Fahrenheit and Celsius thermometers.

Most children acquire these skills by the end of the third grade. By the middle of the third-grade year, if your child seems not to be making normal progress, you should talk with your child's teacher. Perhaps your child is simply developing more slowly than some; perhaps the class is behind where the teacher wishes it to be and will catch up soon; or perhaps your child has a learning problem that needs attention. Explore each of these possibilities with the teacher and obtain her views before jumping to your own conclusion.

Some children progress more rapidly than others. If your child shows unusual proficiency, you may wish to talk to the teacher to see what adjustments, if any, should be made in his program and to obtain suggestions about how you can enrich your child's experience at home.

Addition Table

+	0	1	2	3	4	5	6	7	8	9
0	0	1	2	3	4	5	6	7	8	9
1	1	2	3	4	5	6	7	8	9	10
2	2	3	4	5	6	7	8	9	10	11
3	3	4	5	6	7	8	9	10	11	12
4	4	5	6	7	8	9	10	11	12	13
5	5	6	7	8	9	10	11	12	13	14
6	6	7	8	9	10	11	12	13	14	15
7	7	8	9	10	11	12	13	14	15	16
8	8	9	10	11	12	13	14	15	16	17
9	9	10	11	12	13	14	15	16	17	18

NOTES

1. By the end of the third grade, your child should have mastered the basic addition facts contained in the addition table.

2. The facts should be learned through hands-on experience with real objects, not by rote. However, finding patterns in this table will help your child reinforce previously learned knowledge.

3. Once your child understands the commutative property of addition (that $2 + 4 = 4 + 2$), the number of facts to be learned is reduced from 100 to 55 (the 10 shaded facts on the diagonal and 45 facts to one side of the diagonal).

4. Once your child understands the inverse relationship of addition and subtraction (that $4 + 2 = 6$ and $6 - 2 = 4$), the table can also be used to check subtraction facts.

COMMON ERRORS IN ADDITION AND SUBTRACTION

The following are examples of errors commonly made by children in elementary school. If your child makes such mistakes, follow the suggestions provided after the examples.

Error		*Possible Explanation*
1.	$\begin{array}{r} 65 \\ +73 \\ \hline 158 \end{array}$	Does not know basic addition fact.
2.	$\begin{array}{r} 87 \\ -35 \\ \hline 62 \end{array}$	Does not know basic subtraction fact.

3.
$$\begin{array}{r} 43 \\ +8 \\ \hline \text{④1} \end{array}$$
Forgets to rename tens when regrouping.

4.
$$\begin{array}{r} 43 \\ +8 \\ \hline \text{4⑪} \end{array}$$
Does not understand the place-value system; writes down 11 instead of renaming 4.

5.
$$\begin{array}{r} 43 \\ +2 \\ \hline 65 \end{array}$$
Does not understand the place-value system; adds units to units and tens.

6.
$$\begin{array}{r} 16 \\ ②4 \\ 37 \\ +30 \\ \hline 87 \end{array}$$
Leaves out a number when adding. (Carelessness? Vision?)

7.
$$\begin{array}{r} 42 \\ +30 \\ \hline 70 \end{array}$$
Confuses the role of zero in addition with its role in multiplication.

8.
$$\begin{array}{r} 84 \\ +12 \\ \hline 86 \end{array}$$
Confuses the role of 1 in addition with its role in multiplication.

9.
$$\begin{array}{r} 634 \\ -16 \\ \hline 18 \end{array}$$
Fails to complete subtraction. (Carelessness? Lack of understanding of place-value system?)

10.	462	Subtracts smaller
	−378	digit from larger
	116	digit at all times.

11.	78	Subtracts units from
	−3	units and tens.
	45	

12.	63	Forgets to rename
	−7	tens when
	66	regrouping.

If your child makes errors such as those above, ask him to do a similar exercise and explain to you step by step, in his own words, exactly what he is doing and why. Try to determine whether his error is the result of carelessness, misunderstanding of the problem, inaccurate computation, or lack of knowledge of the correct procedure. Then help your child work on similar problems, explaining carefully the procedure at each step. (*Note:* Give this kind of help only if you can be patient and supportive. Any sign of disapproval on your part will be counterproductive. If you know you can't be patient, go watch television or have an ice cream cone, and resolve to call your child's teacher in the morning.)

FOURTH GRADE

The Fourth-Grade Child as a Learner

The fourth-grade child is not markedly different from the way he was one year earlier. He remains curious and eager to learn and works hard to establish a place for himself in the world of school and friends, as well as in the family.

However, his increasing maturity makes him more sure of his own motives. He knows what he wants to do and what he does not want to do, and he becomes much more autonomous in directing his own actions. Since he is usually not yet ready to challenge adult authority, his growing independence may come as a relief to parents and teachers.

The fourth-grade child is also becoming increasingly social. Both boys and girls may join clubs or cliques (with the sexes always carefully separated), and they engage in many gregarious activities. (At this age, the boy or girl who is "different" and does not have friends may begin to feel left out.) Some friendships may last, but most are likely to be ephemeral. Children are trying out relationships the way they try out clothes or movies.

Academically, the fourth-grade child must make a large adjustment. Now that he has mastered the basic mechanics of reading and arithmetic, he is ready to read for information and enjoyment and to use his developing mathematical ability to solve problems. Personally and socially, the fourth-grade year usually arrives and passes with few growing pains; but academically, it is for many children a year of significant challenge.

Reading in the Fourth Grade

BEYOND BASIC LITERACY

So far, your child in school has been learning to read. Now, beginning in the fourth grade, he will be reading to learn.

This change in emphasis is of profound importance. From society's point of view the health of our economy and our democracy depends upon a public whose literacy extends far beyond the mere ability to recognize words in print. From your child's point of view, the transition in learning purpose and learning style may be one of the most difficult challenges of his elementary schooling.

America can be proud of the progress it has made in achieving basic literacy. According to the National Assessment of Educational Progress, 95 percent of our young adults can read and understand the printed word. However, "in terms of tomorrow's need, there is cause for concern: only a very small percentage can understand complex material." As the Commission on Reading recently wrote,

The world is moving into a technological-information age in which full participation in education, science, business, industry, and the professions requires increasing levels of literacy. What was a satisfactory level of literacy in 1950 probably will be marginal by the year 2000.

In order to prepare children to meet tomorrow's demands, says the commission, reading instruction must emphasize the higher-level skills of comprehension and analysis. Basic literacy is not enough.

PREPARATION FOR THE FOURTH GRADE

By the time your child enters the fourth grade, he should be ready for this challenge. If he has been making normal progress in an effective K–3 program, he should begin the fourth-grade year with most of the word recognition skills he needs to continue to improve as a reader. He should also be accustomed to reading for meaning and to thinking about what he reads.

More specifically, the child entering the fourth grade should

- Have a growing sight vocabulary of common words.
- Be able to use the skills of phonic analysis (initial consonants, ending consonants, medial consonants, consonant blends, short and long vowels, diphthongs, variant spellings) to decode unfamiliar words.
- Be able to use the skills of structural analysis (prefixes, suffixes, compounds, contractions) to determine the meaning of unfamiliar words.
- Understand the meaning of stories and passages written at a third-grade level of difficulty.
- Be able to find the main idea and key details in passages of appropriate difficulty.

- Be able to locate words in a dictionary and books in a library.

    If your child can do these things, he is ready to begin fourth-grade work. If he cannot, you should consult with your child's teacher to determine the cause of his difficulty and to plan for appropriate remediation. *Do not wait until your child has trouble in the fourth grade.* When your child was in kindergarten and the first grade, we advised you to be patient, because children develop at different rates and many early problems tend to disappear as children mature. But at this grade level, with the change in the nature of instruction that is about to occur, the time for waiting is over. Get your child the help he needs *now.*

THE FOURTH-GRADE READING PROGRAM

Word Recognition Skills

In the fourth grade, reading instruction shifts from an emphasis on word recognition skills to an emphasis on comprehension and study skills. Nevertheless, good teachers know that the word recognition skills must be maintained and that some children in the class may need continuing instruction in them. Word recognition skills were described in the chapter "Reading in the Third Grade." If your child has difficulty determining what an unfamiliar word is, you may wish to reread that chapter. (There is a difference between not knowing what a word is and not knowing what it means. The child may not know what the word *debenture* means because he has no knowledge of finance. However, if the fourth-grade child cannot both pronounce the printed word *adventure* and know its meaning, he probably has a reading problem.)

Comprehension Skills

The purpose of reading is to construct meaning from printed text. Recognition of the words and syntactical patterns is not enough. The reader must comprehend what he is reading—the main idea of the essay, the events and mood of the story, the slant of the editorial, the steps and sequence of the recipe or the travel directions. Furthermore, reading is not passive—the good reader does not simply let the writer's words and ideas wash over him. He actively uses his mind to comprehend the writer's meaning, to relate what he is reading to prior knowledge, to interpret what he is reading in light of his past experiences, to vary the speed and closeness of his reading with his purpose.

Good reading instruction helps children become active, competent, thinking readers. Among the comprehension skills commonly taught at this level are the following:

- Identifying the main idea of a paragraph, a short passage, or a short story.
- Making generalizations based on the main ideas of two or more sources.
- Finding key details.
- Relating key details and groups of details to an author's main idea and purpose.
- Determining sequences of time, place, activity, and thought.
- Predicting outcomes of events and action of characters.
- Understanding the implications of a text, as well as its literal meaning.
- Inferring relationships not stated.
- Distinguishing between fact and opinion.
- Recognizing sales and propaganda techniques.
- Discerning an author's point of view.

Good programs help children apply these skills to all kinds of reading matter. They also gradually increase the difficulty of the material to which the skills are applied.

Study Skills

Increasingly, the child uses his developing reading ability to gain information and understanding in other subjects, such as history, geography, science, and health. As he does so, he needs to develop study skills enabling him to make the most of what he reads. Good reading programs help him do so. Among the study skills most commonly taught at this level are the following:

- Following written directions (of increasing complexity).
- Using alphabetical sequence to locate books and other material.
- Understanding and using the various parts of a book (tables of contents, chapter headings, indexes, glossaries, appendixes).
- Using a dictionary (for word meanings, spelling, other information).
- Using simple encyclopedias.
- Locating books and simple reference material in a library.
- Recalling important information.
- Organizing information to facilitate understanding and recall.
- Obtaining information from maps, charts, globes, and drawings.

As with comprehension skills, good reading programs help children apply these study skills to all subject areas and to reading material of gradually increasing difficulty.

TEACHING THE FOURTH-GRADE READING PROGRAM

As we have said, the fourth-grade reading program focuses on the development of comprehension and study skills. However, the ways in which schools and teachers organize their programs vary widely.

Some teachers continue to use basal reading programs, in the manner described in the chapter "Reading in the Third Grade." Some use basal readers occasionally, to review or reinforce a basic skill. Some use them for pupils of lower ability but not for those who are more advanced. Most teachers begin to teach reading through books of literature or through textbooks in the content areas—chiefly social studies, science, and health. (In this way, a lesson may be about social studies and reading simultaneously, and more school time is gained for teaching both content and comprehension skills.) Some teachers teach reading through the content areas exclusively, without the use of basal readers.

In the lower grades, most of the reading material is in story form. (It may or may not be literature; that is another matter.) Research has shown that narrative text (stories) is easier for children to understand than expository text (nonfiction). Gradually, however, good programs introduce children to expository writing. By the fourth grade, some experts say, half or more of the reading instruction that children receive should involve expository writing.

Whether the material that children are reading is in their basal readers, in social studies or science textbooks, or in trade books selected by the teacher or the child, the general form of the comprehension lesson is apt to be the same. First, there is a stage of *prereading*, in which the teacher introduces the children to the text to be read. She provides relevant background information, elicits interest, sets purposes for reading, raises pertinent questions, and helps children focus their attention. Then comes the stage of *guided reading*. The children read the assigned passage, usually silently, remembering the questions that the teacher had raised. (Sometimes teachers give written study questions to provide additional guidance at this stage.) When the children finish the passage, the teacher questions them about it. Good teachers ask questions at different levels of thinking—from the literal (What happened? What did it say?) to the evaluative (How useful was it? Was it fair?). Sometimes, alas, the questions simply belabor the obvious or ask the child to confirm what the teacher is thinking. Effective teachers ask questions that truly get children to think on their own.

Finally, there is the stage of *post-reading*, in which the teacher helps the children to reflect on what they have read, to remember important information, and to make connections between what they have read and other reading they have done or other experiences they have had. She may also provide feedback on how well they have done the lesson, with an eye toward motivating or helping them in their next effort.

If the process is effective, the child should not only understand and appreciate what he has read for its content, he should also be acquiring valuable comprehension and study skills as well. He is learning to read for a specific purpose: to monitor his own progress in accomplishing that purpose (called *meta-cognition* by some educators) and to think about what he has read and relate it to other knowledge and experience.

Some teachers make such teaching and learning explicit and overt; that is, they teach specific techniques for improving reading comprehension. One such study method, often used when reading is taught through the content areas, is SQ3R (survey-question-read-recite-review). This technique, proposed by F. P. Robinson in 1961, provides a systematic method for reading and learning text material as follows:

- *Survey:* The child previews the material, noting its organization, looking at the table of contents, chapter or section headings, illustrations.
- *Question:* Working alone, in pairs, or in groups, the children pose questions about the information they expect to find. The questions should be appropriate to the purpose for reading the text.
- *Read:* The child reads the text, trying to answer the questions that had been raised.
- *Recite:* The child puts the text away and tries to answer his own (or the teacher's) questions orally or in writing.
- *Review:* The child rereads the text in order to check the accuracy of his answers.

This technique, and variations of it, may be a bit advanced for some children of this age, but some children are able to use it, and they profit by doing so.

WHAT TO LOOK FOR IN A GOOD FOURTH-GRADE READING PROGRAM

There is no one best way to teach reading. Studies have shown that good teaching can occur with many methods. Unhappily, poor teaching can occur with many methods as well. From the parents' point of view, the method that works best is the one that works with your child.

Fortunately, you don't need to be a trained reading teacher to know whether your child is receiving effective instruction or not. If the answers to most of the following questions are yes, chances are your child is participating in an effective reading program. If many of the answers are no, you should talk to your child's teacher and, perhaps, the principal to see what changes can be made.

- Does the teacher have a plan for reading instruction? Can she describe clearly and specifically how her program is organized? Can she list the comprehension and study skills she is trying to teach?
- Does the teacher know your child's instructional level? Can she tell you not only what book he is in, but exactly what skills he is working on?
- Does the teacher provide time for reading instruction each day? Is there time for both reading for pleasure and working on skills?
- Does the teacher provide reading instruction in the content areas—social studies, science, health, and the like?
- Does the teacher frequently read aloud to the children, to share her enthusiasm and to motivate the children to read?
- Are books, magazines, and other reading materials abundantly available in the classroom?
- Do the children make frequent use of the school and/or community library?
- Does your child like to read at home?
- Does your child score at least on grade level on standardized reading tests?

HOW TO HELP YOUR CHILD AT HOME

Most parents should not try to teach their children to read. Teaching reading requires special skill and knowledge, and even when a parent is a trained reading teacher, he or she may do more harm than good by creating tension with the child or by conflicting with the teacher's methods. However, there are things that you can do at home in order to create an atmosphere that will encourage your child to read.

- Praise and encourage your child's successful efforts to read.
- Continue to read to your child, every day if possible, but frequently no matter what. Don't think that your child is too old to be read to now that he can read by himself—most children this age still love the time they spend with their parents this way.
- Encourage your child to read to you when he feels comfortable doing so.
- Continue to give your child books as presents. Make them special.
- Visit the library with your child and help him choose books that he may like.
- Limit the amount of television your child is allowed to watch. Research has shown that viewing television for about ten hours per week may actually aid reading achievement. Beyond this amount, achievement tends to decline.
- Make constructive use of the television your child does watch. Be selective about the programs he sees; talk with him about the content of the programs; find reading material related to matters that interest him on television.
- Talk often with your child to help him enlarge his vocabulary and to use language to think and to express himself.
- Confer periodically with your child's teacher to learn about his progress at school.

THE SIGNS OF PROGRESS

No single test can measure accurately your child's annual progress in reading, and surely no single set of questions can do so. However, the following section of a unit test on comprehension, taken from the Ginn and Company Grade 4 program *Barefoot Island* (1982, p. 41), may give you some idea of the kind of passage your child should be able to read and the kinds of questions he should be able to answer by the end of the fourth grade.

Read each story. Fill in the circle next to the best answer to each question.

Neal gathered together everything that he would need. He had his brushes and watercolors, but he couldn't find his pad. He ran upstairs to his bedroom. When he came back down, he took everything outside. He set up everything next to the flower garden. He studied the flowers very carefully before he began.

1. According to the story, which sentence is most likely true?

- (a.) Neal likes to stay indoors.
- (b.) Neal takes pictures of his dog.
- (c.) Neal can never find his brushes.
- (d.) Neal likes to paint pictures.

2. What did Neal probably get upstairs?

- (a.) his brushes
- (b.) his watercolors
- (c.) his pad
- (d.) his flowers

Literature in the Fourth Grade

"I thought Oz was a great head," said Dorothy.

"And I thought Oz was a lovely Lady," said the Scarecrow.

"And I thought Oz was a terrible Beast," said the Tin Woodman.

"And I thought Oz was a Ball of Fire," exclaimed the Lion.

"No, you are all wrong," said the little man meekly. "I have been making believe."

"Making believe!" cried Dorothy. "Are you not a Great Wizard?"

. . . "Not a bit of it, my dear. I'm just a common man."

. . . "I think you are a very bad man," said Dorothy.

"Oh, no, my dear! I'm really a very good man, but I'm a very bad Wizard, I must admit."

What more need a person know about puffery in high places? About the need we have to invent the wonderful and the terrible? About the power of simple truth to transcend bombast and pretense? L. Frank Baum's magical story of *The Wonderful Wizard of Oz* has delighted people of all ages throughout the twentieth century. It is part of the rich tradition to which your child is heir, the literary tradition of English-speaking people. Much of your child's education should be devoted to exploring this tradition.

In the fourth grade, works of literature occupy a central place in the child's reading program. In an individualized reading program, they constitute the bulk of the child's reading. In a basal reading program, they are used by good teachers as enrichment and as motivation for learning to read. Whatever the program, good teachers spend much time reading aloud to their children (in some classes for a certain portion of each day), finding appealing books of appropriate difficulty for children to read, talking about stories and poems, and sharing their pleasure and enthusiasm with the class.

There is no end to the variety and number of things to be read. Children should read or listen to folktales, fairy tales, fables, myths, legends. They should explore stories of all kinds—adventure stories, fantasy stories, realistic stories, animal stories, stories about science, stories about the past, stories about other people in other lands, stories and biographies about famous men and women. They should read and hear poetry of all kinds—story poems, nonsense poems, nursery rhymes, song lyrics, poems about nature and animals and space travel and people and children like themselves.

Some of this literature should be old—the children's classics of our tradition. Children should not grow up without experiencing the great works that have entertained and instructed generations—works like *Aesop's Fables*, Grahame's *The Wind in the Willows*, the inspired nonsense of Edward Lear. But some of the literature should be new, with a more contemporary ring and feel. Most fourth-grade children enjoy such works as *Charlotte's Web* by E. B. White, *Sounder* by William H. Armstrong, and *Blubber* by Judy Blume, and the poetry of David McCord and Eve Merriam.

Good teachers employ many techniques to introduce their children to such literature and to motivate them to read it. They read aloud to the class, making the story hour a warm and special time. They bring new books to class, show them to children, talk about them. They create displays of books and book jackets on counters, bulletin boards, door frames. They arrange reading corners in their classrooms—snug nooks with a rug for lying on, a special lamp, and dozens of new books, waiting to be tried. They provide time for children to read in class. They distribute book lists to children and parents. They call attention to films and movies based on books and make the books available to their classes. They organize book clubs. They take their children to the library often, and they bring books from the library to class. They make every effort to create an environment in which reading is made fun, important, and easy to do.

Obviously, when children read literary works and discuss them with their teachers or with others in the class, they are improving their reading skills. Indeed, as we have said, in some classes such works constitute the bulk of the reading that children do. In any program, however, good teachers never forget that the basic reason for reading literature is to enjoy it. Whatever other benefits may be derived—reading skill, human understanding, enlarged vocabulary, ability to write—they are secondary to the sheer pleasure that comes from reading a well-written piece that has something to say.

For this reason, good teachers do not make children reduce everything they have read to the form of a standard book report. Sometimes they simply ask the child what he has read, noting the title and the author in their records. Sometimes they ask the child two or three questions to test comprehension and to help the child think about what he has read. (Why was Big John happy at the end? Could the ending have been different? What other book was this most similar to?) Sometimes they have the child write something about the book, discussing a favorite character, an exciting scene, a question not answered. Sometimes, when more than one child has read the same book, they arrange for group reports in the form of a play, pantomime, or group painting to be shared with the rest of the class. The trick is to capitalize on the child's natural urge to share with other people something he has enjoyed. In good classrooms, the atmosphere of the literature program is always one of discovery and joy. Good teachers dread the drudgery that led to that most deadly book report of all: "This book told me more about penguins than I wanted to know."

The literature program is one part of the school curriculum in which parents *can* play an important role. Because the purpose at this level is not so much to teach children about literature as to immerse them in it, parents can be very helpful simply by encouraging children to read, finding books for them to read, and reading to them at home. Establish your own story hour—even once or twice a week, if you are busy—and make it special and important. Balance the familiar works that your child wants to hear again and again with works that are new to him (and you). Talk with your child about what you have read. And, since in the end it is your behavior and not the teacher's that your child is more likely to emulate, spend time reading for enjoyment yourself.

Writing in the Fourth Grade

As children progress through the upper elementary grades, writing becomes essential to the study of other disciplines. The child is asked to write science and social studies reports, and thus his comfort with the writing process facilitates report writing. The techniques the child has learned in the personal writing he did in the early grades carries over into the content writing he does in the middle grades.

Many teachers, but by no means all, help their pupils step by step with the writing process. There are still many schools where the teacher provides little help between the assignment of the topic and the correction of the final product. Your child is fortunate if he has a teacher who has adopted a process approach, one who works with the children through all stages of the writing process, from the very beginning (topic selection) through the drafting, conferencing, revising, editing, and publishing stages.

THE WRITING PROCESS

Works of literature, magazine articles, and newspaper feature stories are not created in the final form we see published. By the time of publication, both the writer and the work have gone through several stages.

All writers spend time thinking about their topic. Whether writers choose subjects themselves or are assigned one, they must think of an approach. Sometimes in the search for a topic or a novel way to treat it, writers speak to other people (*rehearsing, pre-writing,* or *brainstorming* step). At this point, the writer may make a brief outline or notes, but no actual writing takes place. And yet, it is perhaps the most creative moment of the entire process.

The very first written version is called *drafting.* It resembles the artist's first rough rendition of what will eventually be the finished work. In the need to record what has been only spoken or thought about, the writer pays little attention to the mechanics of writing—handwriting, usage, spelling, and punctuation. Content is primary.

When drafting, the writer is alone. Some writers draft and redraft, spending much solitary time with their work. During this process, some writers continue to work alone. Others want help. They need an audience. They want a reaction. They want feedback, and they look to an editor, a friend, or a relative. The feedback stage is sometimes called *conferencing* or *critiquing.* Editors are trained to be helpful audiences. They listen carefully and ask good questions. An audience needs to learn to ask good questions and to be supportive but critical in a helpful way. In the world of poetry, a good editor can enhance a poet's talent. T. S. Eliot's "Wasteland" owes much of its power and beauty to Ezra Pound's editing.

The writer digests the comments and *revises* the work. When the work says what the writer wishes it to say, the final touches are added by *editing*. Spelling and punctuation are checked, and the final copy is prepared.

Since writing is a creative process, not all writers follow this procedure in a lock-step way. Nevertheless, in broad terms this is a fairly accurate description of the process many writers go through when they work.

THE FOURTH-GRADE WRITER

Children in fourth grade are not experienced writers. They have much to learn. They are more similar to third-grade writers than they are different, particularly at the beginning of the school year. They are aware that they write for an audience, and they themselves are becoming better audiences. They understand the need for detail; they know when a classmate's piece makes sense and when it doesn't. They know good writing is "a story that makes you feel like you're there" because of the details included. It is easier for them to see when someone else's writing is not clear than to see confusion in their own. Often they know exactly what they want to say and assume the reader will understand as well. Reading work to a group of classmates and the teacher results in revision suggestions to the writer.

The good writing teacher acts as a role model, asking good questions of the writer and teaching good writing techniques. She may speak about more active verbs that add life to a sentence, leading the writer to think of a more descriptive verb than *run* such as *dash* or *race*. "How did the man run?" She might ask the cause of a particular event in a student's story. "What happened before the fight between you and your brother? Did he tease you?" She may call attention to the lead, the opening sentence or paragraph. "Does the first sentence of the story make the reader want to know more? Do you have any other ideas about how to start the story?" She may help the writer draw tighter limits to a story, to focus on a particular topic. Many fourth graders have difficulty focusing on a topic and are inclined to tell long chronological stories in their first drafts.

Without a teacher's guidance, many children simply change single words when revising. Revision is a thinking and organizing skill that requires much teacher guidance, often taking two weeks to two months.

After revision, the final piece is recopied. Often a cover is made. Even in the final version there may be spelling errors, omissions of words, and the like. Even though the fourth grader's final piece is almost always less than perfect, he is usually very proud of it. Writing is always a work in progress—it can always be improved. At some point the writer declares a piece finished and goes on to the next project. Encouragement, interest, and praise on the part of the parent rather than criticism will help the fourth grader develop a positive feeling about writing.

The fourth grader's personal writing deals with his private life, family pets, and vacations, as well as with class activities (the birth of chicks or a class trip). Many teachers ask their pupils to keep a daily diary, which often serves as a good source for topics.

The fourth-grade writer continues to be interested in writing about his own experiences. The steps he has gone through in his personal writing remain valid for "research writing." He still brainstorms with his classmates, drafts his first pieces, confers with his teachers and other students, revises, and edits. However, writing is beginning to take on a new significance because the child is starting to write in-depth reports. He enjoys collecting facts from books, magazines, films, and his own experiences but needs help organizing the material.

Children in one fourth-grade class in a suburban school are working on their first serious research project. The project is part of a unit on pond life. Their writing has grown out of a field trip they had made to a pond, where they collected pond animals. Back in the classroom they examined the animals under microscopes, recorded their observations, and shared their findings with the rest of the class. With the help of their teacher and reference books, they identified the animals. They talked about the animals with one another and chose a particular animal to study.

The teacher helped them to brainstorm topics about their animal. They made a circle with their animal's biological name in it after identification in books and then drew lines with questions emanating from it. They returned to the reference books to make notes that would answer their questions. The teacher showed them how to organize their material. They could use note cards if they wished, or they could color-code their material, for example, by coloring one of their questions in their brainstorming cluster red and then underlining in red all the information answering that question.

Some children are drafting their first copy, while others are still gathering information. The writing process allows children to proceed at their own speed. The teacher monitors each child's progress closely so that she may help whenever a problem arises.

At the conferencing table, the teacher sits with three children. All three have finished their first draft; they have all chosen the scud, a tiny pond creature, as their animal. They read their drafts to one another. The teacher asks, "What do you think is your most interesting sentence? Why did you arrange your material in this order? Does your important sentence show up as well as it might or should you begin with it? Should it be the lead in your paragraph?" The teacher continues, encouraging the other two children to ask questions. "Do you think the scud's movement has anything to do with its eating? Should those sentences go near each other? What's a good word for the way the scud moves?"

The child decides that one sentence fits better in the third paragraph than in the first. The child returns to her desk, cuts the sentence out, and secures it with tape to the new place.

Over the next few weeks, the children will work hard on their conferencing and revisions, finally editing their work, correcting grammar and spelling, and recopying. The end product will be a class book on pond life with a contribution from each child.

The fourth-grade writer recognizes that writing serves many purposes. He may write a letter to a friend he met in camp, he may write a story about his new puppy, or he may write an interesting report about a social studies or science topic. He is learning to organize and digest material and to create a new product from his experience.

SPELLING IN THE FOURTH GRADE

Most fourth-grade teachers use a spelling curriculum as the basis for their programs. Good teachers enrich the list with words selected from current events, everyday class activities, and other areas of the curriculum. Spelling activities usually follow a weekly routine, with pretesting, discussion of words, use of words in sentences, study, and testing. Often spelling activities are assigned as homework. Most children's spelling skills improve as they grow older. The improvement is probably more a result of reading and seeing words applied correctly than a formal spelling program. Nevertheless, spelling continues to be part of our elementary school curriculum and is probably helpful.

Some children will always have difficulty in spelling. Poor spelling skills are not a sign of poor intelligence or poor education—some people simply have trouble with spelling.

Spelling isn't writing, and the two should never be confused. One of the authors, a teacher of writing, is reminded of the adult who told her, "I can't write, I can't even spell," as if spelling were a function of writing.

When a child drafts and revises, he should not be criticized for misspelled words. When he edits, his spelling errors should be pointed out to him so that he may correct them.

WORD PROCESSING

Today's elementary-school children do not fear computers as do many of their parents. Computers are part of their lives. Many families have computers at home, and many elementary schools do as well. Word processing can be a liberating force for the child who has bad handwriting or whose coordination impedes writing. Once he has composed a first draft on the computer, the child is free to insert and delete information and to move sentences and paragraphs around. There is no recopying. The computer simply changes the material according to the writer's directions and prints out revised material. The writer is more willing to revise because the onerous chore of recopying is gone. Spelling errors can be eliminated because most word-processing programs have a spell-check that identifies misspelled words and typographical errors.

A GOOD WRITING PROGRAM

A good writing program is one that

- Understands the writing process.
- Values children's experience and their perception of it.

- Helps children to be good observers, to listen to sounds, to notice smells, to see detail.
- Helps children transfer their skills from their personal writing to their content writing.
- Provides time for the entire writing process and time for children to listen to and read their classmates' writing. Some classrooms have libraries of "books" by classroom authors. Some schools have parent volunteer programs with parents editing and typing books by children.
- Teaches children how to be good editors, to ask the right questions, to be specific, to be positive and encouraging and yet helpful, to be committed to helping others create a better piece.
- Recognizes the difference between handwriting and writing, helping children whose handwriting is an overwhelming task by allowing them occasionally to dictate stories or use a word processor.
- Recognizes that spelling should be correct in the finished draft (without overemphasizing it in working drafts).
- Values literature, encourages children to read, and provides time for reading aloud to them.
- Recognizes that writing, like speaking, is a trial-and-error skill and needs encouragement and nurturing.
- Displays children's writing prominently and attractively.
- Stresses the specifics of what is good about some writing samples.
- Shows interest in every child's writing.
- Uses models for writing techniques from literature.
- Encourages each child to develop his own writing voice.
- Teaches children how to organize factual material and observations.

The Pink Worm

Russ Korins

At the stream, I caught a pink worm. It is called a Tubifex. It has a long, thin red line down its back. It had little lines crossing it.

I brought it back to the classroom and looked at it under a microscope. It looked a lot bigger. I couldn't even see the whole thing. The red line (probably a blood vessel) was gigantic. The lines crossing it looked twice their size. I could see little hairs sticking out. I saw a "tail". It would not stay still. It kept swirling and curling up like a snake. It was fun watching it in Room 3.

Mathematics in the Fourth Grade

By the time your child enters the fourth grade, he should already have a solid foundation in basic mathematical skills and knowledge. He should be able to count, read, and write cardinal numbers to 10,000 or more and to apply them to real phenomena—numbers of objects, amounts of money, spatial dimensions, temperature. He should understand the concept of place value in our base ten number system and the use of decimal points in counting money. He should understand the idea of a fraction as part of a whole or as some part of a number of objects in a set. He should understand addition and subtraction as inverse operations, know addition and subtraction facts through 24, and be able to add and subtract four-digit numbers both with or without regrouping (carrying or borrowing). He should be familiar with basic two- and three-dimensional geometric shapes and accustomed to making rough measurements of common objects and phenomena. He should be able to supply his knowledge in the solution of simple word problems and to use skills of estimation to check the reasonableness of his answers.

Above all, he should be gaining confidence in his ability to use his mind to solve problems mathematically. The mathematics that children acquire during their elementary school years is much more than a collection of skills and knowledge—it is a problem-solving capacity, an ability to quantify phenomena and relationships and to use mathematics to extract new meaning from a situation. Thinking mathematically is a mindset to be acquired early in childhood; it is not something that should come later, after the child has acquired the basics. Thinking is itself the basic skill; without it, number facts and procedures have little meaning.

If your child is progressing normally, he probably enjoys learning math in school and using it there and at home. However, if your child considers mathematics hard or if he lacks confidence in his ability to solve problems or to do the work the teacher gives him, you should talk to your child's teacher early in the fourth-grade year. Given proper time, attention, and encouragement, most children can master the mathematics taught at this level. But the attitude toward mathematics that may develop because of a sense of failure now may haunt your child for a lifetime. Ask the teacher what you and she can do together to make your child's experience in mathematics more rewarding. As you do so, remember that at this age it is still more important that the child succeed at what he can do than to try to cover material that is beyond him. And often a little bit of personal attention from the teacher will help your child remove a stumbling block and open the way for rapid progress.

THE FOURTH-GRADE MATHEMATICS CURRICULUM

Schools establish their mathematics curricula in various ways. In some cases, a textbook or series of textbooks is adopted for use in a given school, community, or state, and the teacher is required to follow the text or series as the basis of the curriculum. In other cases, a course of study, or *scope and sequence*, is developed by the school system or the state, and the teacher is free to choose from a variety of books and other instructional materials. Whatever their origin, fourth-grade mathematics curricula throughout the United States are much more similar to one another than they are different. Typically, the fourth-grade mathematics curriculum comprises five parts, or *strands:*

> Numbers and numeration
> Operations with whole numbers
> Operations with fractions
> Probability and statistics
> Geometry and measurement

Some curricula include a sixth part—problem solving. In the authors' view, however, problem solving is the goal of all mathematics and should be incorporated into the teaching and learning of each part of the curriculum.

The five strands of the mathematics curriculum are taught throughout the elementary grades. Skills and topics are often repeated from grade to grade; material may be introduced at one grade level, taught and practiced extensively at the next, and reviewed and "mastered" at the third. Such overlapping is not inefficient; it is a deliberate teaching strategy to ensure that the child gains a secure foundation in the subject. For this reason, you may wish to look at the chapters on mathematics in the third and fifth grades.

In the fourth grade, the skills and knowledge on which children typically concentrate are discussed in the following.

Numbers and Numeration

- Cardinal numbers: Read and write whole numbers to hundred millions.
- Ordinal numbers: Read and write ordinal numbers to hundred millions.
- Numerals: Read and write notation for fractions, including mixed numbers. Read and write Roman numerals from I to C (1 to 100).

- Place value: Learn the concept of place value to hundred millions and hundredths:
  Example   153,472,918.06.
- Even, odd: Consider the sum, difference, or product of two or more whole numbers as even or odd.
- Prime numbers: Discover the prime numbers between 1 and 100. A prime number is a natural number greater than 1 the only factors of which are 1 and itself:
  Examples   2, 3, 5, 7, . . .
- Negative numbers: Develop an understanding of positive and negative numbers on a number line:

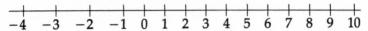

- Rounding: Learn to round (or round off) numbers to the nearest tenth, whole number, hundred, or thousand:

  Examples   6.46 becomes 6.5
  28,892 becomes 29,000

- Estimation: Estimate large quantities by applying mathematical skills and knowledge. Develop the habit of estimating answers to problems as a means of checking reasonableness of answer.
- Patterns: Perceive patterns in sequence of numbers:

Examples

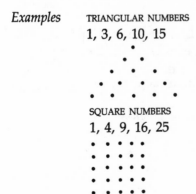

TRIANGULAR NUMBERS
1, 3, 6, 10, 15

SQUARE NUMBERS
1, 4, 9, 16, 25

Operations With Whole Numbers

- Addition and subtraction: Learn addition and subtraction facts through 24. Add and subtract two-, three-, or four-digit numbers, with or without regrouping (carrying or borrowing), including subtraction involving regrouping with zeros:

Examples	698	6000
	1712	−2917
	+4952	3083
	7362	

Use addition and subtraction as inverse operations to check accuracy:

Examples	5421	4698
	−723	+723
	4698	5421

Use rounding to estimate sums and differences:

Examples	412	500	400
	893	900	800
	127	200	100
		1600	1300

(The sum is less than 1600 but more than 1300.)
- Multiplication and division: Learn multiplication facts through 12 × 12. Learn written and mental multiplication by 10, 100, and 1,000. Learn to use the standard algorithm (procedure) for multiplying three-digit numbers by two-digit numbers:

Example	264
	×57
	1848
	1320
	15048

Understand division as the inverse operation of multiplication:

$$Example \qquad 32 \times 6 = 192$$
$$192 \div 6 = 32$$

Learn division facts through $144 \div 12$. Learn to divide two- and three-digit numbers by a one-digit number; find both quotient and remainder (if any):

$$Examples \quad 114 \qquad 41\tfrac{6}{7}$$
$$4\overline{)456} \quad 7\overline{)293}$$

Identify factors and prime factors:
Example   24 has the factors 1, 2, 3, 4, 6, 8, 12, and 24. Find the average of two, three, or four numbers.

Properties of operations: Learn that addition and multiplication both have the commutative property (the order of two numbers in addition and multiplication can be reversed without changing the answer):

$$Examples \quad 2 + 4 = 4 + 2$$
$$2 \times 3 = 3 \times 2$$

Learn that multiplication has the commutative property and that division does not:

$$Examples \quad 12 \times 6 = 6 \times 12 \quad \text{YES}$$
$$12 \div 6 = 6 \div 12 \quad \text{NO}$$

Learn that addition and multiplication both have the associative property (given a series of whole numbers to be added or multiplied, the order in which they are added or multiplied can be changed without changing the answer).

Examples
$$4 + 6 + 3 = 4 + 6 + 3$$
$$10 + 3 = 4 + 9$$
$$13 = 13$$
$$2 \times 3 \times 4 = 2 \times 4 \times 3$$
$$6 \times 4 = 2 \times 12$$
$$24 = 24$$

Learn that multiplication has the distributive property over addition and subtraction. If two numbers are added together and the sum multiplied by a third number, the same result is obtained if each of the first two is first multiplied by the third and the two products added.

Examples
$$4 \times (3 + 2) = (4 \times 3) + (4 \times 2)$$
$$4 \times 5 = 12 + 8$$
$$20 = 20$$

$$5 \times (6 - 4) = (5 \times 6) - (5 \times 4)$$
$$5 \times 2 = 30 - 20$$
$$10 = 10$$

Use distributive property of multiplication over subtraction to compute mentally:

Example
$$6 \times 99 =$$
$$(6 \times 100) - (6 \times 1) =$$
$$600 - 6 = 594$$

Learn that the identity property for addition is the special number 0 and that the identity property for multiplication is the number 1:

Examples
$$159 + 0 = 159$$
$$273 \times 1 = 273$$

• Word problems: Use addition, subtraction, multiplication, and/or division to solve word problems, including multiple-step problems: *Example* An airplane traveled from New

York to Los Angeles by way of Denver. There were 170 passengers when it left New York. In Denver, half the 170 passengers got off and 20 more got on. How many passengers did the plane carry from Denver to Los Angeles?

Operations With Fractions

- Order, inequality: Compare and order halves, thirds, fourths, fifths, sixths, etc., using such terms as *greater than*, *less than*, and *between*.
- Relationship to division: Understand the relationships between fractions and division:

$$Example \qquad 9 \div 4 \text{ may be written } \tfrac{9}{4}$$
$$\tfrac{9}{4} = \tfrac{8}{4} + \tfrac{1}{4} = 2\tfrac{1}{4}$$
$$9 \div 4 = 2\tfrac{1}{4}$$

- Relation to multiplication and division: Understand the inverse relationship between multiplication and division involving fractions:

$$Example \qquad \tfrac{36}{6} = \tfrac{1}{6} \times 36.$$

- Addition and subtraction: Locate fractions and mixed numbers on a number line. Add and subtract fractions with like denominators:

$$Example \qquad \tfrac{3}{8} + \tfrac{4}{8} = \tfrac{7}{8}.$$

Add and subtract mixed numbers with like denominators:

$$Example \qquad 2\tfrac{1}{4} + 3\tfrac{3}{4} = \tfrac{8+1}{4} + \tfrac{12+3}{4} = \tfrac{9}{4} + \tfrac{15}{4} = \tfrac{24}{4} = 6$$

Develop sets of equivalent fractions:

Example $\frac{1}{2} = \frac{2}{4} = \frac{3}{6} = \frac{4}{8}$ ...

Add and subtract fractions with unlike denominators:

$$\textit{Example} \quad \frac{1}{2} \times \frac{1}{3} = \frac{1}{6}$$
$$\frac{1}{2} \times \frac{3}{3} = \frac{3}{6}$$
$$\frac{3}{6} + \frac{2}{6} = \frac{5}{6}$$
$$\frac{1}{3} \times \frac{2}{2} = \frac{2}{6}$$

• Factoring: Find prime factors in numerators and denominators:

$$\textit{Example} \quad \frac{6}{10} = \frac{3 \times 2}{5 \times 2}$$

Determine common denominators of two or more fractions:

$$\textit{Example} \quad \frac{1}{2} + \frac{1}{3} = \frac{3 + 2}{6}$$

Find the greatest common factor (GCF) and least common multiple of numbers (LCM):

Examples   GCF (21, 27, 30) = 3
LCM (2, 7, 8) = 56

• Decimals: Add and subtract decimals to thousandths:

Example
$$\begin{array}{r} 16.124 \\ -8.310 \\ \hline 7.814 \end{array}$$

Multiply and divide decimals to tenths.

Example
$$\begin{array}{r} 4.2 \\ \times 2.3 \\ \hline 126 \\ 84 \\ \hline 9.66 \end{array}$$

Rename decimals as fractions:

$$Example \quad 6.3 = 6\frac{3}{10}$$

Compare and order sets of fractions and sets of decimals.

$$Examples \quad \frac{1}{2}\frac{2}{3}\frac{3}{4} \quad or \quad \frac{6}{12}\frac{8}{12}\frac{9}{12}$$
$$0.3 \ 0.36 \quad or \quad 0.30 \ 0.36$$

- Word problems: Solve word problems involving fractions and decimals:
  Example   Carol took one bicycle trail and Bill took another. Carol's trail was $1\frac{2}{5}$ miles long and Bill's was $\frac{4}{5}$ mile long. How much longer was Carol's trail?

Probability and Statistics

- Data gathering and graphing: Make graphic records of statistical data drawn from newspapers, magazines, polls, or school activities.
- Frequency tables: Make frequency tables from tallied data.
- Average: Determine the average of a collection of data:
  Example   Roll two dice five times and record the results. What is the average of the five sums?
- Range: Determine the range of a collection of data and organize the data within the range.
- Fractions: Use fractions to express the results of chance happenings.
- Arrangements: Find orderly ways to count the number of arrangements within a set.
- Predictions: Predict outcomes of experiments and compare results with predictions.

Problem Solving

The reason for learning mathematics is to be able to use mathematical thinking to solve real problems. Unfortunately, too many children who do acquire facility in computation are unable to apply their skill to problem situations. Tests such as those given by the National Assessment of Educational Progress show that many of today's children are unable to solve simple arithmetic word problems; that is, they cannot use their computational skills when they are required to think.

There are several reasons for this distressing state of affairs. One is that in most real-life situations, and in some problems posed in classrooms, there is more information than needed to answer the question. The child must exercise his judgment in selecting only the data needed. Consider this problem: *The school library is open 6 hours a day. There are 180 days in the school year. How many hours is the library open each week?*

If the child answers 1080 (180 × 6), as many do with problems of this kind, he is either not reading the question carefully or not thinking.

Another reason is that many problems require more than one step for their solution, and children have trouble selecting and sequencing the steps. Consider this problem: *Carol and John bought two slices of pizza for 60 cents each and shared one large cup of soda for 35 cents. How much money did they spend in all?*

The solution requires two simple steps: (1) 60 cents × 2 = $1.20; (2) $1.20 + 35 cents = $1.55. Even so, many children find this kind of problem difficult.

A less likely reason for children's difficulty with word problems may be that they have difficulty reading the words and extracting meaning from the sentences. Unless the child has a specific learning disability, however, the problem is more apt to be with thinking than with reading. This is probably because he has not been *taught* to solve problems. Too often the teacher assumes that her job is to teach computational skills and that the child will somehow be able to apply these skills to problems entirely on his own, without benefit of instruction. Good teachers do not make this mistake. They involve children in problem solving at every step in the curriculum. They constantly challenge their pupils to think, to use what they are learning to solve problems.

Good teachers also teach the skills of problem solving directly.

Most problem-solving methods involve four steps:

1. *Understanding the problem.* The child should repeat the problem in his own words, identify the key questions, and select and, if necessary, write down the relevant facts. He should estimate a reasonable answer before trying to find the exact answer.
2. *Making a plan.* Different problems require different plans. The child should draw upon his skills and knowledge to devise a plan that may work. He may sort and classify, make tables or graphs and look for patterns and relationships, use diagrams or models to visualize the problems, and manipulate objects. He may need to use measurement or computational skills. The trick is to make use of what he knows and not to jump to an easy answer or to give up because the problem seems hard.
3. *Carrying out the plan.* Once the plan is made, it must be carried out. Often this is the step that requires measurement or written computations.
4. *Checking the answer.* Children should acquire the habit of first checking the *reasonableness* of the answer. (If a rabbit eats 2 pounds of food each week and you want to know how much 2 rabbits will eat in a 14-day period, 56 pounds [$2 \times 2 \times 14$] is not a reasonable answer. All you have to do is visualize what 56 pounds would look like to know that that is so). Then they should check the *accuracy* of their answer.

Many good teachers teach this four-step problem-solving method to their children and give them practice in following it.

TEACHING THE FOURTH-GRADE MATHEMATICS CURRICULUM

The typical mathematics lesson in the fourth grade resembles the typical lesson in the third grade. The content gradually changes, but the form of the activity is much the same.

Most elementary schools schedule time each day for the study of math. (The lessons are often taught in the morning, when the children are the most alert.) Most commonly, the fourth-grade teacher works with the class as a whole. The lesson may begin with a review of what the class did the previous day, or the teacher may help the class go over a seatwork or homework assignment from the day before. Then the teacher will introduce the new concept or skill for the day, often using individual children and manipulative materials (blocks, counters, chips, buttons, and rods), as well as the blackboard, to illustrate and explain. The bulk of the lesson is spent discussing this new concept or skill, with the teacher asking questions, helping the children make observations and see relationships, and providing encouragement and explanation where needed. Toward the end of the lesson, the teacher may assign some related exercises or other work to be done in class (*seatwork*) or at home (*homework*).

If your child is functioning at grade level, this standard approach should work well. However, individual children vary in their ability and rates of development. Perhaps your child is more advanced than most of the class and is insufficiently challenged. Or perhaps your child needs more time and help to master what many of the other children already know.

Teachers cope with these problems in various ways. Many provide enrichment activities for the more mathematically able children, to be done in school or at home when they have finished the regular work. (Such enrichment activities should genuinely stretch children's minds—they should not be just more of the same.) Teachers also work with small groups of children at other times during the day, going over the morning lesson, helping with the seatwork, or providing remedial instruction.

In some classes, teachers group children for mathematics instruction just as in the earlier grades children are grouped for reading instruction. For example, in a class of twenty-five children, there may be a group of eight doing more advanced work, a group of ten doing grade-level work, and a group of seven working at more basic material. The teacher will assign seatwork (or projects in another subject) to two groups while working individually with the third group.

In other classes, such grouping may not be permanent, but the teacher may occasionally form small groups for specific purposes. For example, a teacher whose review of children's seatwork assignments shows that six children need help in performing the division algorithm may call these six together for special help while the rest of the class is busy with other assignments.

Teachers also work with individual children, of course. But few programs are so organized as to make individual instruction the main form of activity, and in most schools, the amount of time available for individual instruction is limited.

PRINCIPLES OF EFFECTIVE MATHEMATICS TEACHING

However their classes may be organized, effective mathematics teachers follow certain fundamental principles.

Children Must Develop Understanding as Well as Skill

The point of learning mathematics is to be able to solve problems requiring mathematical thought. Basic skills are required to solve problems, but if the child does not understand the problem, cannot extract the relevant information from the problem situation, or cannot choose the right mathematical skill or principle to apply, then the basic skills alone will be of little use. For this reason, good teachers make sure that children understand the concepts underlying basic facts and skills.

Consider the child who knows his multiplication facts but makes this error:

$$\begin{array}{r} 29 \\ \times 2 \\ \hline 68 \end{array}$$

Chances are the child does not think that $2 \times 2 = 6$ or that $4 + 1 = 6$. Instead, he is making a logical mistake. He knows that when you add $29 + 2$, you carry the 1 and add it to the 2, as follows:

$$\begin{array}{r} 1 \\ 29 \\ +2 \\ \hline 31 \end{array}$$

Why, then, does it not make sense to carry the 1 and add it to the 2 when multiplying?

$$\begin{array}{r} 1 \\ 29 \\ \times 2 \\ \hline 68 \end{array} \quad (9 \times 2 = 18; 1 + 2 = 3; 3 \times 2 = 6)$$

So long as the multiplication algorithm is simply a formula to follow mechanically without any understanding of the principles involved, such mistakes are bound to happen—indeed, they may be a credit to the child's intelligence. Good teaching prevents such errors by providing numerous experiences for the child with concrete objects, which must be counted and sorted into groups of ten, then regrouped (or carried) as made necessary by multiplication. (Also, the child who has learned to estimate solutions to problems would know that this solution would have to be less than $30 \times 2 = 60$.)

In general, the concept is developed first, usually through actions performed on physical objects, then the notation associated with the concept, then the skill itself. Both understanding and skill are necessary, with understanding preceding skill.

Learning Proceeds From the Concrete to the Representational to the Abstract

In order to learn mathematical concepts thoroughly, children should experience the concept first in concrete physical form and then in representational or pictorial form before finally progressing to the use of abstract notation or doing mental arithmetic. Good teachers have children manipulate a wide variety of objects—blocks, chips, buttons, beans, Cuisenaire rods, balance beams—in order to have them observe firsthand the mathematical effect of their actions. Consider the following example.

The teacher is introducing the class to division. On the table at the front of the room she stacks twelve large books. "How many books are there in the pile?" she asks. The children count them, 1 to 12. Then the teacher asks a child to remove two books from the stack and place them in a separate pile.

"How many books are left?" she asks.

"Ten," say the children without counting.

"Right," says the teacher. "What did we just do?"

"Subtracted," says a child.

"Right," says the teacher. On the board she writes "12 − 2

= 10." Then the teacher has another child remove two more books.

"How many are left now?" she asks.

"Eight," says the class. The teacher writes "10 − 2 = 8."

"How many times do you think we can subtract two?" she asks. The class gives various answers. "Well, let's see," says the teacher. She asks the children to keep removing books two at a time until only two are left. "How many piles are there now?" she asks.

A child counts them quickly and says, "Six."

"How many twos did you subtract?" asks the teacher.

"Six."

"If I wanted to know how many books there are, I could count each one. What might be a faster way?"

"Multiply," says a child.

The teacher has her write "6 × 2" on the blackboard. "Good," says the teacher. "Just as multiplication is a shortcut for addition, so division is a shortcut for subtraction. When we subtract 2 six times from 12, it is the same as dividing 12 by 2. We have discovered that we could make six piles of 2 from our stack of 12. We write it like this: 12 ÷ 2 = 6. Or we can write it like this: $2\overline{)12}^{\,6}$." And so the lesson continues, with other examples of division, first making use of concrete objects, then involving pictures and diagrams, and finally involving arithmetic notation on the blackboard. This progression from the concrete to the representational to the abstract is standard in most good classrooms.

Skills and Knowledge Are First Introduced, Then Developed, Then Mastered

The study of mathematics is sequential, with each successive step building on the one before it. However, in a good mathematics program, skills and knowledge are not taught just once. Children are first introduced to a topic, then they are given extensive practice in developing it and applying it to problem situations, and finally they are expected to master it.

Most mathematics curriculum guides, or *scope and sequence charts*, reflect this approach. Topics like place value or division by one-digit numbers are apt to appear in the guides for grades 3, 4, and 5. Good teachers do not assume that because something has been taught, it has been learned; nor do they assume that once something has been grasped, it will necessarily be retained, unless the child is given frequent practice in using the pertinent skill or knowledge.

Skills and Knowledge Are Taught Sequentially

Although repeated practice is usually necessary for true mastery, mathematics curricula still follow a logical progression from more simple to more complex skills and knowledge. In learning multiplication, for example, the child may follow a progression such as the following:

$$\begin{array}{r} 7 \\ \times 2 \\ \hline 14 \end{array}$$

• Multiplication of single-digit numbers by single-digit numbers. Learning the multiplication table.

$$\begin{array}{r} 214 \\ \times 2 \\ \hline 428 \end{array}$$

• Multiplication of two-, three-, or four-digit numbers by single-digit numbers without regrouping.

$$\begin{array}{r} 645 \\ \times 3 \\ \hline 1935 \end{array}$$

• Multiplication of two-, three-, or four-digit numbers by single-digit numbers with regrouping.

$$\begin{array}{r} 21 \\ \times 42 \\ \hline 42 \\ 84 \\ \hline 882 \end{array}$$

• Multiplication of two-digit numbers by two-digit numbers without regrouping.

$$\begin{array}{r} 64 \\ \times 35 \\ \hline 320 \\ 192 \\ \hline 2240 \end{array}$$

• Multiplication of two-digit numbers by two-digit numbers with regrouping.

$$\begin{array}{r} 764 \\ \times 326 \\ \hline 4584 \\ 1528 \\ 2292 \\ \hline 249,064 \end{array}$$

• Multiplication of three-digit numbers by three-digit numbers with regrouping.

In good programs, such a progression is not pursued in isolation from other topics. Children do not first learn all there is to know about addition, then all there is to know about subtraction, then multiplication, then division. Rather, these operations are taught together as they reinforce and relate to one another. (Addition and subtraction are seen as inverse operations; division may be regarded as repeated subtraction; and so on.) But within each operation, the level of difficulty is carefully controlled until the child acquires mastery.

Skills and Knowledge Are Applied Constantly

In many mathematics programs (and in many mathematics textbooks), children are first taught a concept or skill, then given extensive practice in it, then led to apply it. The disadvantage of this approach is that when children reach the application stage—often the word problems at the end of the chapter—they may encounter difficulty because they have had no practice in the use of that skill or concept.

Good teachers circumvent this potential problem by constantly having children use what they are learning in ways that seem natural and fun. They use classroom situations (the arithmetic involved in planning the class trip), classroom studies (the geometry involved in building a stockade for social studies), the news and weather (charts, graphs, and computations of temperature and rainfall), games, and puzzles—any activity that requires children to think and to apply what they are learning. For children so instructed, mathematics is not something to be learned for its own sake—its natural and inevitable use is problem solving.

The Teacher Helps Each Child Learn

At the elementary school level, the teacher's job is not limited simply to presenting material. Her job is to ensure that children learn. With appropriate help from the child, the parent, and the school's support staff, the teacher should see that each child acquires the skills and knowledge considered important. Good teachers know what each child is learning and where each may be having difficulty, and they adapt their teaching accordingly and provide such help as may be needed.

For example, in one class a group of four children was asked to total the cost of various items they had selected on their makebelieve menus and to determine what each child should pay if the cost was shared equally. Knowing that the problem would be simple for one child, the teacher asked him to determine how much each of the other four children would have to pay if he paid one more dollar than the others.

WHAT TO LOOK FOR IN A GOOD FOURTH-GRADE MATHEMATICS PROGRAM

Like younger children, most fourth graders enjoy learning mathematics. If the program is one that stimulates their thinking without overtaxing their abilities, they respond readily to the challenge. If the answers to most or all of the following questions are yes, chances are your child is participating in an effective program. If many of the answers are no, you may want to inquire further by talking with your child's teacher and, possibly, the principal.

What to Look for in the Classroom

When you visit your child's classroom, do you see

- Number lines displayed on the walls or on the floor?
- Various graphs on various subjects, reflecting work that the teacher and the class has done?
- Chips, counters, Cuisenaire rods, and similar objects used for counting and sorting?
- Rulers, scales, thermometers, and other measuring devices?
- Pictures of two-dimensional shapes and three-dimensional objects used for exploring geometric properties?
- Worksheets showing good work done by children?

What to Look for From the Teacher

Does your child's fourth-grade teacher

- Describe clearly what the class has been doing in mathematics and what she plans for it to do?
- Provide time each day, or at least most days, for mathematical activity?
- Provide a program that follows the principles of effective mathematics teaching described above?
- Know your child's individual abilities and feelings about mathematics?
- Show enthusiasm about teaching mathematics?

What to Look for From Your Child

When you talk to your child during the fourth-grade year, does he

- Seem interested in using his mind for numbers, quantities, and mathematical relationships?
- Show a sense of excitement and confidence in using his mind for math?
- Describe math activities he has done in class?
- Bring home papers or worksheets reflecting work that he has done?
- Seem able to do the kind of work listed in the section "The Signs of Progress" (p. 161).

HOW TO HELP YOUR CHILD AT HOME

By the time your child is in fourth grade, he is no longer at the beginning of his formal study of mathematics. He has already spent several years in a planned program, with its own terminology, procedures, and expectations. For this reason, unless you are very sure of your ground, you should be wary about confusing your child by trying to teach him yourself. However, after consulting with the teacher, there are things you can do at home to reinforce what your child is learning at school.

Do's

- Talk to your child's teacher to find out about your child's math program and to ask what you can do at home.

- Praise and encourage your child's efforts to use mathematics: to do the arithmetic involved in shopping or traveling, to see patterns in numbers and shapes, to quantify phenomena in daily experience, and to think logically about them.
- Continue to estimate and measure with your child. Estimate the time it will take and the amount of gasoline you will use to get to Grandma's. Keep graphs of the temperature each day. Chart the shape and location of the moon at bedtime each night.
- Get your child to use mathematics in everyday situations. Ask him to check the grocery bill; have him make a budget for his Christmas shopping; get him to figure out how much soda and how many cookies will be needed for the birthday party and how much money.
- Play math games with your child. Games can be fun, and they improve the child's ability to think quantitatively and spatially. Games involving cards and dice are fun and can sharpen a child's skills of computation, short-term memory, and probability estimation. One good source is the book *Arithmetic Skill Development Games* by Michael Schiro (Belmont, Calif.: Fearon Pitman Publishers, 1978).
- Ask the teacher what kinds of mistakes your child makes in arithmetic. Find old workbooks that contain similar problems, and help your child with them. Do easy problems first, to build confidence.
- Help your child solve word problems (see the section "Problem Solving" earlier in this chapter). Be sure that your child understands the problem; have him state it in his own words. Be sure to estimate the answer beforehand and check it afterward.
- Help your child use a pocket calculator to assist in learning number facts and to check accuracy in computation (see the section "The Use of Calculators" in the chapter "Mathematics in the Third Grade").

Don'ts

- Don't be impatient. Your time with your child should be loving and supportive, not tense and anxiety-provoking.
- Don't persist with an activity if your child becomes frustrated or inattentive.
- Don't confuse your child or shake his confidence by criticizing the teacher's methods. Talk to the teacher if necessary, but work together, not at odds.
- Don't say that you (or some people) are "no good at math." Almost everyone can learn fourth-grade mathematics. Don't promote a defeatist attitude.
- Don't suggest that girls aren't as good in math as boys.

THE SIGNS OF PROGRESS

No single test can fully measure your child's progress in mathematics. Curricula vary somewhat from state to state and school to school. All tests merely sample a child's skill and knowledge and are thus subject to error; no tests satisfactorily measure such important traits and attitudes as persistence, imagination, and the willingness to use mathematical knowledge.

Nevertheless, by the time your child is in the fourth grade, his responses on written tests are usually the most readily available means of determining progress. Thus, by the time he finishes the fourth grade, he should be able to answer accurately the kinds of questions given below. Although these questions do not reflect the entire fourth-grade curriculum, they should give you a fair idea of your child's progress. If he can answer them easily and accurately, chances are that he is at least acquiring the minimum expected skills and knowledge. If he has trouble, he may need special help. Talk to his teacher and, if necessary, the principal. (You may want to assess your child's ability to answer questions like these in about April of his fourth-grade year.)

1. In which number is 8 in the millions place?

    a. 2,867.403
    b. 8,413,536
    c. 84,775,402
    d. 3,686,119

2. What is the place value of 6 in the number 16,902,000?

3. Which symbol belongs in the □? 483,903 □ 438,215.

    a. <
    b. >
    c. =
    d. +

4. What is 5313 rounded to the nearest thousand?

5. What is the sum?

    618
    4736
    +698

6. Add the following:

    25.703
    +92.829

7. What is the difference?

    7314
    −836

8. Subtract the following:

    40,230
    −32,541

9. What is the product?
4033
<u>×5</u>

10. Multiply the following:
6184
<u>×7</u>

11. What is the quotient?
4⟌3783

12. Which number sentence can be used to check the division?

```
    142          a. 142 + 568 = □
 4⟌568          b. 142 + 4 = □
  −400          c. 142 × 4 = □
    168          d. 142 × 568 = □
  −160
      8
    −8
      0
```

13. Add the following:
$17.99
<u>+0.86</u>

14. Subtract the following:
$20.00
<u>−9.98</u>

15. Multiply the following:
$0.85
<u>×9</u>

16. Which fraction pair names the shaded part?

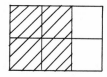

    a. $\frac{2}{3}$ $\frac{1}{6}$

    b. $\frac{2}{3}$ $\frac{1}{3}$

    c. $\frac{4}{6}$ $\frac{2}{3}$

    d. $\frac{4}{6}$ $\frac{1}{3}$

17. Which is a fraction for $2\frac{1}{2}$?

    a. $\frac{4}{2}$

    b. $\frac{5}{5}$

    c. $\frac{5}{4}$

    d. $\frac{5}{2}$

18. Complete the following number sentence:
$\frac{3}{4}$ of $12 = \square$

19. Add the following: $\frac{7}{12} + \frac{4}{12} = \square$.

20. One thousand milliliters is the same as how many liters?

21. How would the first figure look from the top?

a.

    a.   b.   c.   d.

22. The Grand Hotel has 20 floors. There are 10 large rooms and 15 small rooms on each floor. There are 50 balconies. How many rooms are there in the hotel?

23. The bus makes 12 trips daily between 9:00 A.M. and 5:00 P.M. If there are no stops between trips, how long is each trip?

Multiplication Table

×	0	1	2	3	4	5	6	7	8	9	10	11	12
0	0	0	0	0	0	0	0	0	0	0	0	0	0
1	0	1	2	3	4	5	6	7	8	9	10	11	12
2	0	2	4	6	8	10	12	14	16	18	20	22	24
3	0	3	6	9	12	15	18	21	24	27	30	33	36
4	0	4	8	12	16	20	24	28	32	36	40	44	48
5	0	5	10	15	20	25	30	35	40	45	50	55	60
6	0	6	12	18	24	30	36	42	48	54	60	66	72
7	0	7	14	21	28	35	42	49	56	63	70	77	84
8	0	8	16	24	32	40	48	56	64	72	80	88	96
9	0	9	18	27	36	45	54	63	72	81	90	99	108
10	0	10	20	30	40	50	60	70	80	90	100	110	120
11	0	11	22	33	44	55	66	77	88	99	110	121	132
12	0	12	24	36	48	60	72	84	96	108	120	132	144

NOTES

1. By the end of the fourth grade, your child should have mastered the basic multiplication facts contained in the multiplication table.
2. The facts should be learned through hands-on experience with real objects, not by rote. However, finding patterns in this table will help your child reinforce previously learned knowledge.
3. Once your child understands the commutative property of multiplication (that 2 × 4 = 4 × 2), the number of facts to be

learned is reduced from 169 to 91 (the 13 shaded facts on the diagonal and 78 facts on one side of the diagonal). Once the child knows that any number multiplied by zero is zero and any number multiplied by 1 is the number, the 91 facts are reduced to 66.

4. Once your child understands the inverse relationship of multiplication and division (that $4 \times 2 = 8$ and $8 \div 2 = 4$), the table can also be used to check division facts.

COMMON ERRORS IN MULTIPLICATION AND DIVISION

The following are examples of errors commonly made by children in elementary school. If your child makes such mistakes, follow the suggestions provided after the examples.

Error		Possible Explanation
1.	$\begin{array}{r} 67 \\ \times 8 \\ \hline 529 \end{array}$	Does not know basic multiplication fact; thinks $7 \times 8 = 49$.
2.	$54 \div 9 = 5$	Does not know basic division fact.
3.	$6 \times 0 = 6$	Does not understand role of zero in multiplication.
4.	$\begin{array}{r} 22 \\ \times 4 \\ \hline 68 \end{array}$	Confuses addition with multiplication; thinks $2 \times 4 = 8$, $2 + 4 = 6$.

5.
$$\begin{array}{r} 43 \\ \times 6 \\ \hline 58 \end{array}$$
Renames 4 in tens column but does not multiply (thinks $3 \times 6 = 18$, $1 + 4 = 5$).

6.
$$\begin{array}{r} 245 \\ \times 23 \\ \hline 735 \end{array}$$
Multiplies only by ones column. (Carelessness? Unfamiliarity with algorithm? Not bothering to estimate?)

7.
$$\begin{array}{r} 27 \\ \times 8 \\ \hline 166 \end{array}$$
Does not add regrouped number.

8.
$$\begin{array}{r} 2 \\ 8\overline{)40} \end{array}$$
Reverses divisor and dividend (thinks $8 \div 4$ instead of $40 \div 8$).

9.
$$\begin{array}{r} 15^{\text{rem } 4} \\ 24\overline{)384} \\ \underline{24} \\ 1\cancel{2}4 \\ \underline{120} \\ 4 \end{array}$$
Makes subtraction error within division algorithm.

10.
$$\begin{array}{r} 82^{\text{rem } 8} \\ 27\overline{)2322} \\ 2\cancel{2}6 \\ \hline 062 \\ -54 \\ \hline 8 \end{array}$$
Makes multiplication error within division algorithm.

11.
$$\begin{array}{r} 90 \\ 7\overline{)633} \\ \underline{630} \end{array}$$
Ignores remainder (perhaps doesn't know what to do with it).

12.
$$\begin{array}{r} 204 \\ 2\overline{)4008} \end{array}$$
Confuses place value in division algorithm.

If your child makes errors such as those above, ask him to do a similar exercise and explain to you step by step, in his own words, exactly what he is doing and why. Try to determine whether his error is the result of carelessness, misunderstanding of the problem, inaccurate computation, or lack of knowledge of the correct procedure. Then help your child work on similar problems, explaining carefully the procedure at each step. (*Note:* Give this kind of help only if you can be patient and supportive. Any sign of disapproval on your part will be counterproductive. If you know you can't be patient, go watch television or have a hot fudge sundae, and resolve to call your child's teacher in the morning.)

FIFTH GRADE

The Fifth-Grade Child as a Learner

The typical fifth-grade child has reached a serene plateau. He has come to terms with his body, his family, his teachers, his friends; he knows his world well and has a secure place in it. The ten-year-old has completed the struggles of childhood and pauses now before the storms of adolescence. As the psychologist David Elkind says, the age of ten is a "halcyon period in human development."

During this year, the child should consolidate the gains he has made in school thus far. He should master fully the basic skills of reading and mathematics and be well launched into reading in the content areas and into mathematical problem solving. Now that his perception of time and space is more like that of an adult, he should greatly expand his factual knowledge of history and geography. He should be at home performing simple science experiments. If he is musically inclined, he should begin to acquire technical proficiency.

In general, fifth grade is a wonderful year for your child to acquire more knowledge, memorize facts (the typical baseball statistics nut is a ten-year-old), and sharpen skills. The time for ambiguity and introspection and doubt and rebellion will come later. This happy time is the time to soak up knowledge. Help your child make the most of it!

Reading in the Fifth Grade

Literacy: Profiles of America's Young Adults, a 1986 study compiled by the National Assessment of Educational Progress, measured the literacy skills of young adults between the ages of twenty-one and twenty-five according to three literacy scales representing distinct and important aspects of literacy:

- *Prose literacy*—the knowledge and skills needed to understand and use information from texts that include editorials, news stories, poems, and the like.
- *Document literacy*—the knowledge and skills required to locate and use information contained in job applications or payroll forms, bus schedules, maps, tables, indexes, and so forth.
- *Quantitative literacy*—the knowledge and skills needed to apply arithmetic operations, either alone or sequentially, that are embedded in printed materials, such as in balancing a checkbook, figuring out a tip, completing an order form, or determining the amount of interest from a loan advertisement.

Among the study's major findings and conclusions were the following:

- While the overwhelming majority of young adults adequately perform tasks at the lower levels on each of the three scales, sizable numbers appear unable to do well on tasks of moderate complexity.
- "Illiteracy" is not a major problem for this population. It is also clear, however, that "literacy" *is* a problem. Sizable numbers of individuals are estimated to perform within the middle range on each of the scales. Within these broad ranges, individuals are neither totally "illiterate" nor fully "literate" for a technologically advanced society.
- The overwhelming majority of America's young adults are able to use printed information to accomplish many tasks that are either routine or uncomplicated. It is distressing, however, that relatively small proportions of young adults are estimated to be proficient at levels characterized by the more moderate or relatively complex tasks.

This study and others like it have prompted a reexamination of the way reading has been taught in the schools. In the view of most educators today, the emphasis placed on lower-level skills during the back-to-basics movement of the 1970s is too limited. New emphasis needs to be placed on the higher-order thinking skills of reading comprehension, interpretation, and analysis. Your child's fifth-grade program should reflect this approach.

PREPARATION FOR THE FIFTH GRADE

By the time your child enters the fifth grade, he should be ready for this emphasis. If he has been making normal progress in the lower grades, he should begin the fifth-grade year with most of the word recognition skills he needs to continue improving as a reader. He should also be accustomed to reading for meaning and to thinking about what he reads. More specifically, the child entering the fifth grade should

- Have an ample sight vocabulary of common words.
- Be able to use the skills of phonic analysis (initial consonants, ending consonants, medial consonants, consonant blends, short and long vowels, diphthongs, variant spellings) to decode unfamiliar words.
- Be able to use the skills of structural analysis (prefixes, suffixes, compounds, contractions) to determine the meaning of unfamiliar words.
- Be able to understand the meaning of stories and passages written at a fourth-grade level of difficulty.
- Be able to find the main idea and key details in passages of appropriate difficulty.
- Be able to determine sequences of time, place, activity, and thought.
- Be able to predict outcomes of events and actions of characters.
- Be able to understand the implications of a text, as well as its literal meaning.
- Be able to locate words in a dictionary and books in a library.

If your child can do these things, he is ready to begin fifth-grade work. If he cannot, you should consult with your child's teacher to determine the cause of his difficulty and to plan for appropriate remediation. Any reading problems that exist with children of this age should be diagnosed immediately and an appropriate remedial program begun at once.

THE FIFTH-GRADE READING PROGRAM

A complete fifth-grade reading program consists of developmental reading, recreational reading, and reading in the content areas. Developmental reading involves instruction in word recognition skills, comprehension skills, and study skills. Recreational reading is reading for pleasure; it entails growth in reading power, vocabulary, and human understanding as well. In content area reading, children are taught the skills necessary to read and learn effectively from textbooks and other materials in social studies, science, health, and other subjects.

Good fifth-grade teachers pay attention to each of these kinds of reading, adjusting their emphasis in order best to meet the needs of individual children in the class. Some children may need to continue work in the basic skills. Others may need continuing help in making the adjustment from learning to read to reading to learn in the content areas. Still others may need only occasional help or encouragement in the skills of reading; they are rapidly becoming effective readers, and the teacher can spend more time discussing with them the substance of what they read. The span of reading abilities in most fifth-grade classes is extensive. What should matter to you is that your child is receiving instruction at a level appropriate for him.

Word Recognition Skills

In the fifth grade, the emphasis of reading instruction is on comprehension and study skills. Nevertheless, good teachers know that the word recognition skills must be maintained, and that some children in the class may need continuing instruction in them. Word recognition skills were described in the chapter "Reading in the Third Grade." If your child has difficulty determining the meaning of an unfamiliar word, you may wish to reread that chapter.

Comprehension Skills

The purpose of reading, Jana M. Mason and Kathryn H. Au remind us, is to construct meaning from printed text. Recognition of words and syntactical patterns is not enough. The reader must comprehend what he is reading—the main idea of the essay, the events and mood of the story, the slant of the editorial, the steps and sequence of the travel directions. Furthermore, reading is not passive—the good reader does not simply let the writer's words and ideas wash over him. He actively uses his mind to comprehend the writer's meaning, to relate what he is reading to prior knowledge, to interpret what he is reading in light of his past experiences, to vary the speed and closeness of his reading with his purpose.

Good reading instruction helps children become active, competent, thinking readers. Among the comprehension skills commonly taught at this level are the following:

- Identifying the main idea of a paragraph, a short passage, or a short story.
- Making generalizations based on the main idea of two or more sources.
- Finding key details.
- Relating key details and groups of details to an author's main idea and purpose.
- Determining sequences of time, place, activity, and thought.
- Predicting outcomes of events and action of characters.
- Understanding the implications of a text, as well as its literal meaning.
- Inferring relationships not stated.
- Distinguishing between fact and opinion.

- Recognizing sales and propaganda techniques.
- Discerning an author's point of view.

These skills are the same as those in grade 4, but they are applied to increasingly difficult reading material. Good programs help children apply these skills to all kinds of reading matter.

Study Skills

Increasingly, the child uses his developing reading ability to gain information and understanding in other subjects, such as history, geography, science, and health. As he does so, he needs to develop study skills enabling him to make the most of what he reads. Good reading programs help him do so. Among the study skills most commonly taught at this level are the following:

- Following written directions (of increasing complexity).
- Using alphabetical sequence to locate books and other material.
- Understanding and using the various parts of a book (tables of contents, chapter headings, indexes, glossaries, appendixes).
- Using a dictionary (for word meanings, spelling, other information).
- Using simple encyclopedias.
- Locating books and simple reference material in a library.
- Recalling important information.
- Organizing information to facilitate understanding and recall.
- Obtaining information from maps, charts, globes, and drawings.

As with comprehension skills, these skills are the same as the skills in grade 4, but are applied to increasingly difficult reading material. Good programs help children apply these study skills to all subject areas.

TEACHING THE FIFTH-GRADE READING PROGRAM

As we have said, the fifth-grade reading program focuses on the development of comprehension and study skills. However, the ways in which schools and teachers organize their programs vary widely.

Some teachers continue to use basal reading programs, in the manner described in the chapter "Reading in the Third Grade." Some use basal readers occasionally, to review or reinforce a basic skill. Some use them for pupils of lower ability but not for those who are more advanced. (It is not uncommon for many levels of readers to be used in the same class.) Most teachers also teach reading through books of literature or through textbooks in the content areas—chiefly social studies, science, and health. (In this way, a lesson may be about social studies and reading simultaneously, and more school time is gained for teaching both content and comprehension skills.) Some teachers teach reading through the content areas exclusively, without the use of basal readers.

In the lower grades, most of the reading material is in story form. (It may or may not be literature; that is another matter.) Research has shown that narrative text is easier for children to understand than expository text. Gradually, however, good programs introduce children to expository writing. By the fifth grade, some experts say, half or more of the reading instruction that children receive should involve expository writing.

Whether the material that children are reading is in their basal readers, in social studies or science textbooks, or in trade books selected by the teacher or the child, the general form of the comprehension lesson is apt to be the same. First, there is a stage of *pre-reading*, in which the teacher introduces the children to the text to be read. She provides relevant background information, elicits interest, sets purposes for reading, raises pertinent questions, and helps children focus their attention.

Then comes the stage of *guided reading.* The children read the assigned passage, usually silently, remembering the questions that the teacher had raised. (Sometimes teachers give written study questions to provide additional guidance at this stage.) When the children finish the passage, the teacher questions them about it. Good teachers ask questions at different levels of thinking—from the literal (What happened? What did it say?) to the evaluative (How useful was it? Was it fair?). Sometimes, alas, the questions simply belabor the obvious or ask the child to confirm what the teacher is thinking. Effective teachers ask questions that truly get children to think on their own.

Finally, there is the stage of *post-reading,* in which the teacher helps the children to reflect on what they have read, to remember important information, and to make connections between what they have read and other reading they have done or other experiences they have had. She may also provide feedback on how well they have done with the lesson, with an eye toward motivating or helping them in their next effort.

If the process is effective, the child should not only understand and appreciate what he has read for its content, he should also be acquiring valuable comprehension and study skills as well. He is learning to read for a specific purpose: to monitor his own progress in accomplishing that purpose (called *metacognition* by some educators) and to think about what he has read and relate it to other knowledge and experience.

Some teachers make such teaching and learning of comprehension skills explicit and overt; that is, they teach specific techniques for improving reading comprehension. One such study method, often used when reading is taught through the content areas, is SQ3R (survey-question-read-recite-review). This technique, introduced by F. P. Robinson in 1961, provides a systematic method for reading and learning text material as follows:

- *Survey:* The child previews the material, noting its organization, looking at the table of contents, chapter or section headings, illustrations.

- *Question:* Working alone, in pairs, or in groups, the children pose questions about the information they expect to find. The questions should be appropriate to the purpose for reading the text.
- *Read:* The child reads the text, trying to answer the questions that had been raised.
- *Recite:* The child puts the text away and tries to answer his own (or the teacher's) questions orally or in writing.
- *Review:* The child rereads the text in order to check the accuracy of his answers.

This technique, and variations of it, can be useful in helping motivate children of this age.

WHAT TO LOOK FOR IN A GOOD FIFTH-GRADE READING PROGRAM

There is no one best way to teach reading. Studies have shown that good teaching can occur with many methods. Unhappily, poor teaching can occur with many methods as well. From the parents' point of view, the method that works best is the one that works with your child.

Fortunately, you don't need to be a trained reading teacher to know whether your child is receiving effective instruction or not. If the answers to most of the following questions are yes, chances are your child is participating in an effective reading program. If many of the answers are no, you should talk to your child's teacher and, perhaps, the principal to see what changes can be made.

- Does the teacher have a plan for reading instruction? Can she describe clearly and specifically how her program is organized? Can she list the comprehension and study skills she is trying to teach?

- Does the teacher know your child's instructional level? Can she tell you not only what book he is in, but exactly what skills he is working on?
- Does the teacher provide time for reading instruction each day? Is there time for both reading for pleasure and working on skills?
- Does the teacher provide reading instruction in the content areas—social studies, science, health?
- Does the teacher frequently read aloud to the children, to share her enthusiasm and to motivate the children to read?
- Are books, magazines, and other reading materials abundantly available in the classroom?
- Do the children make frequent use of the school and/or community library?
- Does your child like to read at home?
- Does your child score at least on grade level on standardized reading tests?

HOW TO HELP YOUR CHILD AT HOME

Most parents should not try to teach their children to read. Teaching reading requires special skill and knowledge, and even when a parent is a trained reading teacher, he or she may do more harm than good by creating tension with the child or by conflicting with the teacher's methods. However, there are things that you can do at home in order to create an atmosphere that will encourage your child to read.

Do's

- Praise and encourage your child's successful efforts to read.
- Continue to read to your child, every day if possible, but frequently no matter what. Don't think that your child is too

old to be read to now that he can read himself—most children this age still love the time they spend with their parents this way.

- Encourage your child to read to you when he feels comfortable doing so.
- Continue to give your child books as presents. Make them special.
- Visit the library with your child and help him choose books that he may like.
- Limit the amount of television your child watches. Research has shown that viewing television for about ten hours per week may actually aid reading achievement. Beyond this amount, achievement tends to decline.
- Make constructive use of the television your child does watch. Be selective about the programs he sees; talk with him about the content of the program; find reading material related to matters that interest him on television.
- Talk often with your child to help him enlarge his vocabulary and to use language to think and to express himself.
- Confer periodically with your child's teacher to learn about his progress at school.

THE SIGNS OF PROGRESS

No single test can measure accurately your child's annual progress in reading, and surely no single set of questions can do so. However, the following poem by Langston Hughes and the questions taken from the teacher's guide to *Standing Strong*, Allyn and Bacon, Inc. (1978, pp. 275–76), may give you some idea of the material your child should be reading and how he is asked to respond to it:

Mother to Son

Well, son, I'll tell you:
Life for me ain't been no crystal stair.
It's had tacks in it,
And splinters,
And boards torn up,
And places with no carpet on the floor—
Bare.
But all the time
I'se been a-climbin' on,
And reachin' landin's,
And turnin' corners,
And sometimes goin' in the dark
Where there ain't been no light.
So, boy, don't you turn back.
Don't you set down on the steps
'Cause you finds it kinder hard.
Don't you fall now—
For I'se still goin', honey,
I'se still climbin',
And life for me ain't been no crystal stair.
—Langston Hughes

Discussion After Reading

1. To what is the poet comparing life in this poem?
2. Why do you think the poet uses the idea of a long hard climb to describe life?
3. Have you had any experiences that seemed like a hard climb or a hard struggle? What were they?
4. If you were to describe your own life in terms of something else, as the poet has done here, what would you use?

5. What kind of woman do you think the mother was?
6. What kinds of bad experiences do you think she has had in her life?
7. What is she telling her son?
8. What does the mother mean when she speaks of life being "no crystal stair"?

Literature in the Fifth Grade

"I don't know what you mean by 'glory,' " Alice said.

Humpty Dumpty smiled contemptuously. "Of course you don't—till I tell you. I meant 'there's a nice knock-down argument for you!' "

"But 'glory' doesn't mean 'a nice knock-down argument,' " Alice objected.

"When *I* use a word," Humpty Dumpty said, in rather a scornful tone, "it means just what I choose it to mean—neither more nor less."

"The question is," said Alice, "whether you *can* make words mean so many different things."

"The question is," said Humpty Dumpty, "which is to be master—that's all."

Perhaps the full import of this lesson in semantics is lost on most fifth-grade children when first they read or hear it, although the interplay of personalities couched in polite language is apt not to be. But the memory of Alice and the March Hare and the Mad Hatter and the Red Queen shrieking "Off with their heads" and all the wonderful other characters of Lewis Carroll's invention is likely to carry the reader back to the text again, and each rereading may be rewarded with surprise and fresh understanding. For so it is with classics, and so it must be with readers who would be masters of their language and its literary tradition.

In the fifth grade, works of literature occupy a central place in the child's reading program. In an individualized reading program, they constitute the bulk of the child's reading. In a basal reading program, they are used by good teachers as enrichment and as motivation for improving their reading ability. Whatever the program, good teachers spend much time reading aloud to their children (in some classes for a certain portion of each day), finding appealing books of appropriate difficulty for children to read, talking about stories and poems, and sharing their pleasure and enthusiasm with the class.

There is no end to the variety and number of things to be read. Children should read or listen to folktales, fables, myths, legends. They should explore stories of all kinds—adventure stories, fantasy stories, realistic stories, animal stories, stories about science, stories about the past, stories about other people in other lands, stories and biographies about famous men and women. They should read and hear poetry of all kinds—story poems, nonsense poems, nursery rhymes, song lyrics, poems about nature and animals and space travel and people and children like themselves.

Some of this literature should be old—the children's classics of our tradition. Children should not grow up without experiencing the great works that have entertained and instructed generations, works like Carroll's *Alice in Wonderland*, J. M. Barrie's *Peter Pan*, Rudyard Kipling's *Just So Stories*, and Mary Mapes Dodge's *Hans Brinker and the Silver Skates*. But some of the literature should be new, with a more contemporary ring and feel. Most fifth-grade children enjoy such works as *Zeely* by Virginia Hamilton, *James and the Giant Peach* by Roald Dahl, *Harriet the Spy* by Louise Fitzhugh, and the poetry of Carl Sandburg and Langston Hughes.

Good teachers employ many techniques to introduce their

children to such literature and to motivate them to read it. They read aloud to the class, making the story hour a warm and special time. They bring new books to class, show them to children, talk about them. They create displays of books and book jackets on counters, bulletin boards, and doorframes. They arrange reading corners in their classrooms—snug nooks with a rug for lying on, a special lamp, and dozens of new books, waiting to be tried. They provide time for children to read in class. They distribute book lists to children and parents. They call attention to films and movies based on books and make the books available to their classes. They organize book clubs. They take their children to the library often, and they bring books from the library to class. They make every effort to create an environment in which reading is made fun, important, and easy to do.

Obviously, when children read literary works and discuss them with their teachers or with others in the class, they are improving their reading skills. Indeed, as we have said, in some classes such works constitute the bulk of the reading that children do. In any program, however, good teachers never forget that the basic reason for reading literature is to enjoy it. Whatever other benefits may be derived—reading skill, human understanding, enlarged vocabulary, ability to write—they are secondary to the sheer pleasure that comes from reading a well-written piece that has something to say.

For this reason, good teachers do not make children reduce everything they have read to the form of a standard book report. Sometimes they simply ask the child what he has read, noting the title and the author in their records. Sometimes they ask the child two or three questions to test comprehension and to help the child think about what he has read. (Why was Big John happy at the end? Could the ending have been different? What other book was this most similar to?) Sometimes they have the child write something about the book, discussing a favorite character, an exciting scene, a question not answered. Sometimes, when more than one child has read the same book, they arrange for group reports in the form of a play, pantomime, puppet show, or mural to be shared with the rest of the class. The trick is to capitalize on the child's natural urge to share with other people something he has enjoyed. In good classrooms, the atmosphere of the literature program is always one of discovery and joy. At the fifth-grade level, children are encouraged to read widely—historical and current fiction, biographies, nonfiction, and poetry.

At this level, some teachers talk to children about elements· of fiction—plot, setting, character, theme, even point of view. Teachers ask questions to help children focus their attention, notice details, interpret motives, predict outcomes, and understand implications. (What was the hero's chief conflict? What would have happened if —? What would you have done in that situation? Why do you suppose the author made the story happen in springtime? Suppose you were the author and you had written this, what would you have happen next?) Sometimes the discussion is related to the children's own writing. The teacher uses selections from good literature as a model for what the child may write. For example, a writing lesson may be about a good lead or a good beginning, and the teacher may use good leads from literature as examples.

In good classrooms at this level, however, such discussions are always conducted for the purpose of heightening appreciation and enjoyment. Learning the terms and methods of literary criticism is not yet essential. There will be time for literary criticism later in your child's school career. Now is the time for literary enjoyment.

The literature program is one part of the school curriculum in which parents *can* play an important role. Because the purpose at this level is not so much to teach children about literature as to immerse them in it, parents can be very helpful simply by encouraging children to read, finding books for them to read, and reading to them at home. Suggest old favorites of yours for your child to try. Read a book your child particularly likes so you may discuss it together. Establish your own story hour—even once or twice a week, if you are busy—and make it special and important. Balance the familiar works that your child wants to hear again and again with works that are new to him (and you). Talk with your child about what you have read. And, since in the end it is your behavior and not the teacher's that your child is more likely to emulate, spend time reading for enjoyment yourself.

Writing in the Fifth Grade

The fifth-grader writer is growing up and is more comfortable with writing than he was in fourth grade. He is willing to take chances and takes pleasure in expanding his vocabulary with the use of a thesaurus. Fifth graders are more skillful at integrating dialogue, action, and description in their writing than children in the lower grades. Many fifth graders know how to use a word processor and find it helpful. They write personal essays and news articles for classroom and school newspapers, as well as reports in other disciplines.

A fifth-grade class in a small town is in the middle of a writing lesson. On the bulletin board is a display of books with illustrated covers by classroom authors. Gay-colored letters announce VISIONS AND REVISIONS above the display. Titles include "Avis Rent a Wreck," "The Unwelcome Surprise," and "The Unbelievable Car Ride." Two children are sitting in a corner. One is reading his story and the other listens carefully. Several children are at their desks, writing. A few are illustrating covers. At a round table, six children and the teacher are conferring. The teacher says to one child, "What can we help you with?"

"I'd like to know what everybody thinks of my lead,"

says a girl with a red bow. The teacher motions for her to read it. "Lizzie walked into the bathroom at three in the morning with frosted flakes in her hair."

The children and teacher laugh. "Did that get your attention?" the teacher asks the pupils. They all nod affirmatively.

Another child is having difficulty with his lead. The teacher suggests, "Why don't you try beginning with a piece of conversation?"

One boy has written his whole piece but was having trouble with the ending. He read the two endings he had composed. The group pointed out what they thought was good about each ending. He finally decided to write an ending that included portions of both.

Under a good teacher's guidance, fifth-grade children work well in a workshop situation. They are enthusiastic about their writing and about that of their classmates. They show a high degree of interest in each other's work and nothing is more encouraging than when a child's peers and teacher are interested in his work.

Personal experience continues to be a major source of the fifth grader's writing. At this level, that experience can and should be expanded to include reactions to and evaluations of films, books, field trips, and even classroom discussions.

Gaining skill in particular writing techniques occupies an important part in the fifth-grade curriculum. *Voice, point of view, focus, dialogue,* and *lead* are common terms used in writing lessons and conferences. Children discover from their teacher that professional writers often delete adjectives and adverbs during the editing process and that good writing depends on strong verbs and nouns. Teachers help children discover the power of verbs. A teacher may write *walk* on the blackboard and then elicit verbs from the children that illustrate a specific kind of walking, like *slink, limp,* and *amble.* Later, during a conference with a child about his composition, the teacher or another child may remind the writer that *amble* is a stronger way of saying *walk slowly*.

Awareness of this writing technique is equally valuable in content writing. A child writing a science report about a porcupine or a tiger may want to use strong verbs when describing the animal's behavior.

Good teachers of writing encourage children to develop their own voice. Some children use humor. Others write with a sensitivity unique to them. Some experiment with poetry.

Writing is usually the last step in a long, laborious process of thinking, organizing, reorganizing, inserting, and deleting. The professional writer is only too aware that the words on the paper represent a small portion of his labor.

During the past decade, educators and researchers have examined and reexamined the intricacies of the writing process. Books have been published about writing, studies conducted, and courses given in universities and in school districts across the country. Terms like *brainstorm, rehearse, draft, confer, revise,* and *edit* have been assigned to the routines that writers have followed unconsciously over the ages.

Just as in the earlier grades, some adaptation of the writing process continues to serve as the basis of many fifth-grade writing programs. Children who have been exposed to writing during the earlier years are comfortable with it and understand the process and the terms. The U.S. Department of Education 1986 publication *What Works: Research About Teaching and Learning* unequivocally states that "the most effective way to teach writing is to teach it as a process of brainstorming, composing, revising, and editing." The report also suggests that good writing assignments "are often an extension of class reading, discussion, and activities; not isolated exercises."

Many school districts offer writing workshops to their teachers as part of their professional development programs. When teachers themselves write and become conscious of their own process, they are apt to be better teachers of writing. If your school district does not offer writing workshops or encourage teachers to participate in workshops in local colleges or adult schools, you might encourage the Board of Education and the administration to consider doing so.

A March 1985 report by James Howard from the Council of Basic Education ("A Report on Writing as a Key to Improving Academic Learning") strongly urges that the writing process not be limited to the subjects of writing, language arts, or English but be used when children write in the areas of social studies, science, health, and even math. Reports written by children familiar with the writing process approach come alive with personal observations and reactions to research. The techniques learned in writing from personal experience have strong applications in writing in the content areas.

Tammy Moore   Mrs. Voltmer
Grade 5   <u>My</u> <u>Week</u> <u>Without</u> <u>Any</u> <u>T V</u> !   3/26/

It all started when Aaron Handelman gave his current
events. A sixth-grade boy had bet his mother $500 that
he wouldn't watch T.U. for an entire year and he did-
n't which was even more surprising! He of course
got paid his $500 as the reward.

. Mrs. Voltmer got the interesting idea that our
class could something like that but only for
a week. She thought it would be interesting to see
it we could last for a whole week which she
wasn't sure if we could all do.

A couple of days later Mrs. Voltmer gave us a
piece of paper saying that our class was going to
try to not watch T.U. for a week starting March
9 - March 16. We had to bring it home to get signed
by our parents and we had to sign it ourselves. When
I first gave my mother the notice she wasn't
too sure I would make it through the week but
I told her I might be able to.

I thought Monday was my easiest yet still
the hardest day because I had things to keep me
busy but I was used to watching a good deal
of TV so it was hard for me to give it up just
like that. As the days went on it got a bit easier

because I wasn't as hung up on T.V., but it also got a bit harder because I was running out of things to keep me busy during the extra time. The weekend of the pledge I went skiing so that helped me keep busy. At the place where I was staying there was a couple I could play games with. Not to drift off the subject; I found lots of things to keep me busy such as playing games with my sister, taking longer with my homework, reading a bit more and using the phone with my friends a lot more.

I think the pledge was a good idea. For one it saved my mom some money for electricity bills and it showed me that T.V. wasn't an absolute necessity. It also was a good idea because kids who thought they couldn't do it now know they can do things that they try to do. I think the pledge was a real challenge!

After the pledge was over I watched a lot less T.V. That's another good thing that came out of the experiment. The pledge was kind of hard but 2 things kept me going; "WILLPOWER" & the thought of CHEESY PIZZA!

by
Tammy Moore

A GOOD WRITING PROGRAM

A good writing program is one that

- Understands the writing process.
- Values children's experience and their perception of it.
- Helps children to be good observers, to listen to sounds, to notice smells, to see detail.
- Helps children transfer their skills from their personal writing to their content writing.
- Provides time for the entire writing process and time for children to listen to and read their classmates' writing. Some classrooms have libraries of "books" by classroom authors. Some schools have parent volunteer programs with parents editing and typing books by children.
- Teaches children how to be good editors, to ask the right questions, to be specific, to be positive and encouraging and yet helpful, to be committed to helping others create a better piece.
- Recognizes the difference between handwriting and writing, helping children for whom handwriting is especially difficult by allowing them occasionally to dictate stories or use a word processor.
- Recognizes that spelling should be correct in the finished draft (without overemphasizing it in working drafts).
- Values literature, encourages children to read, and provides time for reading aloud to them.
- Recognizes that writing, like speaking, is a trial-and-error skill and needs encouragement and nurturing.
- Displays children's writing prominently and attractively.
- Stresses the specifics of what is good about some writing samples.
- Shows interest in every child's writing.
- Uses models for writing techniques from literature.
- Encourages each child to develop his own writing voice.
- Teaches children how to organize factual material and observations.

Mathematics in the Fifth Grade

The study of mathematics is cumulative. Year after year, as your child's mental abilities develop and as he uses them to acquire and apply mathematical skills and knowledge, the concepts and operations in the mathematics curriculum become increasingly complex. The scope of fifth-grade mathematics is still well within the capacities of most children and parents, but it is no longer the simple matter it was in the earlier grades. In the fifth grade, your child will be expected to master most common arithmetic operations involving whole numbers, to understand and use fractions, to be familiar with the properties and order of arithmetic operations, to find the area, volume, and perimeter of simple plane and solid geometric figures, and more. Given a good foundation, good instruction, and proper encouragement at school and at home, he should have no lasting trouble. But ideally, each of these conditions should be present.

If your child has developed a solid foundation of mathematical skills and knowledge in the earlier grades, he should be thoroughly familiar with our system of counting and writing numbers (including decimals, fractions, mixed numbers, and negative numbers), understand the inverse relationships of addition/subtraction and multiplication/division, know basic addition and multiplication number facts, be familiar with the common algorithms (procedures) for arithmetic operations, arrange data logically in simple graphs and charts, know the standard units and tools of common measurements, recognize common two- and three-dimensional geometric shapes, and apply his mathematical knowledge to the solution of simple word problems. If your child has not acquired these skills, you should see his teacher early in the fifth year to ask her help in diagnosing the existing difficulty and work out a plan to provide the necessary remedial help.

The material presented in this chapter should provide the necessary information to help you determine whether your child is receiving effective mathematics instruction or not. Elementary-school teachers vary in their ability to teach mathematics, especially in the upper grades. A small number may have that special gift to spark children's enthusiasm and to stimulate them to think mathematically. Most will be competent. A few may not be versed well enough in the subject to feel comfortable teaching it and to vary instruction so as to meet all the needs of the class. If you think that the last may be true, talk to your child's principal. Perhaps with some supervisory help, the teacher can improve. Perhaps a team teaching arrangement can be devised, as in some schools. (If there are two fifth-grade classes in the school, Teacher A can teach math to both classes and teacher B can teach social studies to both classes.)

As you assess your child's program, remember that the main goal of the mathematics program is to get your child to use mathematics to solve problems. Basic skills and knowledge are essential, but in themselves they are useless unless the child is motivated and knows how to use them. Praise him when he uses his mind, even if a given conclusion is inaccurate. Accuracy is to be prized, but it will come later. The goal of the program now is not to transmit inert knowledge but to stimulate informed activity of mind.

THE FIFTH-GRADE MATHEMATICS CURRICULUM

Schools establish their mathematics curricula in various ways. In some cases, a textbook or series of textbooks is adopted for use in a given school, community, or state, and the teacher is required to follow the text or series as the basis of the curriculum. In other cases, a course of study, or *scope and sequence*, is developed by the school system or the state, and the teacher is free to choose from a variety of books and other instructional materials. Whatever the origin, fifth-grade mathematics curricula throughout the United States are much more similar to one another than they are different.

Typically, the fifth-grade mathematics curriculum comprises five parts, or *strands:*

> Numbers and numeration
> Operations with whole numbers
> Operations with fractions
> Probability and statistics
> Geometry and measurement

Some curricula include a sixth part—problem solving. In the authors' view, however, problem solving is the goal of all mathematics and should be incorporated into the teaching and learning of each part of the curriculum.

The five strands of the mathematics curriculum are taught throughout the elementary grades. Skills and topics are often repeated from grade to grade; material may be introduced at one grade level, taught and practiced extensively at the next, and reviewed and "mastered" at the third. Such overlapping is not inefficient; it is a deliberate teaching strategy to ensure that the child gains a secure foundation in the subject. For this reason, you may wish to look at the chapter on mathematics in the fourth grade. In the fifth grade, the skills and knowledge on which children typically concentrate are discussed in the following.

Numbers and Numeration

- Cardinal numbers: Read and write cardinal numbers to one billion.
- Ordinal numbers: Read and write ordinal numbers to one billion.
- Numerals: Read and write Roman numerals from I to MM (1 to 2000).
- Place value. Learn the concept of place value to billions and thousandths:
  Example   6,472,900,102.167.
- Prime numbers: Discover the prime numbers between 1 and 100. (A prime number is a natural number greater than 1, the only factors of which are 1 and itself:) *Examples*   2, 3, 5, 7, 11, . . .
- Decimals and fractions: Learn the concept that a number may be symbolized by many different numerals:
  Example $\frac{1}{4} = \frac{2}{8} = \frac{4}{16} = \frac{25}{100} = 0.25$.
- Negative numbers: Learn to use positive and negative numbers in real situations and in educational games:
  Example   At bedtime, the temperature was -2 degrees Celsius. Overnight it went down 3 more degrees. What was the temperature in the morning?
- Exponents: Learn to use exponents as an alternate way of naming numbers, especially large numbers:

Examples $10^1 = 10$
$$10^2 = 10 \times 10 = 100$$
$$10^3 = 10 \times 10 \times 10 = 1000$$
$$10^4 = 10 \times 10 \times 10 \times 10 = 10,000$$
$$10^5 = 10 \times 10 \times 10 \times 10 \times 10 = 100,000$$

$10^6 = 10 \times 10 \times 10 \times 10 \times 10 \times 10 = 1,000,000$
$10^7 = 10 \times 10 \times 10 \times 10 \times 10 \times 10 \times 10 = 10,000,000$
$10^8 = 10 \times 10 \times 10 \times 10 \times 10 \times 10 \times 10 \times 10 =$
100,000,000
$10^9 = 10 \times 10 \times 10 \times 10 \times 10 \times 10 \times 10 \times 10 \times 10$
$= 1,000,000,000$

- Rounding: Learn to round (or round off) numbers to the nearest hundredth, tenth, whole number, hundred, thousand, and ten thousand:

  Examples   6.467 becomes 6.47
  128,892 becomes 130,000

- Estimation: Estimate large quantities by applying mathematical skills and knowledge, including rounding:
  Example   The product of 54 × 78 is greater than 50 × 70 and less than 60 × 80. Develop the habit of estimating answers to problems as a means of checking reasonableness of answer.
- Patterns: Explore sequences in patterns of numbers.

Operations With Whole Numbers

- Addition and subtraction: Master addition and subtraction facts through 24. Add up to four six-digit numbers, with or without regrouping. Subtract up to six-digit numbers, with or without regrouping. Use addition and subtraction as inverse operations to check accuracy. Use rounding to estimate sums and differences:

Example	412	500	400
	893	900	800
	127	200	100
		1600	1300

(The sum is less than 1600 but more than 1300.) Use the
estimate-compute-check routine in all computation.
- Multiplication and division: Master multiplication facts
through 12 × 12. Learn to use the standard algorithm
(procedure) for multiplying up to a three-digit number:

$$\begin{array}{r} \textit{Example} \quad 24615 \\ \times 345 \\ \hline 123075 \\ 98460 \\ 73845 \\ \hline 8492175 \end{array}$$

Understand division as the inverse operation of multiplication:

$$\textit{Example} \quad \begin{aligned} 32 \times 6 &= 192 \\ 192 \div 6 &= 32 \end{aligned}$$

Master division facts through 144 ÷ 12. Learn to divide up to
six-digit numbers by one-, two-, and three-digit numbers;
find both quotient and remainder (if any):

$$\textit{Examples} \quad \begin{array}{r} 2893 \\ 24\overline{)69432} \\ \underline{48} \\ 214 \\ \underline{192} \\ 223 \\ \underline{216} \\ 72 \\ \underline{72} \\ 0 \end{array} \qquad \begin{array}{r} 20\frac{10}{112} \\ 112\overline{)2250} \\ \underline{224} \\ 10 \\ \underline{0} \\ 10 \end{array}$$

Identify factors and prime factors:
Example   24 has the factors 1, 2, 3, 4, 6, 8, 12, and 24; 2 and 3 are the prime factors. Find the average of a set of up to six two-digit numbers.

- Properties of operations: Learn that addition and multiplication both have the commutative property (the order of the two numbers in addition and multiplication can be reversed without changing the answer):

$$\begin{aligned} \textit{Examples} \quad & 2 + 4 = 4 + 2 \\ & 2 \times 3 = 3 \times 2 \end{aligned}$$

Learn that multiplication has the commutative property and that division does not:

$$\begin{aligned} \textit{Examples} \quad & 12 \times 6 = 6 \times 12 \quad \text{YES} \\ & 12 \div 6 = 6 \div 12 \quad \text{NO} \end{aligned}$$

Learn that addition and multiplication both have the associative property (given a series of whole numbers to be added or multiplied, the order in which they are added or multiplied can be changed without changing the answer.)

$$\begin{aligned} \textit{Examples} \quad & 4 + 6 + 3 = 4 + 6 + 3 \\ & 10 + 3 = 4 + 9 \\ & 13 = 13 \\[6pt] & 2 \times 3 \times 4 = 2 \times 3 \times 4 \\ & 6 \times 4 = 2 \times 12 \\ & 24 = 24 \end{aligned}$$

Learn that multiplication has the distributive property over addition and subtraction. If two numbers are added together and the sum multiplied by a third number, the same result is obtained if each of the first two is first multiplied by the third and the two products added.

Examples $4 \times (3 + 2) = (4 \times 3) + (4 \times 2)$
$4 \times 5 = 12 + 8$
$20 = 20$

$5 \times (6 - 4) = (5 \times 6) - (5 \times 4)$
$5 \times 2 = 30 - 20$
$10 = 10$

Use the distributive property of multiplication over subtraction to compute mentally:

Example $6 \times 99 =$
$(6 \times 100) - (6 \times 1) =$
$600 - 6 = 594$

Learn that the identity property for addition is the special number 0 and that the identity property for multiplication is the number 1:

Examples $159 + 0 = 159$
$273 \times 1 = 273$

• Order of operations: Learn the conventional rule for the order of operations: (1) All exponentiations first; (2) all multiplications and divisions next; (3) all additions and subtractions last:

Example $3^2 + 8 \div 2 - 3 \times 4 = \Box$
(1) Exponentiation:
$9 + 8 \div 2 - 3 \times 4 =$
(2) Multiplication and division:
$9 + 4 - 12 =$
(3) Addition and subtraction:
$13 - 12 = 1$

- Word problems: Use addition, subtraction, multiplication, and/or division to solve word problems, including multiple-step problems:
  Example The car wash washed twice as many cars on Saturday as on Friday. Fifty-seven cars were washed altogether. How many cars were washed each day?

Operations With Fractions

- Relationship to multiplication and division: Understand the inverse relationships between multiplication and division involving fractions:
  Example $\frac{36}{6} = \frac{1}{6} \times 36$.
- Addition and subtraction: Locate fractions and mixed numbers on a number line. Develop sets of equivalent fractions:
  Example $\frac{1}{2} = \frac{2}{4} = \frac{3}{6} = \frac{4}{8}$ etc.
  Add and subtract fractions with like and unlike denominators:

$$\text{Examples} \quad \frac{3}{8} + \frac{4}{8} = \frac{7}{8}$$
$$\frac{1}{2} + \frac{1}{3} = \frac{5}{6}$$
$$\frac{1}{2} \times \frac{1}{3} = \frac{1}{6}$$

Add and subtract mixed numbers with like and unlike denominators:

$$\text{Examples} \quad 2\frac{1}{4} + 3\frac{3}{4} = \frac{8+1}{4} + \frac{12+3}{4} = \frac{9}{4} + \frac{15}{4} = \frac{24}{4} = 6$$
$$2\frac{1}{4} + 1\frac{1}{3} = \frac{9}{4} + \frac{4}{3} =$$
$$\frac{27}{12} + \frac{16}{12} = \frac{43}{12} = \frac{36}{12} +$$
$$\frac{7}{12} = 36\frac{17}{12}$$

- Factoring: Find prime factors in numerators and denominators.

Example: $\frac{6}{10} = \frac{3 \times 2}{5 \times 2}$

Determine common denominators of two or more fractions:

Example $\frac{1}{2} + \frac{1}{3} = \frac{3 + 2}{6}$

Find the greatest common factor (GCF) and least common multiple (LCM) of sets of whole numbers:

Examples GCF (21, 27, 30) = 3
LCM (2, 7, 8) = 56

Rename fractions to lowest terms:

Example $\frac{9}{12} = \frac{3}{4}$.

- Multiplication and division: Understand the inverse relationship between multiplication and division involving fractions:

Examples $\frac{36}{6} = \frac{1}{6} \times 36$
$\frac{1}{3} \div 2 = \frac{1}{3} \times \frac{1}{2} = \frac{1}{6}$

Multiply fractions by whole numbers:

Example $\frac{3}{4} \times 3 = \frac{3}{4} \times \frac{3}{1} = \frac{9}{4} = 2\frac{1}{4}$.

Multiply one proper fraction by another:

Example $\frac{1}{2} \times \frac{2}{3} = \frac{2}{6} = \frac{1}{3}$

- Decimals: Add and subtract decimals to thousandths:

Example
$$\begin{array}{r} 16.124 \\ -8.31 \\ \hline 7.814 \end{array}$$

Multiply and divide decimals to hundredths:

$$
\begin{array}{r}
\textit{Example} \qquad 4.24 \\
\times 2.15 \\
\hline
2120 \\
424 \\
848 \\
\hline
9.1160
\end{array}
$$

Rename decimals as fractions:

$$\textit{Example} \qquad 6.3 = 6\frac{3}{10}$$

Compare and order sets of fractions and sets of decimals:

$$\textit{Examples} \qquad \frac{1}{2} \quad \frac{2}{3} \quad \frac{3}{4} \quad \textit{or} \quad \frac{6}{12} \quad \frac{8}{12} \quad \frac{9}{12}$$
$$0.3 \quad 0.36 \quad \textit{or} \quad 0.30 \quad 0.36$$

Round to nearest tenth, hundredth, or thousandth. Obtain equivalent decimal fractions and use them in division:

$$\textit{Examples} \qquad \frac{8.0}{0.4} \times \frac{10}{10} = \frac{80}{4}$$
$$0.4\overline{)8.0} = 4\overline{)80}$$

- Word problems: Solve word poroblems involving fractions and decimals:
  Example   A store clerk whose hourly wage is $6.00 earns time and a half for working overtime (more than 8 hours a day). How much does he earn for working $11\frac{1}{2}$ hours on a given day?

Probability and Statistics

- Graphs and tables: Continue to organize data in bar graphs, line graphs, frequency tables, pie charts, and the like.

- Average and range: Determine the range and average of a collection of data.
- Fractions: Use fractions to express the probability of an event. *Example* (1) What is the probability that a blue marble will be drawn from a bag containing one red, one white, and one blue marble? (*Solution:* P (blue) = the number of blue marbles = $\frac{1}{3}$ the number of marbles in the bag.) (2) If a die is tossed, what is the probability that the number that comes up will be less than 6? (*Solution:* P (6) = $\frac{1}{6}$; P (<6) = $1 - \frac{1}{6}$ = $\frac{5}{6}$.)
- Random sample: Understand concept of a random and unbiased sample (one in which every member of the group has an equal chance of being chosen).
- Probability and space: Relate probability to ratios of areas: *Example*

What is the probability that the spinner will stop on green?

Geometry and Measurement

- Measurement: Use both customary and metric units of measurement in measuring length, distance, mass, capacity, temperature. Be thoroughly familiar with the prefixes *milli-*, *centi-*, and *kilo-* and with such symbols as g, mg, kg, mL, L, mm, km, and cm.
- Volume, area, perimeter: Find the area, volume, and perimeter of specific figures, first by counting units and then by identifying more efficient procedures. Use graph paper to

develop formulas for determining the area and perimeter of rectangles and squares.

- Plane shapes: Use rulers, compasses, and protractors to construct precise circles, squares, triangles, polygons, and the like. Explore the concepts of similarity, symmetry, and congruence in plane figures. Use a protractor to construct acute, obtuse, and right angles. Use graph paper to develop the concept of scale drawing. Relate scale to ratio.

- Solids: Construct models of three-dimensional shapes (spheres, pyramids, cylinders, cones) and investigate their properties (including edges, faces, vertices). Identify the intersection of planes and three-dimensional figures.

- Terminology: Understand and use such terms as *parallel, perpendicular, line, line segment, intersecting lines, polygon, radius, face, edge, vertex, angle, ray,* and *point.*

- Coordinates: Locate positions on a grid using coordinates. Use positive, negative, and fractional numbers.

- Patterns: Explore the patterning in tables and in related shapes.

Problem Solving

Mathematical skill and knowledge is of little use to those who cannot apply it effectively to problem situations. Many of our children, however, have trouble in doing so. In a recent test given by the National Assessment of Educational Progress, nearly 90 percent of thirteen-year-old students were unable to answer correctly a problem such as the following: *Orange soda costs 70 cents for a 36-ounce bottle. At the school fair, Betty's class sold 50 cups holding 9 ounces each for 30 cents apiece. How much profit did the class make on each bottle?*

In order to solve this problem correctly, the child must first understand the exact nature of the question and then select that information that is relevant and reject that information that is not. (In this case, the fact that the class sold 50 cups is not relevant.) He must then plan and carry out a sequence of three steps: (1) 36 ÷ 9 = 4; (2) 4 × 30 cents = $1.20; (3) $1.20 − 70 cents = 50 cents. The computation involved is simple; what is apparently more difficult is the ability to read carefully and to think in mathematical terms.

Good teachers make problem solving the heart of the mathematics curriculum. Problem solving is not an activity to be reached at the far end of a unit of instruction; it is part and parcel of all mathematics teaching and learning. For example, the child learning fractions does not learn the multiplication and division algorithms in the abstract, by rote. Rather, he learns by manipulating and counting parts of a whole or elements of a set in order to answer questions posed by his teacher. In this way, he relates knowledge to practical experience and develops skill in using his knowledge to solve problems.

Good teachers also teach problem-solving skills directly. Most problem-solving methods involve four steps:

1. *Understanding the problem.* The child should repeat the problem in his own words, identify the key questions, select and, if necessary, write down the relevant facts. He should estimate a reasonable answer before trying to find an exact answer.

2. *Making a plan.* Different problems require different plans. The child should draw upon his skills and knowledge to devise a plan that will work. He may use sorting and classification, make tables or graphs and look for patterns and relationships, use diagrams or models to visualize problems, or manipulate objects. He may need to use measurement or computational skills. The trick is to think with what he knows, not to jump to an easy answer or to give up because the problem seems difficult.

3. *Carrying out the plan.* Once the plan is made, it must be carried out. Often this is the step that requires measurement or written computations.

4. *Checking the answer.* Children should acquire the habit of first

checking the *reasonableness* of the answer. Consider the following problem: *Of all the books sold at the fair, three fourths were paperbacks. One half of the paperbacks were mysteries. What part of the books sold were paperback mysteries?* If the child answers $1\frac{1}{2}$ ($\frac{3}{4} \times 2$), the answer is not reasonable. Then children should check the *accuracy* of their answer.

Many good teachers discuss this four-step problem-solving method with their children and give them practice in following it.

TEACHING THE FIFTH-GRADE MATHEMATICS CURRICULUM

The typical fifth-grade mathematics lesson resembles the typical fourth-grade mathematics lesson. The content gradually changes, but the form of the activity is much the same.

Most elementary schools schedule time each day for the study of math. (The lessons are often taught in the morning, when the children are most alert.) Most commonly, the fifth-grade teacher works with the class as a whole. The lesson may begin with a review of what the class did the day before, or the teacher may help the class go over a seatwork or homework assignment from the day before. Then the teacher will introduce the new concept or skill for the day, often using individual children and manipulative materials (blocks, counters, chips, buttons, rods), as well as the blackboard, to illustrate and explain. The bulk of the lesson is spent in discussing this new concept or skill, with the teacher asking questions, helping the children make observations and see relationships, and providing encouragement and explanation where needed. At the end of the lesson, the teacher may assign some related exercises or other work to be done in class (*seatwork*) or at home (*homework*).

If your child is functioning at grade level, this standard approach should work well. However, individual children vary in their ability and in their rates of development. Perhaps your child is more advanced than most of his class and is not sufficiently challenged. Or perhaps your child needs more time and help to master what many of the other children already know.

Teachers cope with these problems in various ways. Many provide enrichment activities for the more mathematically able children, to be done in school or at home when they have finished the regular work. (Such enrichment activities should genuinely stretch children's minds—they should not be just more of the same.) Teachers also work with small groups of children at other times during the day, going over the morning lesson, helping with the seatwork, or providing remedial instruction.

In some classes, teachers group children for mathematics instruction just as in the earlier grades children are grouped for reading instruction. For example, in a class of twenty-five children, there may be a group of eight doing more advanced work, a group of ten doing grade-level work, and a group of seven working at more basic material. The teacher will assign seatwork (or projects in another subject) to two groups while she works individually with the third.

In other classes, such grouping may not be permanent, but the teacher may occasionally form small groups for specific purposes. For example, a teacher whose review of children's seatwork assignments shows that six children need help in dividing a fraction by a fraction may call these six together for special help while the rest of the class is busy with other assignments.

Teachers also work with individual children, of course. But few programs are so organized as to make individual instruction the main form of activity, and in most schools, the amount of time available for individual instruction is limited.

PRINCIPLES OF EFFECTIVE MATHEMATICS TEACHING

However their classes may be organized, effective mathematics teachers follow certain fundamental principles.

Children Must Develop Understanding as Well as Skill

The point of learning mathematics is to be able to solve problems requiring mathematical thought. Basic skills are required to solve problems, but if the child does not understand the problem, cannot extract the relevant information from the problem situation, or cannot choose the right mathematical skill or principle to apply, then the basic skills alone will be of little use. For this reason, good teachers make sure that children understand the concepts underlying basic facts and skills.

Consider the child who when dividing a fraction by a fraction makes this error: $\frac{3}{4} \div \frac{1}{4} = \frac{1}{3}$. The child's problem is not that he lacks the knowledge of basic multiplication facts. He has been taught that when you divide a fraction by a fraction, you invert and multiply. And so he did: $\frac{4}{3} \times \frac{1}{4} = \frac{4}{12} = \frac{1}{3}$. Since the rule is perfectly arbitrary to him, having no basis in his experience with real phenomena, it makes as much sense to invert the first fraction as the second.

Had the child been properly taught, the following mental image might have recurred to him from long practice with similar images, with Cuisenaire rods, or with other objects:

$$\frac{3}{4} \div \frac{1}{4} = 3$$

A child who thus understands the *meaning* of dividing three-fourths by one-fourth cannot make the kind of error shown above.

In general, the concept is developed first, usually through actions performed on physical objects, then the notation associated with the concept, then the skill itself. Both understanding the skill are necessary, with understanding preceding skill.

Learning Proceeds From the Concrete to the Representational to the Abstract

In order to learn mathematical concepts thoroughly, children should experience the concept first in concrete physical form and then in representational or pictorial form, before finally progressing to the use of abstract notation or doing mental arithmetic. Good teachers have children manipulate a wide variety of objects—blocks, chips, buttons, beans, Cuisenaire rods, balance beams—in order to have them observe firsthand the mathematical effect of their actions. The child learning to divide properly a fraction by a fraction (see above) is a good example.

Skills and Knowledge Are First Introduced, Then Developed, Then Mastered

The study of mathematics as sequential, with each successive step building on the one before it. However, in a good mathematics program, skills and knowledge are not taught just once. Children are first introduced to a topic, then they are given extensive practice in developing it and applying it to problem situations, and finally they are expected to master it.

Most mathematics curriculum guides, or *scope and sequence*

charts, reflect this approach. Topics like addition and subtraction of decimals or measuring perimeter of polygon are apt to appear in the guides for grades 4, 5, and 6. Good teachers do not assume that because something has been taught, it has been learned; nor do they assume that once something has been grasped, it will be retained, unless the child is given frequent practice in using the pertinent skill or knowledge.

Skills and Knowledge Are Taught Sequentially

Although repeated practice is usually necessary for true mastery, mathematics curricula still follow a logical progression from more simple to more complex skills and knowledge. In learning fractions, for example, the child may follow a progression such as the following:

$= \frac{1}{4}$ Identify fractional parts of a whole object or picture.

$= \frac{2}{3}$ Identify fractional parts of a collection of objects or pictures.

$\frac{1}{6} + \frac{2}{6} = \frac{3}{6}$
$\frac{6}{7} - \frac{5}{7} = \frac{1}{7}$ Add and subtract fractions with the same denominator

$\frac{3}{6} = \frac{6}{12} = \frac{12}{24}$ Find equivalent fractions.

$\frac{12}{16} = \frac{3}{4}$ Reduce (simplify) fractions to lowest terms.

$\frac{9}{7} = 1\frac{2}{7}$ Change improper fractions to mixed numbers.

$2\frac{2}{3} = \frac{8}{3}$ Change mixed number to improper fractions.

$$3\tfrac{2}{3}$$ $$3\tfrac{2}{3}$$ Add and subtract mixed
$$-1\tfrac{1}{3}$$ $$+1\tfrac{1}{3}$$ numbers with like
$$\overline{2\tfrac{1}{3}}$$ $$\overline{4\tfrac{3}{3}} = 5$$ denominators.

$$\tfrac{1}{2} \times \tfrac{2}{3} = \tfrac{2}{6} = \tfrac{1}{3}$$ Multiply fractions.

$$\tfrac{7}{8} \div \tfrac{1}{2} = \tfrac{7}{8} \times \tfrac{2}{1} = \tfrac{14}{8} =$$ Divide fractions.
$$1\tfrac{6}{8} = 1\tfrac{3}{4}$$

$$\tfrac{2}{5} + \tfrac{3}{4} = \tfrac{8}{20} + \tfrac{15}{20} = \tfrac{23}{20} = 1\tfrac{3}{20}$$ Add and subtract fractions with unlike denominators.

$$\tfrac{7}{8} - \tfrac{1}{2} = \tfrac{7}{8} - \tfrac{4}{8} = \tfrac{3}{8}$$

In good programs, such a progression is not pursued in isolation from other topics. Children do not first learn all there is to know about addition, then all there is to know about subtraction, then multiplication, then division. Rather, these operations are taught together as they reinforce and relate to one another. (Addition and subtraction are seen as inverse operations; division may be regarded as repeated subtraction; and so on.) But within each operation, the level of difficulty is carefully controlled until the child acquires mastery.

Skills and Knowledge Are Applied Constantly

In many mathematics programs (and in many mathematics textbooks), children are first taught a concept or skill, then given extensive practice in it, then led to apply it. The disadvantage of this approach is that when children reach the application stage—often the word problems at the end of the chapter—they may encounter difficulty because they have had no practice in the use of that skill or concept.

Good teachers circumvent this potential problem by constantly having children use what they are learning in ways that seem natural and fun. They use classroom situations (the arithmetic involved in planning the class trip), classroom studies (the geometry involved in building a stockade for social studies), the news and weather (charts, graphs, and computations of temperature and rainfall), games, and puzzles—any activity that requires children to think and to apply what they are learning. For children so instructed, mathematics is not something to be learned for its own sake—its natural and inevitable use is problem solving.

The Teacher Helps Each Child Learn

At the elementary school level, the teacher's job is not limited simply to presenting material. Her job is to ensure that children learn. With appropriate help from the child, the parent, and the school's support staff, the teacher should see that each child acquires the skills and knowledge considered important. Good teachers know what each child is learning and where each may be having difficulty, and they adapt their teaching accordingly and provide such help as may be needed. If a particular child is having difficulty learning to add fractions, she will work individually with the child (in class while the other children are busy, at the end of the lunch hour, or after school), giving him enough practice at manipulating concrete objects and enough written practice exercises until the child gets the idea. Her assumption is always that the child wants to know and is capable of learning; her job is to see that he does.

WHAT TO LOOK FOR IN A GOOD FIFTH-GRADE MATHEMATICS PROGRAM

Like younger children, most fifth graders enjoy learning mathematics. If the program is one that stimulates their thinking without overtaxing their abilities, they respond readily to the challenge. If the answers to most or all of the following questions are yes, chances are your child is participating in an effective program. If many of the answers are no, you may want to inquire further by talking with your child's teacher, and possibly, the principal.

What to Look for in the Classroom

When you visit your child's classroom, do you see

- Number lines displayed on the walls or on the floor?
- Various graphs on various subjects, reflecting work that the teacher and the class have done?
- Chips, counters, Cuisenaire rods, and similar objects used for counting and sorting?
- Rulers, scales, thermometers, and other measuring devices?
- Pictures of two-dimensional shapes and three-dimensional objects used for exploring geometric properties?
- Worksheets showing good work done by children?

What to Look for From the Teacher

Does your child's fifth-grade teacher

- Describe clearly what the class has been doing in mathematics and what she plans for it to do?
- Provide time each day, or at least most days, for mathematical activity?
- Provide a program that follows the principles of effective mathematics teaching described above?
- Know your child's individual abilities and feelings about mathematics?
- Show a sense of enthusiasm about teaching mathematics?

What to Look for From Your Child

When you talk to your child during the fifth-grade year, does he

- Seem interested in using his mind for numbers, quantities, and mathematical relationships?
- Show a sense of excitement and confidence in using his mind for math?
- Describe math activities he has done in class?
- Bring home papers or worksheets reflecting work that he has done?
- Seem able to do the kind of work listed in the section "The Signs of Progress" (p. 221).

HOW TO HELP YOUR CHILD AT HOME

By the time your child is in fifth grade, he is no longer at the beginning of his formal study of mathematics. He has already spent several years in a planned program, with its own terminology, procedures, and expectations. For this reason, unless you are very sure of your ground, you should be wary about confusing your child by trying to teach him yourself. However, after consulting with the teacher, there are things you can do at home to reinforce what your child is learning at school.

Do's

- Talk to your child's teacher to find out about your child's math program and to ask what you can do at home.
- Praise and encourage your child's efforts to use mathematics: to do the arithmetic involved in shopping or traveling, to see

patterns in numbers and shapes, to quantify phenomena in daily experience, and to think logically about them.

- Continue to estimate and measure with your child. Help him make a floor plan of your house and yard. If you are wallpapering his room, have him determine how much wallpaper will be needed.
- Get your child to use mathematics in everyday situations. Have him plan a budget—travel, lodging, meals—for your summer vacation. How much money will he need to save for his new skates if you share the expenses equally and if he sells his old skates for ten dollars?
- Play math games with your child. Games can be fun, and they improve the child's ability to think quantitatively and spatially. Games involving cards and dice are fun and can sharpen a child's skill of computation, short-term memory, and probability estimating. One good source is the book *Arithmetic Skill Development Games* by Michael Schiro (Belmont, Calif.: Fearon Pitman Publishers, 1978).
- Ask the teacher what kinds of mistakes your child makes in arithmetic. Find old workbooks that contain similar problems, and help your child with them. Do easy problems first, to build confidence.
- Help your child solve word problems (see the section "Problem Solving" earlier in this chapter). Be sure that your child understands the problem; have him state it in his own words. Be sure to estimate the answer beforehand and check it afterward.
- Help your child use a pocket calculator to assist in learning number facts and to check accuracy in computation (see the section "The Use of Calculators" in the chapter "Mathematics in the Third Grade").

Don'ts

- Don't be impatient. Your time with your child should be loving and supportive, not tense and anxiety-provoking.

- Don't persist with an activity if your child becomes frustrated or inattentive.
- Don't confuse your child or shake his confidence by criticizing the teacher's methods. Talk to the teacher if necessary, but work together, not at odds.
- Don't say that you (or some people) are just "no good at math." Almost everyone can learn fifth-grade mathematics. Don't promote a defeatist attitude.
- Don't suggest that girls aren't as good in math as boys.

THE SIGNS OF PROGRESS

No single test can fully measure your child's progress in mathematics. Curricula vary somewhat from state to state and school to school. All tests merely sample a child's skill and knowledge and are thus subject to error; no tests satisfactorily measure such important traits and attitudes as persistence, imagination, and the willingness to use mathematical knowledge.

Nevertheless, by the time your child is in the fifth grade, his responses on written tests are usually the most readily available means of determining progress. Thus, by the time he finishes the fifth grade, he should be able to answer accurately the kinds of questions given below. Although these questions do not reflect the entire fifth-grade curriculum, they should give you a fair idea of your child's progress. If he can answer them easily and accurately, chances are that he is at least acquiring the minimum expected skills and knowledge. If he has trouble, he may need special help. Talk to his teacher and, if necessary, to the principal. (You may want to assess your child's ability to answer questions like these in about April of his fifth-grade year.)

1. In which number is 7 in the thousandth place?
   a. 7,412.143
   b. 92,702.12
   c. 74,913.82
   d. 1,416.927

2. What is 846.143 rounded to the nearest hundredth?

3. the product of 76 × 24 is probably
   a. greater than 1400
   b. less than 1400
   c. about 140
   d. about 100.

4. Add the following:

$$238,103$$
$$918,412$$
$$689,596$$
$$+18,568$$

5. Subtract the following:

$$932,104$$
$$-576,925$$

6. Multiply the following:

$$64,932$$
$$\times 263$$

7. Divide the following: $219\overline{)932,107}$

8. Find the average of this set of numbers: 18, 26, 47, 32, 11, 59.

9. Express this decimal as a fraction: 0.125.

10. Express this fraction as a decimal: $\frac{3}{4}$.

11. Express this mixed number as a decimal: $26\frac{943}{1000}$.

12. Add $\frac{2}{3} + \frac{3}{5}$.

13. Subtract $9\frac{7}{8} - 6\frac{3}{4}$.

14. Multiply $\frac{7}{8} \times \frac{1}{4}$.

15. Multiply $20 \times \frac{3}{4}$.

16. If a die is tossed, what is the probability that a number lower than 3 will come up?

17. Find the perimeter of a rectangle whose length is 24.6 inches and whose width is 9.3 inches.

18. Locate the ordered pair (3, 5) on a grid.

19. Sam had ten candles on his birthday cake. With his first breath he blew out $\frac{4}{5}$ of the candles. With his next breath he blew out $\frac{1}{2}$ of the candles that were still lighted. After his two breaths, how many candles were still lighted?

20. A man rented a truck for 6 hours on one day and $3\frac{1}{2}$ hours on the next day for a total cost of $237.50. What did it cost to rent the truck per hour?

COMMON ERRORS IN FRACTIONS

The following are examples of errors commonly made by children in elementary school. If your child makes mistakes of this kind, follow the suggestions listed below.

Error   *Possible Explanation*

1. $\frac{5}{3} = 5\frac{1}{3}$ Does not understand notation for improper fraction.

2. $6\frac{3}{4} = \frac{9}{4}$ Does not understand notation for mixed numbers.

3. $\frac{2}{5} + \frac{1}{3} = \frac{3}{8}$ Adds both numerators and denominators.

4. $\frac{7}{8} - \frac{3}{5} = \frac{4}{3}$ Subtracts both numerators and denominators.

5. $\frac{3}{5} - \frac{1}{3} = \frac{2}{15}$ Subtracts numerators and multiplies denominators.

6. $\begin{array}{r} 3\frac{3}{4} = \frac{15}{20} \\ +2\frac{2}{5} = \frac{8}{20} \\ \hline \frac{23}{20} = 1\frac{3}{20} \end{array}$ Fails to add whole numbers.

7. $\frac{2}{3} \times \frac{5}{3} = \frac{10}{3}$ Fails to multiply denominators.

8. $\frac{2}{3} \times \frac{1}{5} = \frac{10}{15} \times \frac{3}{15} = \frac{30}{15}$ Mixes procedures for addition and multiplication.

9. $3 \times 2\frac{1}{2} = 6\frac{1}{2}$ Multiplies whole numbers and adds fractions.

10. $\frac{3}{4} \div \frac{1}{3} = \frac{4}{3} \times \frac{1}{3} = \frac{4}{9}$ Inverts first fraction rather than second.

Sometimes children have difficulty with fractions because they are shaky in basic arithmetic number facts (for example, 9 × 7, 12 ÷ 4). More commonly, however, their trouble is caused by the kind of instruction they have had. If a child thinks of operations on fractions as moving symbols around according to an arcane set of rules with little or no connection to reality, then one complicated procedure is as good as another. The solution is to get your child to work with real objects and think about them in real situations. (If you divide the pile of 100 poker chips into 10 stacks of 10 and then subtract $\frac{3}{10}$ of the piles, how many stacks of 10 are left? If you had subtracted twice as many of the piles, how many stacks of 10 would have been left?) A child who is grounded in reality and common sense could not believe that $\frac{1}{5}$ of $\frac{2}{3}$ could be greater than $\frac{2}{3}$, as in Error 8 above.

THE
INTERMEDIATE
YEARS

Science in the Intermediate Years

ELEMENTARY SCIENCE: STEPCHILD IN THE CURRICULUM

In many of our nation's elementary schools, science is the stepchild of the curriculum. Attention is lavished—properly so—upon the language arts and upon mathematics. Exciting work is done in the arts, in the social studies, with computers. But little time is devoted to science. Whatever children do in that subject is regarded almost as incidental, the happy outcome of an individual teacher's interest or the byproduct of studying nature or animals. As a result, too many of our young people are not acquiring the skills, knowledge, and attitudes they need if they are to become scientifically literate participants in a world that is increasingly shaped by science and its applications.

No doubt there are reasons for this state of affairs. It is only within the last generation or so that science has been generally regarded as an appropriate subject for systematic study in the curriculum for all children in the United States. Many teachers are not well educated in science and feel uncomfortable teaching it. Teaching science well is hard work, requiring much preparation, considerable skill, and a certain amount of risk taking on the part of the teacher because you cannot always predict the outcome of an experiment or activity. Because there is no agreed-upon national curriculum and because the goals of teaching science are diffuse, children's progress is difficult to assess. Moreover, the attitudes of many parents toward the importance of science are often ambivalent.

Whatever the reasons, the result is unfortunate. Like it or not, the world that our Western tradition has created is one largely shaped by science. (Indeed, the development of the scientific method may be our culture's most lasting contribution to mankind.) The child who fails to become comfortable with the methods of science in his early years may never feel fully at home in the world he will inhabit as an adult. A society that fails to train well a sufficient number of its young people in science will surely be at a disadvantage in an increasingly science- and technology-oriented world.

Meanwhile, children possess an innate desire to "do science"—to observe natural phenomena, to raise interesting questions, to seek answers to perplexing problems, to explore their environment in an effort to experience and understand it thoroughly. Children in the intermediate years are scientists by nature. When they are stimulated to use their minds and senses to explore the world that is still so new to them, their enthusiasm leads them to marvelous discoveries and deepening understanding. Why do the seasons change? Why does the wind blow? How does television work? When adults (or textbooks) give brief, definitive answers to questions like these (for example, "The seasons change because the earth revolves around the sun"), curiosity may be stifled and attention directed elsewhere. But when the question serves as a springboard to stimulate the child to discover more on his own (for example, "Why do you think the seasons change? Let's list some possibilities and see what we can do to check them out"), the child begins to use his mind as a scientist would. The process is natural to children this age and should be encouraged whenever possible.

Fortunately, there are schools and teachers throughout the country who do understand the nature of science and the nature of children and who give science an important place in the elementary school curriculum. From them we can learn what more we should be doing in all science classrooms.

CONTENT AND PROCESS

First, we must understand what science is. Many people regard it as a collection of facts, laws, and theories to be memorized—the table of elements, the laws of thermodynamics, the classification of plants and animals. Many others confuse it with some of its technological applications—spaceflight, genetic engineering, wonder drugs. Educated people know that science is both the *process* of conducting rational inquiry into the nature of things and the *content* of understanding that is gained from such inquiry. It is both a way of looking at the world and the knowledge derived therefrom.

In the decades prior to the 1960s, the emphasis of most elementary school science programs was upon content (information). In the 1960s and the 1970s, the focus changed to process (scientific thinking)—to *doing* science rather than reading or learning about it. In the 1980s, leading educators agree that a good science program combines both content and process. Children should pursue knowledge and understanding in the same way that scientists do, and they should also begin to learn some of the salient facts and broad principles that help us to see order in the universe and our everyday world. As with social studies, there is more to be learned than can possibly be taught in the few years of elementary school. For that reason, it is not important that all children have exactly the same experience or learn the same facts or principles. What is important is that all children be helped to think as scientists and that they begin to acquire an understanding of some of the important principles governing natural phenomena. As *First Lessons: A Report on Elementary Education in America* (U.S. Office of Education, 1986) recently said,

> We need a revolution in elementary-school science. . . . Science is a way of thinking, a way of understanding the world. . . . The scientific method is the method of thought, of reasoning, which applies not only to explorations of the physical universe but to all the realms of intellectual inquiry that require hypotheses, inference, and other tools of brainwork. As Bertrand Russell explained: "A fact, in science, is not a mere fact, but an instance."

SCIENCE PROCESS SKILLS

Science curricula throughout the United States vary widely from school to school. However, most programs designed to teach children science attempt to develop skills like those listed below (this list is based on the skills taught in *Science . . . A Process Approach II*, 1981, developed by the Commission on Science Education of the American Association for the Advancement of Science, or AAAS):

- *Observing:* Children learn to use sight, touch, smell, taste, and hearing to gather information about objects. They learn to increase the power of their senses by using instruments, such as microscopes and telescopes.
- *Using space/time relationships:* Children learn that spatial relationships change with time and that these changes can be

described in terms of shape, direction and arrangement, motion and speed, symmetry, and rate of change.

- *Classifying:* Children learn to sort and classify objects or events in order to observe similarities and differences. They learn to choose a basis for classification that makes sense for a given purpose. (For example, a child who is trying to determine the properties of a collection of rocks may sort them according to texture rather than size.)
- *Measuring:* Children learn to quantify their observations by informed and standard measurement devices. They learn to use numbers to make their measurements more precise.
- *Recording and communicating data:* Children learn to use written notes, numbers, drawings, diagrams, maps, photographs, charts, graphs, and the like to record data about objects and their relationships. They learn to communicate their observations clearly to others.
- *Predicting:* Children learn to predict results on the basis of what they have observed. They learn to distinguish between a reasonable prediction and a guess.
- *Inferring:* Children learn to make inferences to describe observations. For example, a child may record each day the level of the water left in a jar over a period of weeks. He may infer that the level of water drops over time.

Once the child has become familiar with these basic processes, he is introduced to the more formal processes of the scientific method, described below:

- *Controlling variables:* Children learn to identify variables and to control them in conducting an experiment. For example, if a child hypothesizes that a wet cloth will dry faster if hung outdoors in the sun, he learns to hang a wet cloth outdoors in the shade as well, so that he can distinguish between the effect of the sun and the effect of the shade.
- *Interpreting data:* Children learn to observe, collect, and clas-

sify data: to discern patterns and relationships in the data:
and to describe and make inferences about the data.

- *Formulating hypotheses:* Children learn to formulate hypotheses based on their observations and inferences.
- *Defining operationally:* Children learn to define a term according to what they actually see and do.
- *Experimenting:* Children learn to use previous skills to test hypotheses, solve problems, and raise new questions.

The skills described above are taught at increasing levels of sophistication as the child progresses through the grades.

SCIENCE CONTENT

Although there is no standard science curriculum in use throughout America's elementary schools, most science programs do provide children with experiences in the physical, life, and earth sciences. Physical science is concerned with such topics as heat, light, electricity, magnets, machines, motion, and energy. Think of it as *physics.* The life sciences are concerned with such topics as life cycles, seeds, the needs of plants and animals, and changes in plants and animals. Think of them as *zoology, biology, botany,* and *ecology.* The earth sciences are concerned with such topics as the weather, the seasons, the sun and the moon, rocks, and erosion. Think of them as *astronomy, meteorology,* and *geology.* The elementary-school child, of course, may not know that he is studying geology. He may think he is examining rocks. And, indeed, there is an advantage in keeping terminology simple at this level—it helps both the child and the teacher to focus on the phenomena being studied, without pretentiousness or academic clutter.

The following examples illustrate the topics children may study in science in the intermediate years:

- A Midwestern suburb: Grade 3—Stream Tables
  Clay Boats
  Aquarium
  Solar System

  Grade 4—Batteries and Bulbs I
  Colored Solutions
  Pond Water
  Body Systems
  Trees and Growing Plants

  Grade 5—Batteries and Bulbs II
  Microbes and Microscope
  Bridges and Structures
  Human Growth and
  Development
  Plants and Seeds
  Maps and Geology

- An Eastern city: Grade 3—Electricity in Everday Life
  The Earth and the Sun
  The Needs of Plants and
  Animals
  How Sounds Are Made
  Observing and Measur-
  ing Weather Changes
  Friction, Gravity, and
  Motion
  Rocks and How We Use
  Them

  Grade 4—Finding Directions With a
  Compass
  Our Nearest Neighbor in

Space: The Moon
Getting New Plants
Sounds Travel
Weather and Climate
From Season to Season
Moving Things More
Easily
The Water We Use

Grade 5—How Man Changes
Materials
Little Environments
The Sun's Family
Climate
Mirrors and the Reflection
of Light
Making It Go
Batteries and Bulbs III

• A Southern county:

Grade 3—*Life Sciences*
Where Do Plants and
Animals Live?
Groups of Living Things
A Community
What Do We Eat?
How We Use What We
Eat

Matter and Energy
Using Electricity

Earth/Space
Water Cycle
The Changing Land
Stars

Man and Technology
Machines at Work
Biographies

Grade 4—*Life Sciences*
The Insect World
Bones and Muscles
Sunshine and Green
Plants

Matter and Energy
Matter

Earth/Space
The Solar System
The Earth's Atmosphere
The Earth's Rocks
The Earth's Resources

Man and Technology
Machines and Force
Traveling Through the
Solar System
Career Information
Biographies

Grade 5—*Life Sciences*
Animal Behavior
Cells
Life in the Ocean
Human Body Systems
Making Choices About
Your Body's Needs

Matter and Energy
How Much Matter?
Heat Energy
The Changing Earth

Earth/Space
The Weather Around Us
What Will the Weather
Be?

The Moon and Beyond

Man and Technology
Career Information
Biographies

SCIENCE ATTITUDES

Typically, science curricula do not specify the attitudes they intend to teach as clearly as they do the process skills and the content. However, the development of positive attitudes toward science at this level is important. Among the attitudes that good programs attempt to develop are the following:

- Science is a human activity—it is something people do to understand themselves and their world.
- Doing science is fun. Raising questions and using your mind and senses in order to answer them is fun.
- Doing science well requires accuracy, objectivity, and open-mindedness.
- When doing science, you can learn from your mistakes as well as from your successes.
- Scientific knowledge is constantly changing and expanding.
- Scientific knowledge can be used both for human welfare and for destruction.

HOW SCIENCE PROGRAMS ARE TAUGHT

The methods used to teach elementary science are as varied as the curricula themselves. In some schools, textbooks serve as the basis of the curriculum, and most science activity consists of reading and writing. (Such programs are necessarily limited in their effectiveness; as *What Works*, the 1986 report of the U.S. Department of Education, maintains, "Children learn science best when they are able to do experiments, so they can witness 'science in action.' ") Some teachers supplement the textbooks by engaging children in activities (not "experiments" in the true sense) that illustrate the points made in the text.

Some schools use a *text-kit* approach, which recognizes the importance of hands-on activity. The book provides structure for the program, background information, and instructions, but the child must do the activities involving the materials in the kit in order to learn the concepts.

Still other programs use a laboratory approach. The children are given (or they originate) a problem, and then they attempt to solve it. They learn by actually doing activities or experiments. The role of the pupil in such programs is different from that of the pupil in the teacher-dominated classroom. Children raise questions, seek ways of answering them, collect data, observe objects and events, interpret their findings, and confirm or disconfirm hypotheses. They are not only active participants in the learning process, they actually control its direction and depth. The teacher's role is also different in such programs. She refrains from giving answers and directions: Her role is that of guide and resource person. She asks questions to stimulate thought, points out phenomena, provides help when needed, but generally remains in the background. Her job is not to teach by telling or showing, but to serve as a catalyst in the child's search for answers.

At present, three excellent laboratory-oriented curricula are in widespread use. One is *Science . . . A Process Approach II*, developed by the AAAS. The second is *The Science Curriculum Improvement Study (SCIS)*, written by Robert Karplus, and its revisions, SCIS I and SCIS II. The third is a collection of individual units published by the Elementary Science Study (ESS) of the Education Development Center. If your child is fortunate enough to be involved in one of these programs, ask your child's teacher for written material about it so that you can better understand its rationale and how it works. If your child is involved in a program that makes little use of laboratory-oriented, hands-on activity or if he spends little or no time doing science at all, ask your child's teacher and principal why this is the case in the face of all knowledgeable professional advice.

One Science Unit: Crayfish

Sometimes science learning occurs spontaneously or serendipitously, as when butterflies emerge from the cocoons in the jar or when a child inquires about the beautiful oil slick he saw in a puddle on the way to school. More frequently in the intermediate grades, teachers plan *units* of instruction in science—a set of related lessons and activities on a given topic. Much of the activity is conducted by individual children working alone or in small groups as they make observations and conduct experiments, although occasionally the entire class is involved in a project.

One fourth-grade class participated in a unit on crayfish. During a trip to a nearby pond, the class became fascinated by the crayfish scuttling about near the water's edge. The teacher suggested that the children collect some crayfish and bring them back to the classroom. For the next hour or so they had great fun catching the crayfish—some by hand, some in nets—and placing them in pails of pond water. They collected twelve live crayfish of assorted sizes—one for each pair of children in the class.

In the classroom, the teacher prepared a suitable habitat—a large shallow pool, aerated with a small pump, containing aquarium gravel and a number of inverted flowerpots with openings so the crayfish could crawl beneath them. The children were excited by the presence of this new life in the classroom. Together with the teacher, they discussed rules for handling and caring for the crayfish ("Don't hurt the crayfish"; "Let water stand before adding it to the pool"; "Don't feed the crayfish in the big pool") and posted these rules in a conspicuous place.

Over the next ten weeks, the children observed closely the crayfish and their behavior and conducted experiments to learn more about them. Working in pairs or small groups while the rest of the class was engaged in other activity, the children marked their own crayfish with an assigned nail polish color and observed it closely. They drew pictures of their crayfish, trying to be as accurate as possible (How many legs? How many legs with claws?), and wrote descriptions. In a notebook they recorded where in the pool they found their crayfish each time they went to observe it and tried to determine patterns in its movement. They fed it different foods, determined what it liked best, established how much (actually, how little) it ate, and observed the way it used its body and mouth to eat. They observed how the crayfish moved when they brought their hands toward them and noted where they liked to hide. They weighed their crayfish once a week (on small balance scales, using metal washers as weights) and made graphs showing the changes in weight. They observed what the crayfish was able to lift and move, noting that the crustacean could lift more than its own weight. They read books about crayfish and about the life forms that live in similar habitats.

Toward the end of the unit, the teacher proposed an experiment to study the interactions between crayfish. The children removed all the flowerpots except one, then each day noted which crayfish hid beneath the remaining pot. They removed this crustacean from beneath the pot, watched another enter the space, and then watched the first one reclaim its spot. They made predictions about which crayfish would claim the pot next once the strongest was removed. Gradually, they manipulated the pots and the crustaceans until they could chart an entire hierarchy of social dominance. They talked about whether human beings behaved in a similar manner—in the classroom, at the playground, in the world news.

By the end of ten weeks, a number of the crayfish had died, and the teacher proposed that the children return the others to the pond. They did so gladly, watching their own fish scuttle away—some quickly, some less so—wondering if they would ever see it again.

In the end, it probably make little difference how much information these children acquired about crayfish—although the exploration of social dominance was a powerful lesson indeed. But surely they had had a good experience in "doing science"—in observing closely, quantifying observations, keeping records, and formulating hypotheses and verifying them with the work of their own hands and minds.

WHAT TO LOOK FOR IN A GOOD INTERMEDIATE SCIENCE PROGRAM

A good science program in the intermediate years involves your child in many hands-on activities through which he learns the fundamental processes of science, expands his knowledge of the natural world, and acquires positive attitudes toward science and its uses. Here are some things you might look for:

- Does your child's teacher devote sufficient time to science? Many experts say that children in these years should spend at least 2½ to 3 hours per week in science activities.
- Does your child's teacher help him learn the processes of science as well as scientific facts and principles?
- More specifically, does your child engage in hands-on activities in which he can observe and think about his own

operations on plants, animals, physical objects, and so forth?

- Is your child stimulated to use his own mind and pursue his own curiosity, or is he asked only to remember facts provided by the teacher or textbook?
- Does your child's classroom contain plants, animals, fish, rocks, stream tables, and other evidence of hands-on scientific activity?
- Does your child's teacher make use of neighborhood resources—trees, plants, animals, rocks, streams, ditches, ponds, whatever?
- Is your child given trade books to read to enrich the program—books about dinosaurs, hurricanes, windmills, polar bears, robots, canyons, waterfalls, and so much more?
- Is your child helped to make connections between what he is learning in science and what he is doing in mathematics, in literature, in social studies, in writing? For example, does he use the math he is learning to quantify his observations in science? Does the science experiment provide material to write about?
- Is your child increasingly aware of social issues involving science and its applications?

If the answers to these questions are yes, your child is involved in a good science program. If the answers are no, you may want to talk to your child's teacher to find out what she has planned for the rest of the school year. If necessary, you may also wish to speak to the principal.

Social Studies in the Intermediate Years

SO MUCH TO LEARN

There is so much to learn. How does the world work? Where do our food and water come from? What was here before these buildings? How do other people live? How are people different from animals? How old is the earth? Who made our country? How does democracy work? How is democracy different from dictatorship? Why are there wars?

The questions about human nature and human history, about who we are and how we came to be this way, tumble over one another, infinite in number. Each answer prompts a new set of questions. Given adequate stimulation, the child's natural curiosity cannot be sated. With help, he follows his mind and his imagination into those realms of knowledge we know by such adult names as history, geography, anthropology, psychology, sociology, political science, economics, civics—the social studies. Because of his age, the depth of his questions and of the answers he will accept may still be limited. But the scope of his interests, and of what his parents and teachers *want* him to know, is as broad as the study of all mankind. Clearly there is more to be taught and more to be learned than can be squeezed into the very best programs in the intermediate years of elementary school.

Small wonder, then, that social studies programs in our nation's elementary schools very so widely in content and approach. There is little consensus on what should be taught and when. Some programs emphasize the great political events in the history of our country and of the child's state and community. Some emphasize social and economic history—how people lived in the past, and why they lived that way—and the shaping influence of climate and geography upon history. Some focus on our own society and its Western European roots, while others introduce cross-cultural studies, both for their own sake and to develop a better perspective of our own culture. Some concentrate on knowledge—facts and ideas—and others on skills, that is, the processes by which man studies and develops knowledge. Some programs are simply more elaborate and better planned than others. A foreign visitor to our schools might well get the idea that anything goes in the social studies.

Over the years, some have voiced concern about this state of affairs. Most recently, for example, U.S. Secretary of Education William J. Bennett has called for a new curriculum based on history, geography, and civics. In the report *First Lessons: A Report on Elementary Education in America*, Bennett says that "social studies in the upper elementary grades should stress the continuity and correlations among these disciplines." Although he does not spell out a specific curriculum, Bennett suggests guidelines for each of these areas. For *history*, he cites the recommendations of the Organization of American Historians that by the end of the eighth grade, children should

- Know the chronology of the main events of U.S. history and be able to place in order and roughly date the major periods of world history.
- Be able to explain the significance of the most important events in U.S. and world history, including social and eco-

nomic developments that have evolved, such as industrialization, slavery, urbanization, women's suffrage, and civil rights.

- Recognize and place in context some of the important men and women in U.S. history.
- Have read and understood the essential significance of at least parts of such documents as the Declaration of Independence, the U.S. Constitution, Lincoln's Second Inaugural Address, and Martin Luther King's "I Have a Dream" speech.

Of *geography*, Bennett says that children "can begin at an early age to learn illustrations of the five basic themes of geography education: location, place, relationships within places, movement, and regions."

And of *civics*, he argues that "American civics, like American history, should be presented without sugar coating but also without apology. . . . The proper first focus of study by American boys and girls, regardless of ancestry or ethnicity, is on the essential facts, the central institutions, and the fundamental principles of the United States and the western civilization whose traditions and culture are our shared inheritance."

In fact, most elementary schools *do* teach history, geography, and civics. The variety stems from *what* history, geography, and civics they teach; from the additional material they teach; from *how much* they teach; and from *how* they teach it. If you wish to understand your child's social studies program, the following mini-lesson about pedagogy may be helpful.

HOW SOCIAL STUDIES PROGRAMS ARE ORGANIZED

When educators list the goals of a given program, they often categorize them into knowledge, skills, and attitudes. *Knowledge* is the information and ideas the child is to learn, like the dates of the Boston Tea Party or the causes of the Civil War. (*Knowledge* is sometimes called *content*.) *Skills* (or *process*) are the abilities the child is to acquire, like reading a Mercator projection map or locating a historical source document in the library. *Attitudes* are the beliefs and values the child is to acquire or reinforce, such as patriotism or tolerance for cultural difference. Most social studies programs attempt to develop knowledge, skills, and attitudes, but the balance among the three may differ markedly.

In some programs, knowledge is emphasized, and whatever skills or attitudes a child acquires are almost accidental. (In such a program, the child would most likely be tested on his ability to recall information, not on his ability to discover information or to reason about it.) In other programs, skills are emphasized, and the knowledge is viewed as an almost incidental vehicle for the development of the skills. (In such a program the child might be tested on his ability to interpret a new set of data or to conduct research on a new topic.) In still other programs, both knowledge and skills are subordinated to the development of attitudes, for example, to ways of minimizing conflict with other people or to seeing one's own society in a favorable light.

Good programs strike a balance between all three sets of goals, and good teachers can tell you what their goals are in each of these three areas.

SOCIAL STUDIES KNOWLEDGE

As we have said, there is no standard elementary school social studies program, even with respect to the knowledge portion of the curriculum. The following three typical examples of how social studies content is organized may give you some idea of the diversity.

- A Southern county:

Grade 3—The local community, emphasizing community services, institutions, occupations, and technology.

Grade 4—State history, geography, and culture, especially in the 17th, 18th, and 19th centuries.

Grade 5—American studies, emphasizing history, geography, government, and economics; focus on the 17th to 19th centuries.

- A Northeastern city:

Grade 3—"Exploring Community: Looking at People in Different Communities." Emphasis on contrasting customs and values of people in different communities.

Grade 4—"In Search of the Past." Studies of American Indians, Vikings, Egyptians, and so on are used as vehicles for developing students' abilities to use artifacts, written records, myths, and the like to reconstruct the past.

Grade 5—"Inquiring About America." Selected aspects of American life and history stemming from problems or issues of today, such as the environment or civil rights. The organization is topical, not chronological.

- A Midwestern city:

  Grade 3—"Our City: Then and Now." A chronological study of the city's political and economic history.

  Grade 4—"Explorers in History." An overview of the development of Western Europe and the New World, seen through the exploits of such historical figures as Alexander the Great, Julius Caesar, Leif Ericson, Christopher Columbus, and Ferdinand Magellan.

  Grade 5—American history, from the early Indians to today in eight units, emphasizing both social and economic developments (like "The Rise of the City") and political developments.

- A New York town:

  Grade 3—Textbook: *The Earth: Regions and Peoples* (Modern Curriculum Press)
  Sequence: Learning about Geography Coastal Regions of the United States
  Grassland Regions of the United States

Desert Regions of the United States and Other Lands

Tropical Regions of the Americas and the World

Mountain Regions of the United States and Other Lands

Northern Forest Regions of the United States and Other Lands

Grade 4—Textbook: *The United States—Past to Present* (D. C. Heath)

Sequence: Reviewing Map and Globe Skills

Newcomers to America

Thirteen English Colonies

Building a New Nation

Moving West

A Time of Trouble

Civil War to Present in a Small City

Grade 5—Textbook: *The United States and the Other Americas* (Macmillan)

Sequence: Learning About Maps and Globes

U.S. Land and People

Northeastern States

Southeastern States

North Central States

South Central States

Rocky Mountain States

Pacific States
Forming a New Govern-
ment
A Modern Nation
American Neighbors

Even these outlines fail to suggest the full diversity of the
program content, because in most situations individual teachers
are free to add as much or as little as they wish in order to flesh
out the curriculum outlines.

SOCIAL STUDIES SKILLS

The skills that are taught in social studies programs also vary
from school to school. In general, however, there are four kinds
of skills that appear regularly, with different degrees of emphasis: map and globe skills, research skills, reading skills, and
interpersonal skills.

Map and Globe Skills

Children in the intermediate grades spend considerable time
learning to read maps, charts, and globes. Most social studies
textbooks are filled with them. Most teachers teach about them
directly; many teachers have children themselves make maps or
charts in order to demonstrate knowledge of a region or to show
the relationship between geography and human activity. Gradually, children learn to use different kinds of maps (physical,
climate, land usage, population distribution, political), to compare flat maps with "round" ones, to understand and use the
concept of scale, to locate latitude and longitude, to select and

construct maps and charts for specific purposes. (You may want to buy your child a well-made globe and take imaginary journeys with him from time to time.)

Research Skills

In general, research skills are skills that are used in seeking information; using libraries, museums, and other resources; analyzing data; testing hypotheses; and presenting information. In some social studies programs, children develop such skills incidentally, as a byproduct of conducting research on the content. In others, they are taught the skills deliberately and systematically, with most skills being introduced in the third grade and reinforced with increasing sophistication each year.

Among some commonly taught research skills are the ability to

- Recognize that a problem or issue exists.
- Raise questions related to the problem or issue.
- Generate hypotheses concerning the problem or issue.
- Identify data needed to test hypotheses.
- Identify possible sources of data.
- Use library resources (including card catalog, indices, and such guides as *Reader's Guide to Periodical Literature*).
- Use tables of contents, appendices, glossaries, bibliographies, and indices.
- Use maps, charts, globes, atlases, diagrams, graphs, and the like.
- Interview resource people.
- Take useful notes, distinguishing important and less important information.
- Categorize data.
- Recognize possible conflicts in data.
- Draw inferences from data.
- Revise hypotheses if necessary.

- Draw conclusions.
- Develop a product or report to share problems, hypothesis, data, and conclusions.

Thus listed, these skills may seem rather ambitious. However, if they are practiced on material that is appropriate to the child's level of maturity, they are well within the grasp of most normal children in grades 3, 4, and 5.

Reading Skills

In the intermediate grades, reading and social studies have a symbiotic relationship. The child's success in learning the social studies material depends largely upon his ability to read; at the same time, teachers use social studies material to teach important reading skills. There is no conflict in this situation if the teacher assigns material to read that is not beyond your child's present abilities and provides appropriate instruction in the new skills to be learned.

Among the reading skills commonly taught or reinforced in grades 3, 4, and 5 in social studies are the following:

- Identifying the main idea of a paragraph or passage.
- Finding and categorizing details according to purpose.
- Following sequences in time, place, and thought.
- Understanding implications and drawing inferences.
- Distinguishing between fact and opinion.
- Recognizing sales and propaganda techniques.
- Following directions.
- Locating information.
- Selecting, evaluating, and organizing information.

If your child is not doing well in social studies, the problem probably lies in poor reading and study skills. The time to address such a problem is now! See your child's teacher to determine the source of the problem and what should be done about it.

Interpersonal Skills

In the primary grades (kindergarten through grade 2) much of the social studies program consisted of teaching children the skills of group membership—listening, taking turns, sharing materials. In the intermediate grades, in many schools, this work continues at a more sophisticated level. One state, for example, recommends that pupils learn to

- Recognize that others may have a different point of view.
- Observe the actions of others.
- Be attentive to causes of conflict.
- Listen to reason.
- Recognize and avoid stereotypes.
- Withhold judgment until the facts are known.
- Assess the reactions of other people to one's own behavior.
- Follow democratic procedures in making group decisions.
- Give constructive criticism.
- Suggest means of group evaluation.
- Suggest ways of resolving group differences.
- Anticipate consequences of group action.
- Assume responsibility for carrying out tasks.

Such interpersonal skills are usually taught indirectly—they are learned from the way the teacher conducts the class, guides the discussion, reinforces appropriate behavior, and generally sets a polite and considerate tone.

SOCIAL STUDIES ATTITUDES

Most social studies programs attempt to develop attitudes, as well as skill and knowledge. Most agree that children should develop positive attitudes toward their own community, state, and country and toward the democratic values that our country represents. Few would dispute that children should feel good about themselves and their homeland, whether they see its occasional warts or not.

Beyond this bedrock consensus, however, lies potential conflict. Attitudes engage the realm of values, and in that realm, political and social viewpoints clash.

Some schools conduct programs intended to develop the child's empathy with minority populations in our own society and a sense of the interpendence of all people around the world. One such program, for example, lists the following goals for children:

- Decrease in egocentric perceptions—see things as others see them and consider the interests of others.
- Decrease in ethnocentric perceptions—understand that one's own group is not a standard by which to judge all others.
- Decrease in stereotypical perceptions—see people as individuals, not as members of a stereotypical group.
- Increase in ability to emphathize.
- Development of constructive attitudes toward diversity, change, ambiguity, and conflict.

Others decry such programs as a betrayal of traditional values. Secretary of Education Bennett warns that "as our schools welcome the children of families who have fled Castro and Duvalier and Pol Pot, we must not abandon the teaching of our American traditions in the name of 'globalism' or 'multiculturalism.' "

In the authors' view, elementary schools should not hesitate to emphasize the values on which our pluralistic, democratic society is founded, values embedded in our Constitution and its Bill of Rights. As a concerned parent, you may want to ask your child's teacher or principal what attitudes or values his school's social studies program attempts to develop, remembering, of course, that the intent and the reality are not always the same.

HOW SOCIAL STUDIES PROGRAMS ARE TAUGHT

The methods used by teachers to teach social studies are as varied as the curricula themselves. In some schools, teachers assign chapters in textbooks, discuss the contents of each chapter with the class, and ask the pupils to take tests or write reports. In others, the textbook is supplemented by a wide assortment of trade books, library books, pictures, films, maps, charts, globes, and other realia. In still others, the teacher uses no textbook at all. The units of study are organized around themes (such as "The Rise of the City," "Work in Colonial Times," "Pioneers"), and the instructional materials are a rich variety of books, periodicals, paintings, prints, photographs, and the like. In such programs the teacher is apt to draw freely upon the literature, folklore, music, and art of the period under study.

In the best programs, teachers involve children in many activities related to the unit of study. Children do much more than read or listen and respond—they investigate, hypothesize, seek information, analyze data, create maps and charts, build models, interview resource people, undertake a myriad of projects, and give reports. Active participation in the process of learning is not only motivating, it ensures better learning. As the ancient Chinese proverb (probably apocryphal) says, "I hear, and I forget; I see, and I remember; I do, and I understand." The watchwords are "doing" words—exploring, discovering, comparing, analyzing, creating, reporting. Which child will remember the Alamo longer: the one who reads a textbook account or the one who constructs a model of the site based on old maps and stories about the battle?

One unit of study we encountered suggests what a good teacher can get children to do. A fifth-grade class in a Northeastern city was studying the great waves of immigration to our Eastern cities in the late 19th and early 20th centuries. It was early spring; the class had been studying topics in U.S. history throughout the year. The teacher and class discussed the idea of family trees, and together drew one on the blackboard. For each individual, they listed the country of origin and, if an immigrant, the year the individual arrived in the United States. They wondered how far back in time they would be able to trace their own family trees and what they would discover about their grandparents, great-grandparents, and other ancestors.

During the next few days the children talked to their parents and other relatives at home and reconstructed their family trees. (Most were able to go as far back as their great-grandparents; some could go back even farther; some had trouble.) Each day a few children would describe their family trees to the rest of the class, and the teacher recorded the countries of origin on the blackboard. In a few days the teacher and class summarized all the trees. Their list of countries looked like this:

Russia	Holland
Poland	South Korea
Lithuania	Germany
Brazil	Scotland
England	Cuba
West Indies	Nigeria
Thailand	Italy
Ireland	Haiti
Austria	Japan

They created a huge pie chart displaying these countries (the teacher later used the chart for a lesson on fractions) and talked about the meaning of the slogan "E Pluribus Unum," which the teacher showed them on some pennies. They made a bar graph showing the number of relatives who had arrived in this country during various ten-year periods at the turn of the century.

The teacher and the class discussed what more they would

like to know about these people. Quickly, the questions tumbled over one another. Why did they come here? What was it like to leave their homes? What work did they do? Where did they live? How did grandmother and grandfather meet each other? How did established Americans treat them? Around these and other questions, the teacher organized study teams to do research. Groups of two to four children were assigned topics like work, leisure, housing, food, and dress. During the next three weeks the children spent much time eagerly seeking information on these topics.

The sources of information were rich and varied. In the classroom the teacher had assembled, with the help of the school librarian, a large stack of books containing stories and pictures about urban immigrant life. In the classroom there were many photographs (showing how locations looked decades earlier and how they looked now), a stack of old magazines, and a display of old posters advertising lectures and theatrical productions. The class spent most of one morning in the school library searching for material with the help of the teacher and librarian. (Many children returned to the library often, and some used the resources of the public library as well.) Each child was asked to interview one of his grandparents and write a report describing what he learned from the interview. (When no grandparent was available, children interviewed another older adult instead.) These reports were shared with the class, and their substance served as another valuable source of information.

While the children were working on their separate projects, the teacher continued to introduce new material to the class. One day they examined a number of old menus taken from restaurants of the period. (They had fun comparing prices as well as meals!) Another day they listened to music of the period (from the show *Tintypes*) and heard an old phonograph record of the opera singer Enrico Caruso. Another day they examined old newspapers. Once they examined two old passports that some children brought to class and made a list of the information and inferences they could make from them. At one point the teacher asked half the class to read the chapter concerning immigration in one fifth-grade textbook and the other half to read the corresponding chapter in another. (The teacher did not have two sets of textbooks for the whole class; she had deliberately asked her principal for twelve copies of each.) The class then reported on what they had read and compared the accounts in the two textbooks.

Toward the end of the unit the teacher and class visited Ellis Island. Prior to the trip, they read about the role that Ellis Island had played in history and prepared a list of questions they hoped to find answers for. On the trip itself, it was hard to say who was more excited or who had more fun—the children or the parent chaperones!

At the end of the unit the children shared these projects with the rest of the class. Some of the projects were presented as written reports, illustrated by charts, maps, and photographs. One study team enacted a play, complete with appropriate costumes and re-created newspapers of the period, on the theme "If Our Grandparents Had Met." Another group prepared a meal, complete with menus, recipes, and shopping lists. A third presented a slide show of old photographs, magazine advertisements, and newspaper articles accompanied by explanatory comments. The teacher kept a large scrapbook of as much as she could retain, to use as resource material for another class the following year.

WHAT TO LOOK FOR IN A GOOD SOCIAL STUDIES PROGRAM

Remember that there is not enough time in elementary school to teach all that might be taught and to learn all that might be learned. Obviously, we want children to learn something of our country's history and of the democratic values and processes by which we live. We also want children to develop an expanding sense of time and place, a growing knowledge of the world's peoples and history, of the interrelationships of history and geography, of politics and economics. But there is no one best set of experiences to convey these ideas. What is more important is the liveliness and thoroughness with which such experiences are taught and the degree to which your child becomes motivated and acquires the skills to learn more.

Here are some questions to consider:

- Does your child like the work he does in social studies?
- Does it seem to be interesting and "alive" to him?
- Does your child engage in study or research projects on topics of special interest or does he just read textbooks?
- Does the teacher use an assortment of books in addition to (or instead of) textbooks?
- Does the teacher introduce a variety of instructional materials into the classroom, including literature, folklore, films, and music?
- Does the teacher discuss current events with the class, especially as noteworthy events or developments occur?
- Does your child seem to be learning and thinking about patterns of history and human behavior, as opposed to learning separate, unrelated facts?

If the answers to these questions are yes, your child is involved in a good social studies program. If the answers are no, you may want to talk to your child's teacher and ask her what else the children will be doing before the end of the school year.

The Arts in the Intermediate Years

In the 1985 report from the Getty Center for Education in the Arts entitled *Beyond Creating: The Place for Art in American Schools*, Elliot W. Eisner of Stanford University writes:

> When a nation is at risk, when from virtually all sides we hear of the vast number of functional illiterates leaving our schools, when remedial course are over-subscribed at even our most selective colleges, the thought of making the case for so seemingly marginal a subject as art in our schools is especially daunting. How can one recommend that the school's most precious resource—time—be directed from what is truly basic in education to the "luxury" of studying art? . . .
>
> The case for art . . . rests upon three major arguments. First, that the arts represent the highest of human achievements to which students should have access. Second, that the school is the primary public institution that can make such access possible for the vast majority of students in our nation. Third, that work in the arts develops unique and important mental skills.

The arts are, or ought to be, as fundamental and as basic to a full education as reading and writing. Our educational tradition has ruptured the link between imagination and intellect; but in real life as we live it, thinking and feeling and imagining are fused. The Council for Basic Education, among others, agrees that the "study of the arts is basic." Not only does such study promote the learning of the basic skills of looking, listening, reading, writing, and computing, but it is important in its own right, helping children perceive and create images that communicate directly through the senses. As more and more of our understanding of the world and one another comes from a television set or a computer screen, these images become powerful indeed!

Unfortunately, in many schools today, tightened budgets and a narrow back-to-basics attitude have limited the attention paid to this part of education. As a concerned parent, you should encourage your school system not to neglect this important aspect of your child's education.

ACTIVITIES IN THE ARTS

Most American schools divide the arts into "Art" (drawing, painting, sculpting, collage-making, weaving, woodworking) and "Music" (singing, dancing, playing instruments, listening to music). Good teachers relate these activities to one another and to other subjects in the curriculum—literature, history, science—as well as to holidays or special events.

Most children continue to enjoy these activities throughout the intermediate years, although some children become more self-conscious as they get older. As *Coming to Our Senses*, a recent report of the Special Projects Panel of the American Council for the Arts in Education (New York, McGraw Hill, 1977), said:

The arts are the natural work of children. The arts are like play—creative, exploratory, purposeful—reality confirming. When painting and constructing, moving and dancing, singing and playing instruments, making and performing plays and stories and poems and songs—when all these are woven into the whole school day, basic subjects are learned more quickly—and are unforgettable.

A good art program in the intermediate years encourages children to express their ideas and feelings in a wide variety of forms and with a wide variety of materials. Children use paints, crayons, clay, watercolors, sand, sawdust, Play-Doh, string, thread, papier-mâché, colored paper, and various found materials, like boxes, buttons, bottle tops, coat hangers, spools, pipe cleaners, shoe laces, egg crates, and scraps of cloth. They use brushes, sponges, scissors, paste, pencils, chalk, and glue. They make drawings, paintings, murals, mobiles, collages, and displays. They discover how these tools and materials work, alone and in combination. Sometimes they create artwork to reflect what they have done or read—they illustrate the story they have been reading or build a model of the Indian village they have been studying. Sometimes they create the art first and then write about it—they draw a picture of their home and then describe it in writing. Sometimes they make art for the sheer joy of doing so—the good teacher treats art as a natural form of expression and communication, not as a subject to be learned.

In a good intermediate art program there is time for learning how to observe the surrounding world more keenly and time for expressing one's observations in visual form. There is time for appreciating what is in the natural environment and what others have made and time for making one's own creations. Whether the aim is appreciation or expression, the teacher always respects the child's individuality. She does not expect all children to react to a visual experience in the same way, and she does not expect their artistic products to look the same or be made the same way. For a class of thirty children to hold up thirty watercolors of a marigold, all made in the same way with the same design and same colors, is a perversion of good art education!

The artwork that children create should adorn and enliven the school. Displays of children's work should spill out of the classroom into the halls, the vestibules, the library, the gym, the principal's office. There should be paintings, drawings, collages, tiled mosaics, papier-mâché sculptures, fanciful kites, enormous dragons, colorful woven flags and banners. A good program creates a warm and inviting atmosphere in the school. Nothing can reduce a building to institutional sterility more quickly than the absence of art.

ACTIVITIES IN MUSIC

In much the same way, a good music program introduces children to a wide variety of musical forms and encourages them to express themselves in these forms. Children sing, march, dance, and move to rhythm, clapping, swaying, stomping, skipping, swinging arms. They experiment with fast and slow, high and low, loud and soft, long and short. Sometimes the teacher plays records. Sometimes she plays the piano or the guitar, and the children sing with her. Sometimes the class sings without accompaniment. Sometimes the children make up a dance to match the mood of a story or a painting; sometimes they paint or write to reflect the feeling of a song.

At this age, singing is still fun for most children. They sing patriotic songs, popular songs, folk songs, lullabies, work songs, show tunes, and seasonal songs. Sometimes the songs are related to another part of the curriculum; for example, children who are learning about the building of the railroads may sing songs like "The Streets of Laredo" and "The Wabash Cannon Ball." More often, the singing is just for fun. Most singing is done in unison, although occasionally two- or three-part harmony is introduced.

In these years, some children in some schools may begin music lessons, usually on string, brass, or woodwind instruments. If there are enough such children, there may be a school band or orchestra, a welcome addition to school life. Also in these years, some teachers begin to acquaint children with basic musical notation and other formal study. For the most part, however, the program emphasizes music making and its dominant key is joy.

Computers in the Intermediate Years

What will your child's world be like? Try as we may, we cannot foretell our children's future, we cannot know what blessings or calamities may befall them. No doubt the eternal human verities will hold sway, but in what context? We cannot predict the pace of social and technological changes. As the sociologist Margaret Mead once said, children are today's immigrants, immigrants to a new age. All we can be sure of about the future world is that it will be different from ours, a world increasingly shaped by the computer.

During our lifetime, computers have begun to change virtually every area of human activity—communications, travel, business, industry, science, medicine, government, even entertainment and the arts. As computer technology develops, new uses and purposes are discovered, which in turn give rise to greater technological advances. Our ancestors who had tamed fire to ward off wolves at the mouths of caves could not have foreseen its uses to smelt ore, forge steel, build bridges, erect skyscrapers. (These changes, of course, occurred over a long period, but today changes can occur within a generation or two, as in microbiology or laser technology.) And those of us who have come of age before the 1980s cannot envision the ways in which the explosive development of computer technology will change the fabric of people's lives. Your child was born at the dawn of a new age, and your job, as well as that of the schools, is to help him feel comfortable in it.

The importance of computers in your child's life and in the educational process itself has not been lost upon the schools. Before 1980 there were virtually no microcomputers in America's schools. The child-to-computer ratio went from about 750 to 1 in 1981 to about 30 in 1 in 1987. The sales of educational software (the programs that tell the computer what to do) have mushroomed, from next to nothing to $150 million in 1985 to a projected $300 million in 1990. Today, computers are as frequently seen in rural schools and in inner cities as they are in the nation's affluent suburbs. In the late 1980s it is as hard to find a school without computers as a home without a television set.

Unfortunately, or perhaps fortunately given the rapid pace of technological change, there is no consensus on how these computers should be used. The available hardware and software have changed so rapidly, and continue to do so, that teachers and principals must constantly shift gears. Complicating matters is the fact that most school personnel have acquired computer training recently, while on the job. Most educators agree that children should acquire "computer literacy," but few can define exactly what it is. It will take time before a generally accepted pattern of use emerges, but in the meantime, we should let "many flowers bloom." However, it is important to note that not all uses of the computer are of equal value. This brief chapter may provide some insights into the difference between imaginative and comprehensive school computer programs and limited or dull ones.

HOW SHOULD YOUR CHILD USE COMPUTERS IN SCHOOL?

In order to get the most from the rest of this chapter, it would help to have some knowledge of what a computer is, how it works, and what it can do. The best way to become familiar with computers is to use them, experimenting with a variety of applications. (Some public libraries have computers for their patrons' use.) If you don't have access to one, reading about them could prove useful. Since this is not a book about computers but a book about children and schools, the following are two computer books that the authors have found helpful: *The Parents' Computer Book* by M. David Stone (New York: Macmillan, 1984) and *Parents, Kids, and Computers* by Lynne Alper and Meg Holmberg (Berkeley, Calif.: SYBEX, 1984).

During the intermediate years children should use computers in a wide variety of ways, to acquaint themselves with their possibilities and limitations and to assist in other subjects, like writing, science, social studies, art, and mathematics. There is no established menu of instruction, but your child will be well served if by the end of the fifth grade he has acquired the computer knowledge described below.

Basic Familiarity

Your child should have a basic understanding of what a computer is, both mechanically and conceptually. He should know how to turn it on, how to select software appropriate for his purpose, and how to load and run a program. He should have a well-developed image of the computer as an input/processing/output system. He should have learned the importance of accurate data and specific instructions. He should feel comfortable using the computer in a variety of situations.

Learning Games

Your child should have an opportunity to experiment with a wide variety of learning games. Many of the earliest computer games of the shoot-em-up variety (the arcade games of the late 1970s) were admittedly mindless (although probably not as harmful as initially reported). Increasingly, however, well-designed software is becoming available. Today, many learning games are truly imaginative, challenging, and intellectually stimulating. There are word games, arithmetic games, games of strategy and logic, and simulation games (in which the player must decide how to act in a simulated situation, such as overcoming dangers while leading a wagon train across the 19th-century United States). These games vary from the simple to the complex; many readily hold an adult's interest. Do not write off well-chosen computer games as mere entertainment—they are a source of much useful learning, both in their content and in the skill required to play them.

Graphics

Your child should have experience using the computer as pen, pencil, paint, and paper. He should use it to draw lines, to construct geometric shapes, and to shade and color areas. In doing so, he will develop some feeling for the way in which architects and draftsmen use computers, and he will gain intuitive knowledge of the geometry he is learning.

Word Processing

Your child should have experience using the computer as a word processor. Word-processing equipment is rapidly making conventional paper and typewriter technology obsolete throughout our society. Your child will almost certainly use it in his later education and his working life. Meanwhile, word processing can be a great help to your child in learning to write well. The ease with which corrections can be made, words and passages rearranged, and clean copy produced encourages children to make successive revisions in their work in order to improve it. (This is particularly true for those children for whom the physical task of writing is laborious.) Word-processing software programs, such as *Story Write*, *Bank Street Writer*, and LOGO's *Text-Editor*, are readily available and highly suitable for children.

Data Base Programs

Your child should know how to use a data base system to sort and select information, and he should have some experience with creating a simple data base system. These skills will become increasingly useful (and perhaps necessary) as he continues his education and enters the working world.

Spreadsheet Programs

Your child should have experience in using spreadsheet programs to analyze related data and perform arithmetic computations upon them. (Probably the best known spreadsheet program is still *Visi Calc*, which was written for the Apple II computer.) In the coming years, such programs will find increased use in schools and businesses.

Programming

Your child should know how to create simple computer programs and have an understanding of how more complex programs are designed and written.

So far we have been discussing ways in which your child can and should use computers without having any knowledge of programming. Some educators believe that such uses are sufficient, that there is no reason for children to learn how to program computers. They point out that one can learn to drive an automobile without studying automobile mechanics.

Others, including the authors, believe that there are important reasons why all children should have some programming experience. Programming a computer, even in rudimentary fashion, removes the mystery and puts the child in charge. It gives him a lively sense of the computer's limitations—"garbage in, garbage out"—and reinforces the idea that the computer does only what you tell it exactly to do. It stresses the need for accuracy. It provides challenging practice in analyzing a problem and designing a sequential process for its solution. (The ability to design a program is crucial; by comparison, learning the specific language involved is almost incidental.) It opens the doors to an intuitive understanding of mathematical and spatial relationships. As Seymour Papert, the Massachusetts Institute of Technology professor who developed the programming language LOGO has written,

> The child programs the computer and, in doing so, both acquires a sense of mastery over a piece of the most modern and powerful technology and establishes an intimate contact with some of the deepest ideas from science, from mathematics, and from the art of intellectual model building.

What programming language should your child learn to use? The three languages in most common use in the schools today are LOGO, BASIC, and PASCAL. (PASCAL, however, is usually not taught below the secondary school level.) As a practical matter, it probably doesn't matter which language your child learns. The point is to have the experience of programming itself; no doubt new languages will appear before long. However, at present, the authors lean toward LOGO because it is a language developed for children but powerful enough to be of use to adults.

It is evident from this discussion that the computer is a powerful tool with many uses. In fact, as educator M. David Stone has written, the computer is more than a single tool—it is a toolbox containing many individual tools or programs. Your child should grow up understanding this variety and should become increasingly proficient in a wide range of the computer's numerous applications.

WHAT TO LOOK FOR IN A SCHOOL COMPUTER PROGRAM

This pattern of widely varying uses of the computer is likely to continue for some time. Schools have not yet had time to adapt to the new technology. Much more thinking and experimentation needs to be done about the role of the computer in instruction. Despite the relatively high volume of computer sales, computers need to become accessible to more children more of the time. Better software needs to be developed. Teachers trained in the pre-computer era need to be reeducated, or gradually to give way to a younger generation, more at home with the computer.

Meanwhile, the technology itself will continue to change. A recent advertisement announced: "In the not-distant future one video disk will hold an entire *Encyclopedia Britannica*, including color photographs; disks occupying the same space as a typical teen's record collection will store the information necessary for a four-year college education." Who knows what other marvels lie behind a layman's imagination and how long it will take the schools to take advantage of the possibilities such marvels will present?

In the meantime, the following are some things you might look for:

- How many computers are there in the school? How are they equipped? How often does each child have access to one?
- What software programs will your child be using? Will he have experiences with learning games, graphics, word processing, data base programs, and spreadsheet programs?
- Do the programs used permit experimentation and creativity, or are they limited to drill and practice exercises?
- Will your child learn to write programs on the computer? What programming language will he be using?
- What are your child's teachers' attitudes toward computers? Are they excited about the learning possibilities they present or do they regard them with apprehension or disdain?
- What special learning experiences has your child had lately involving the use of computers?

HOW TO HELP YOUR CHILD AT HOME

Some time ago, a much-played television commercial showed a young man greeting his drooping parents on his return home from college. It seems that he had just flunked out—because they had not bought him a personal computer.

As people who know how easy it is to become the Bad Parents, even without gratuitous guilt trips of this kind (just ask any adolescent), the authors were appalled. Success in school and later life does not yet depend upon owning a home computer. You can enrich your child's mental growth through the other ways suggested in this book. And should your child need additional hands-on computer time, after-school, week-end, or summer programs are often available at relatively low expense.

Nevertheless, we must admit that ready access to a computer at home can be an educational advantage. If your child is fortunate enough to have such access, be sure that you

- Make the use of the computer a family activity. Use it yourself; use it together; talk about what you do with it.
- Find software programs that respond to your child's interests and that stimulate and challenge his imagination and thinking abilities. Try them out together with your child, the way you might read him the opening chapter of a new book.
- Play computer games with your child. They can be fun for both of you, and worthwhile as well. Particularly good are the games you and your child can play together against the computer.
- Let your child have fun, even if he seems to be wasting time. You can never tell what he might be learning. Besides, who said that children this age are never supposed to have fun? Don't worry about your child becoming a "computer freak" and losing touch with people—when he's ready to be with people, he will be. Some of us have logged a lot of time with comic books and mindless television shows. Granted, we aren't geniuses: Are our lives so stunted?

Health and Physical Education in the Intermediate Years

Most schools throughout the country have health and physical education programs. In some states, they are required by law. Although you may not regard these programs to be as vital as reading and mathematics, they can be a very important part of your child's total development as a healthy, active human being.

HEALTH EDUCATION

Health education should not be confused with health services, concerned with physical examinations, inoculations, school safety, school cleanliness, first aid, and similar matters, and provided by the school nurse or physician. Health education attempts to instill knowledge, attitudes, and habits on such matters as:

- Physical health, including rest and exercise, personal hygiene, nutrition, dental care, substance abuse (tobacco, alcohol, other drugs), and disease prevention.

- Mental health, including understanding of self, awareness of feelings, respect for others, and decision-making (understanding of the consequences of one's actions).
- Safety, including dealing with traffic, talking to strangers, and avoidance of accidents.
- Human growth and development, including bodily systems and functions—respiratory, circulatory, digestive, nervous, reproductive—the human life cycle, and the role of the family.

Health education programs are usually taught by the regular classroom teacher, although the nurse or another special teacher may sometimes be involved. Sometimes the lessons are independent, as when the class examines charts and a model of the human circulatory system. Sometimes they are tied in to other subjects, as when the birth of a new guinea pig in the science corner leads to a discussion of reproduction and infant care. Sometimes they are the by-product of class activities, as when safety precautions are taken on a field trip.

One major concern that many parents have is the possibility of drug or alcohol abuse. Although few children in these intermediate years use drugs or alcohol, the time to establish healthy attitudes is now, before the peer pressures of early adolescence exert their influence. Children need a certain amount of basic information, but more helpful are the discussions and role-playing exercises that build healthy attitudes. Do not hesitate to ask your school officials what they are doing to help deter substances abuse and, if possible, offer your help. Also, if you are concerned about the possibility of such sexually transmitted diseases as AIDS, you should speak to your school officials about that matter as well.

PHYSICAL EDUCATION

Almost all schools provide some sort of physical education program, even if it consists of little more than having children run around outside to let off steam. A good physical education program goes far beyond this simple activity, however. A well-conceived and well-taught program can help your child develop skills and habits that will stand him in good stead for a lifetime.

Partisans of physical education believe that physical fitness is good in itself and that a sound body is a sound mind. They also believe that through individual and team games and activities, children can learn desirable attitudes and values of self-discipline, cooperation, and steadiness under pressure. Among the goals of the program are:

- Physical fitness, including strength, endurance, agility, and vitality.
- Physical skills, including running, jumping, skipping, bending, and skills related to specific sports and activities.
- Desirable social values, including poise, self-respect, respect for others, cooperation, and sportsmanlike conduct.
- Recreational habits, including knowledge and skill at games to play with other children and knowledge and skill at games to play throughout life.

Physical education programs in the intermediate years may be taught by the classroom teacher or by a physical education teacher, who meets with the class several times a week or even once a day. Among the most common activities are

- Games and sports, such as softball, basketball, and soccer.
- Rhythmic activities, such as dancing, pantomime, and creative movement.

- Self-testing and conditioning activities, such as stretching, bending, skipping rope, tumbling, and balancing on a beam.

Good teachers provide a wide variety of activities and make sure that each child is involved, no matter what his physical ability.

Tests in the Intermediate Years

During your child's years in grades 3, 4, and 5 he will probably be given one or more standardized tests. Schools typically administer such tests to determine academic progress, to provide a basis for grouping children, and to assess a child's ability in order to measure his achievement. Although the test results are not yet as important as they will be later (when they may affect your child's choice of college or vocation), they do influence the way in which school personnel think about your child. For this reason, you should know what tests your child takes and have a reasonably clear idea of what the results do and do not mean.

Some schools are very forthcoming about the tests they give and about the scores your child achieved. They will be happy to give you the results and help you interpret them. Other schools may adopt a more guarded or even secretive posture. Don't be deterred; you have a right to know the results of testing done on your child and the right to know what use school personnel plan to make of the results.

STANDARDIZED TESTS

A standardized test differs from the classroom test or quiz the teacher gives to see how well her pupils are mastering the curriculum. It is prepared by test specialists, produced by test publishers who are national in scope, contains explicit instructions about how it should be administered (timing, directions, for example), has machine-scored answer sheets, and provides instructions for interpreting the test results. The test is "standardized" in the sense that it is given under the same conditions and permits comparison of one score or a group of scores with a national sample. Norm-referenced tests compare a child's performance with the performance of other children of the same age. (How do Johnny's scores compare with those of most children his age? How did the kids in our school do compared with the kids in other schools in our county?) Criterion-referenced tests measure your child's performance against a set standard. (Has Johnny mastered basic third-grade arithmetic facts?)

The standardized tests most commonly used in schools are of two types: achievement tests and aptitude tests.

Achievement Tests

Achievement tests measure how much a child has learned in a given subject. A mathematics achievement test, for example, measures how much of the math curriculum a child has learned compared to the program's goal or to what other children his age in his class, his school, his state, or the country have learned. Among the most widely used achievement tests are the following:

California Achievement Tests
California Assessment Program Achievement Series

Comprehensive Tests of Basic Skills (CTBS)
Cooperative Primary Tests
Iowa Tests of Basic Skills
Iowa Tests of Educational Development
Metropolitan Achievement Tests
Science Research Associates (SRA) Achievement Series
Stanford Achievement Series

Aptitude Tests

Aptitude tests measure a child's ability to learn in specific subjects. They are not intended to measure what children have actually learned in class but to assess broad-scale abilities, such as verbal ability, memory, and reasoning ability, which the child needs in order to do schoolwork. Among the most widely used standardized aptitude tests are the following:

California Test of Mental Maturity
Gates-MacGinitie Reading Skills test
Lee-Clark Reading Readiness test
Lorge-Thorndike Intelligence Tests
Metropolitan Readiness Test
Murphy Durrell Reading Readiness Analysis
Stanford-Binet IQ Test
Wechsler Preschool and Primary Scale of Intelligence
Wechsler Intelligence Scale for Children

IQ TESTS

One familiar aptitude test is the IQ (intelligence quotient) test. IQ tests measure basic mental abilities, such as verbal ability, memory, reasoning, and spatial perception. Children are given such tasks as sentence completions, word problems, and problems involving pictures and patterns.

Although IQ tests are in disfavor among knowledgeable educators, they are still used in many schools. Supposedly, such tests can be used to predict how successful a child will be in school. And in a very broad way, they do. The problem is that often parents, teachers, and children themselves think that the score means something it does not.

An IQ score is *not* a measure of a child's fixed innate capacity. All aptitude tests depend in part on what a child has already learned—the distinction between achievement and aptitude tests is not as absolute as it may seem. Research has shown that children can improve their IQ scores given proper instruction and encouragement.

Furthermore, intelligence itself is not a single attribute. There are many different mental abilities involved in the general trait we call intelligence. Dr. Stephen Jay Gould, a Harvard professor and author of *The Mismeasure of Man,* has written that "there's no such thing as a single measure of intelligence. You can't measure intelligence the way you can your foot size or your height."

The scores attained on IQ tests can also vary, depending on, for example, the conditions under which the child took the test or his energy level on that particular day. If you have reason to believe that your child's score is too low and if the school seems to think the matter is important, request that your child be retested.

Finally, an IQ test cannot measure many of the traits we know to be important in determining success in school and in life—traits like common sense, motivation, responsibility, empathy, creativity, and insight.

TEST SCORES

The scores your child receives on standardized tests will probably be reported to you in one of the following forms: raw scores, percentiles, stanines, or grade equivalent scores.

Raw Scores

A raw score is the number of questions your child answered correctly. It doesn't tell you much. For example, what does "23" mean if you don't know how many questions there were in the test and how other children did, let alone what the test was about?

Percentiles

A percentile is *not* the percentage of questions your child answered correctly. It indicates the percentage of people in the norm group (others who took the test) your child scored above. For example, a score of 83 means that your child did better than 83 percent of the children in the norm group (although he may have answered only 70 percent of the questions correctly).

Stanines

Stanines are a statistical measure that groups scores more broadly than percentiles. They range from a low of 1 to a high of 9. Scores of 1, 2, and 3 are below average; scores of 4, 5, and 6 are average; and scores of 7, 8, and 9 are above average. More specifically,

$$
\begin{aligned}
9 &= \text{top } 4\% \\
8 &= \text{next } 7\% \\
7 &= \text{next } 12\% \\
6 &= \text{next } 17\% \\
5 &= \text{middle } 20\% \\
4 &= \text{next } 17\%
\end{aligned}
$$

3 = next 12%
2 = next 7%
1 = lowest 4%

Grade Equivalent Scores

Grade equivalent scores are reported as two digits separated by a decimal. The first digit stands for a grade in school; the second, for a tenth of a year. A grade equivalent score of 2.5 means that the child scored as well on that test as an average child would in the fifth month of the second grade.

Grade equivalent scores are subject to a great deal of misunderstanding. For example, if your third-grade child scores 5.6 on a math test, it does *not* necessarily mean that your child should be doing fifth-grade math. The test may have contained no questions about topics normally covered in grades 4 and 5. What the score means is that your child scored as well on the third-grade test as would an average child on the same test in the sixth month of the fifth grade.

Similarly, if your third-grade child scores 2.4 on a reading test, it does *not* mean that your child should be back in second grade (although it may mean that your child should get special help). It means that your child scored as well on the third-grade test as would an average child in the fourth month of second grade.

Remember that a grade equivalent score is defined as a score that is in the middle for students at a grade level. Half the children in a given population are above and half are below—by definition. Therefore, you should be wary when you are told that your child is performing above or below grade level. Nationally, we shall never be able to bring all of our children up to grade level—because the test makers have *defined* half of our children as being below.

WHAT DO THE TESTS TELL US?

Schools use standardized tests to place and group children for instruction, to determine speed of instruction, to select appropriate learning tasks, to evaluate how well a school or class is achieving, and to determine what children are and are not learning. Such tests tell us how one child's performance compares to that of others in the same grade, and they may be useful in identifying areas of strength and weakness. Because schools must have some way of standardizing the results of instruction from one classroom to another and because they need to provide measures of accountability to the public, standardized tests of some kind are a necessity.

But most standardized tests are too broadly gauged to be of much use. Almost any intelligent, competent classroom teacher can tell you more about your child. Therefore, you should resist making decisions based on test scores alone. Test scores are only one measure of your child's achievement and abilities, and an imperfect measure at that. Help your child to take the tests seriously, but do not overemphasize the results—to him, to the teacher, or to yourself.

The Gifted Child

Who are the gifted? What do we mean by "gifted"? How do we know which child is gifted? How should we help the child who is indeed gifted?

In the authors' experience, there is little consensus on the answers to these questions. On this issue, perceptions and the value systems on which they are based differ so markedly that it is often difficult for people to communicate with one another. In the parents' stereotyped view, the child is gifted, and the school (the teacher, the principal, the rest) is too dull and lazy (and probably jealous) to recognize the fact and do something about it. In the teacher's stereotyped view, the child is bright normal, and the parents are pushing him unrealistically (and probably to great detriment) in order to gratify their own egos. When a school provides special programs for the gifted, some criticize it for catering to the elitist desires of the upper-middle class. When a school lacks such programs, others criticize it for pandering to the egalitarian philosophy of the ignorant masses.

Unhappily, there is too often truth in both assertions. And caught somewhere in the middle of all this is a child—intelligent, creative, ingenious, talented, a bit lonely, probably misunderstood, and not developing his full potential. In individual terms, and from the standpoint of a society whose need for trained intelligence is limitless, the waste of potential is a crying shame.

KINDS OF GIFTS AND TALENTS

Being gifted and/or talented is not an all-or-nothing proposition. People can be blessed in various ways. Some children have an extraordinary capacity for mathematics, others for language. Some have prodigious talent in art or music; some raise questions about science that their teachers never thought of; some can devise creative solutions to almost any intellectual problem. Even intelligence, as we have seen, is not a single trait—there are many kinds of intelligences, many specific intellectual aptitudes. In a 1972 report to Congress, then U.S. Commissioner of Education Sidney Marland identified gifted or talented children as those who were exceptional in one or more of the following areas:

> General intellectual ability
> Specific academic aptitude
> Creative or productive thinking
> Leadership ability
> Visual or performing arts
> Psychomotor ability

Marland's definition, which has been incorporated into federal legislation, has broadly affected many schools.

Another influential definition is that recently proposed by Joseph Renzulli of the University of Connecticut. Renzulli's model emphasizes a child's interest and motivation; it specifies that three interrelated criteria—creativity, above-average ability, and task commitment—must come together in a child's area of interest. The model, which has been adopted by hundreds of school districts, looks like this:

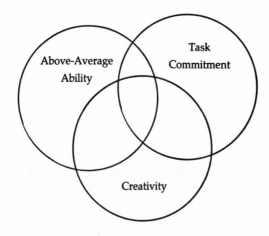

It has proved helpful in avoiding a narrow, IQ-based definition of giftedness and in suggesting characteristics that might be overlooked in traditional school settings.

As a parent, you should treasure whatever is unique about your child, whether others would call the trait gifted or not. But if you suspect that your child does possess unusual gifts or talents—and remember, the range of possible gifts and talents is very broad—you should work cooperatively with the school to support and nurture them. If you suspect unusual ability, arrange for individual testing by a competent professional—a private psychologist or a teacher with special training. You can also ask school personnel to observe your child's behavior and to conduct special testing. Try to determine not only whether your child is gifted, but *how* your child is gifted—exactly what are his unusual aptitudes or talents and how extensive are they?

IDENTIFICATION OF GIFTED CHILDREN

A few children in every generation stand out as truly exceptional. These are the geniuses like Isaac Newton and the prodigies like Mozart, children whose extraordinary gifts no one could fail to recognize. For the most part, however, identification of the gifted and/or talented child is a difficult task. There is no consensus on which traits or abilities are considered gifted and/or talented, on the degree to which a person must possess such traits, or on the procedures that should be used to measure them. Some schools equate giftedness with a high IQ score; for example, a child with an IQ of 125 or more is considered gifted. But there are serious drawbacks to such a view. First, an IQ test measures only a small range of human potential; it ignores whole realms of existence, such as creativity, imagination, persistence, and musical or visual talent. Second, an IQ score is not as "fixed" a measurement as some schools may imply. Any child could score as much as ten points higher or lower on a given day. Furthermore, studies have shown that IQ scores can be improved through effective teaching. Third, whatever the cutoff number is—in this example, 125—it is arbitrary. How can a child with an IQ of 125 be gifted in one school district but not in another, where the cutoff is 130?

Some school districts identify the "top" 2 or 3 percent of their children as being gifted. Forget for a moment the problem of specifying what is meant by *top*. How do we know that gifted children are evenly distributed throughout the population? We don't assume that the "bottom" 2 or 3 percent are handicapped, and in fact, the law rightly forbids our doing so. Might a given child not be in the top 2 or 3 percent in one school district but not in another, with a different pupil population? And what about those children who would rank just below the top—are we so sure of our identification procedures that we can afford not to give *them* special attention?

Some schools identify gifted children on the basis of achievement. For example, a child who has tested two or more levels above his grade level in reading might be considered gifted. Such a criterion only goes so far though. What about the truly gifted child who has *not* achieved because he has been bored and become indifferent or difficult? Do we not have an obligation to identify and nurture *his* special gifts?

Given such problems, most experts agree that rigid criteria or formulas for determining who may be gifted or talented do not work well. Several criteria should be utilized—not a single test but a variety of measures, such as teacher observation, parent interviews, examination of what the child has done or can do, interviews with the child himself or herself. (We deliberately use the cumbersome construction "himself or herself" here because girls have not always received adequate recognition when it comes to being labeled "gifted.") Every effort should be made to identify gifted children who can profit from special attention. Better to cast the net more widely and enrich the lives of a few who may not warrant it than to miss children with special abilities that have not yet bloomed.

How can you tell if your child is gifted and/or talented? As we have said, there is no single test or criterion. However, here are a few signs to look for in intermediate-age children:

- Speaking comfortably in complex sentences with a mature vocabulary for his age.
- Reading all material voraciously and complex material easily.
- Asking questions that reveal an imaginative turn of mind.
- Demonstrating an exceptional ability to solve mathematical problems easily and concisely.
- Making original connections between people, things, events, and ideas.
- Persevering (and becoming expert at) a specific activity (computer games, chess, model building, stamp collecting).
- Displaying an unusual ability at drawing, painting, or music.

This is a short illustrative list; the number of ways in which your child may exhibit a special gift or talent is extensive. Your job, as well as that of the school, is to find that special quality and to help your child develop it.

PROGRAMS FOR GIFTED CHILDREN

Practices for educating gifted children in the intermediate years vary greatly throughout the country. There is no consensus on what *should* be done, and there exist considerable differences in what *is* done. Although the federal government makes available to the states some funding for this purpose, there is no federal legislation stating that schools must provide services for the gifted, as there is for the handicapped. Some states require that local school districts provide such services; some do not. Some local districts provide them whether required or not; others do not. Some schools have pull-out programs, in which children identified as talented are removed from class for a certain time each day or week in order to receive special instruction. These programs may focus on advanced academic skills, provide intellectual stimulation, and stimulate creativity. If conducted well, they can challenge your gifted child's imagination and abilities and help keep him from being bored and losing interest. They also ensure that your child will spend some time with other children of like interests and abilities.

One problem with such progress is that they engage the child for only a portion of his time in school. Gifted children should be challenged continuously throughout the day, not just two or three times a week in small doses. However, if your child is truly a fish out of water among his classmates and if no improvement in the regular class is forthcoming, a special pull-out program can provide welcome stimulation.

Whether or not the school conducts such programs, much can and should be done within the regular intermediate classroom. Capable teachers at this level can individualize their programs sufficiently to provide for the needs of all but the most extraordinary children. Enrichment should not mean more of the same—the teacher should provide activities that permit greater depth and allow more freedom for the child to use his mind. Among the things that teachers can do to offer enrichment is to

- Form reading groups or other activity groups according to the children's interests and abilities.
- Conduct individualized reading programs that allow gifted children to read material well beyond the level of their classmates.
- Teach all subjects in such a way as to provoke thought and imagination—"teach minds, not facts."
- Assign individual projects to be completed at home or in school with a depth and scope appropriate to the child's abilities.
- Make liberal use of the library—in the school, in the community, at home.
- Provide math games and puzzles that challenge thought and creativity.
- Furnish computer software that permits open-ended inquiry.
- Organize trips to science and art museums.
- Establish "mentoring" programs, in which an adult or an older child tutors the intermediate child.
- Arrange visits by resource people who are able to stimulate the gifted child's curiosity and imagination.

Such activities, of course, are desirable for all children. But they can be especially helpful to gifted children because they stimulate mental growth and provide open-ended opportunities for expression.

HOW CAN PARENTS HELP?

Parents play a critical role in nurturing their children's special gifts or talents. Almost every adult who has been recognized for a rare accomplishment can point to a parent or other adult who identified or encouraged his talent when he was young. The attitudes you foster in your child may be as important in the full development of his talent as the native ability itself. Here are some things you can do to help:

- Talk to your child. Listen to him. Answer his questions. Be interested, be interesting, be patient.
- Read to your child, even though he reads for himself. Talk about what you read together.
- Watch television with your child and help him raise thoughtful and critical questions about what he sees.
- Provide a wide variety of books, games, and puzzles that challenge the mind and the imagination.
- Include your child in family discussions. Treat his mind with respect. Give him a real role to play in family activities.
- Take your child to libraries, museums, concerts, and theatrical events.

As you do these things, remember that however special your child's talents may be, he is still a child. He has the same emotional needs as all children—the security of his parents' love and approval, the acceptance of his friends and agemates, and so on. In fact, these needs may be heightened because of his unusual sensitivity and his feeling of being different. At the same time, he must learn to live in a non-gifted world. He must be able to get along with people less capable than he. He should not hide his gifts, but he should not expect preferential treatment in all matters because of his ability in some.

You can help by treating your child normally in most

situations, by helping him relate to other children who may not be as gifted, by openly discussing his feelings of difference if he brings them up, and by making sure he understands that your love is unconditional and not dependent on his abilities. To be loved, as well as to have a special gift, is a wonderful blessing. To go through life feeling that you are worth no more than the gift can be a curse.

HELPFUL RESOURCES

Organizations

> American Association for Gifted Children
> 15 Gramercy Park
> New York, New York 10003
>
> Council for Exceptional Children
> 1820 Association Drive
> Reston, Virginia 22091
>
> National Association for Gifted Children
> 5100 N. Edgewood Drive
> Saint Paul, Minnesota 55112
>
> Program for the Education of the Gifted and Talented
> U.S. Department of Education
> 400 Maryland Avenue, SW
> Washington, D.C. 20202

Books

Ehrlich, Virginia Z. *Gifted Children: A Guide for Parents and Teachers.* Englewood Cliffs, N.J.: Prentice-Hall, 1982.

Little, James Alvino O. *Parent's Guide to Raising a Gifted Child.* Boston, Mass.: Little, Brown, 1985.

Moore, Linda Perigo. *Does This Mean My Kid's a Genius?* New York: New American Library, Plume, 1982.

Vail, Priscilla L. *The World of the Gifted Child.* New York: Penguin, 1980.

The Child With Learning Problems

Most children do reasonably well in school. They like their teachers, get along with their friends, and make normal academic progress. Within this general picture, there is variety. Some children are brighter than others. Some seem to "take" to school activity; some do not. Some are early bloomers; some are slower to develop. Some breeze through the work the school assigns; some have trouble with it. Individual children may experience ups and downs. A child may be happy and productive for a period of several years and then have a bad year because of a poor teacher or because of upsetting circumstances at home. It is well within the normal range for children to have occasional academic or social difficulty.

A minority of children is less fortunate. They have been born with handicapping conditions or have suffered physical or emotional trauma that resulted in such conditions after birth. The parent should know how to detect the presence of such conditions and how and where to seek help for their children.

Some handicaps are apparent at birth or become evident in early childhood. They include severe physical handicaps, blindness, deafness, and mental retardation. However, other handicapping conditions that impede learning may not surface until the child is in school. Among these are less serious visual and hearing impairments, speech problems, emotional disturbances, and a variety of problems known collectively as *learning disabilities*. Your child has certain rights to a free, appropriate education regardless of his handicap. As his parent, you have rights as well. Those rights are enumerated later in this chapter. If you are the parent of a severely handicapped child, your problem is beyond the scope of this book. (You may want to consult the organizations listed at the end of this chapter.) Here we focus on handicapping conditions that are most likely to appear once your child has entered school.

SCHOOL-RELATED PROBLEMS

Each year some third-grade parents receive a message from the school like this: "Mr. Rice, I'm concerned about Mary. She's a sweet girl, and she tries to do everything I ask her to, but somehow she doesn't seem to be making any progress in her reading. Even though she's in the slowest reading group, the other children are beginning to make fun of her. I think perhaps we should talk about having Mary tested."

Each year some fourth-grade parents get a call like this: "Mrs. White, I think you ought to know that it's still not working out with Billy. I thought when we changed his seat he would be less distracted, but he still doesn't do his work and he's always bothering the other children. Frankly, I don't know what to do with him. Can we talk?"

No one likes to receive such messages or worse. If you're normal, you first experience a sick feeling in the pit of your stomach, followed by a rush of anger—at the school, at your child, or at yourself. To help your child, however, you must overcome your anger and distress. You must take charge of yourself and the situation and determine what's wrong and what you're going to do about it.

Problems occur in many forms. Your child may have more than the usual difficulty adjusting to school discipline and routines. He may engage in aggressive or inappropriate behavior with adults or other children. He may be overly shy and withdrawn. He may have great difficulty in learning to read, or he may be able to read but unable to write clearly. He may develop a fear of going to school or a strong dislike for it (a school phobia) and experience chronic headaches or stomach upsets in order to stay home. Or he simply may not be doing as well in school as his apparent intelligence would indicate.

In the past, children with such problems were viewed as slow learners or as being spoiled or lazy. Even today, we encounter some children who learn more slowly than others and some who are spoiled, if not lazy. But in today's world, knowledgeable educators recognize that such behavior is often the sign of a handicapping condition, to which appropriate attention must be paid.

HANDICAPPING CONDITIONS

Among the handicapping conditions that may impede learning and for which help is available under federal law are the following:

> Hearing impairment or deafness
> Speech impairment
> Visual impairment or blindness
> Emotional disturbance
> Autism
> Mental retardation
> Physical impairment
> Chronic or long-term health problems
> Learning disabilities

The condition need not be especially severe to be handicapping (or to warrant help). Even a mild speech, hearing, or vision impairment can affect a child's ability to learn to read and write. An emotional problem need not be incapacitating in order to interfere with normal relationships in a classroom. Today, schools are required to identify such conditions and to help children overcome or cope with them, and to involve you as a parent in the decision-making process.

LEARNING DISABILITIES

Most handicapping conditions are familiar to most parents. Once we are told that a child has a hearing problem, for example, we understand what is meant, even if we may not know exactly what should be done about it. However, one category of handicaps, that of learning disabilities, is not so well understood. It is the most school-related, the newest, and the fastest growing of the commonly recognized handicaps. Experts estimate that from 1 to 30 percent of the school population have a learning disability of some kind and degree.

The U.S. Department of Education defines learning disabilities as follows:

Specific learning disability means a disorder in one or more of the basic psychological processes involved in understanding or in using language, spoken or written, which disorder may manifest itself in imperfect ability to think, read, write, spell, or do mathematical calculations. The term includes such conditions as perceptual handicaps, brain injury, minimal brain dysfunction, dyslexia, and developmental aphasia. The term does not include children who have learning problems which are primarily the result of visual, hearing, or motor handicaps, of mental retardation, of emotional disturbance, or environmental, cultural, or economic disadvantage.

The breadth and imprecision of this definition reflect the confusion that still exists about why some children have difficulty in learning or in performing certain tasks. Experts are still examining such possible causes as neurological impairment and biochemical irregularities in the body. But for the parent and the teacher, the causes of the problem (and the "labels" that are attached once a cause is identified) are much less important than an understanding of what the child can and cannot do and what can be done to help.

Children with learning disabilities have difficulty with schoolwork for no readily apparent physical or emotional reason. They may be very bright, but there is a decided gap between their apparent ability and their actual achievement. They may be restless, hyperactive, easily distractible. They may be disorganized and careless about things, space, time, schoolwork. They may be clumsy and have poor eye-hand coordination. They may have difficulty understanding spoken language, particularly in following directions or understanding requests or questions. They may have difficulty in learning how to read. They may have difficulty in writing about what they know or in processing what they hear or read so that they can write about it. They may be able to solve problems but unable to transfer their knowledge to paper in the form of words. Their work may seem messy and disorganized. They may have unusual difficulty in spelling. They may have trouble in mathematics because they transpose numbers, lack short-term memory, omit steps, or fail to see orderly patterns. The variety of ability combined with disability is limitless. Academically or socially or both, they may seem just a bit off-center.

Until a child is about seven or eight years old, it is sometimes difficult to tell whether he suffers from a learning disability or is merely slow to develop. Many children exhibit some of the problems described above and then outgrow them. However, whenever such problems exist in the intermediate grades, parents and teachers should be aware of them and do what they can to help the child cope, without creating the feeling that something is terribly wrong.

The traditional method of dealing with learning problems is to provide *remediation* in the needed area. For example, if a child has poor small-motor coordination, he is given extensive practice in cutting, tracing, drawing, and the like. Sometimes this focus on a poorly developed skill yields good results. More commonly, however, it leads to increased frustration on the part of all concerned. If the child can't coordinate hand and eye because his nervous system isn't developed that way, no amount of practice will help. We do not ask children who are blind to practice looking at picture books until they can describe the colors. Rather, we help them develop their sense of hearing.

A promising and increasingly prevalent approach is to help the child find a way to compensate for his problem. To this end teachers involve the child in many modes of learning using a wide variety of materials. A child who is not learning from a basal reading series may learn from a phonics-oriented program. A child who finds handwriting too difficult can type his stories on a typewriter or computer or dictate them to the teacher. If the teacher finds what the child can do well and builds upon it, the child can learn without the emotional trauma that often accompanies school failure.

WHEN SHOULD YOU WORRY?

Being the parent of a child with learning problems is not easy. You want to be on top of the situation, to be sure that your child gets whatever help he needs. But you also don't want to make your child distraught by visiting your anxiety upon him—you want to be vigilant but calm. Follow his progress in school closely. Talk with the teacher often. At the first sign of trouble, don't panic. Try to determine the cause, but be sure to be supportive of your child. Build upon the positive. Remember, your child doesn't *want* to have trouble. If *you* don't support him, who will?

Once a potential problem has been called to your attention, talk to the teacher. Ask her to tell you specifically what it is that she perceives. (It doesn't help for her to tell you that your child is dyslexic—find out exactly what he can and cannot do.) If you continue to be concerned, you may want to talk to your pediatrician or arrange for testing by a learning disabilities specialist or a school psychologist. Whatever resource you choose, if your child is still having severe and persistent difficulty in learning at this level, be sure to obtain a full diagnosis and a plan for dealing with the problem.

Raising a handicapped child can be a frustrating, lonely challenge. Many parents of such children have found it helpful to talk to other parents in similar circumstances. By meeting with others through various organizations, you can share information and emotions, learn more about your rights, monitor the quality of the services provided by the school system, lobby for your share of the school budget, and provide assistance to the schools. Find out whether such an organization exists in your school district, and if it does not, consider forming one.

WHAT SHOULD YOU DO? WHAT ARE YOUR RIGHTS?

Federal law gives your child the right to an appropriate education at public expense. The relevant laws are Section 504 of the Rehabilitation Act of 1973, and Public Law 94-142, the Education of All Handicapped Children Act of 1975.

In general, the law requires that your child, regardless of the nature of his handicap, receive a free, appropriate education in as normal a setting as possible (the "least restrictive environment"). Each child must have an Individualized Education Program (IEP), which spells out your child's needs and the specific educational program devised to deal with those needs. Among the services provided are modification in the regular classroom (such as a computer keyboard or the help of an aide), placement in a resource-room program or special class, counseling and psychological services, social work services, speech and language therapy, medical diagnostic services, transportation, and parent counseling and training. A full evaluation and a new IEP are mandated every three years, and more frequently if you or the teacher requests it.

The law also requires that you as the parent be fully informed of these proceedings and given the opportunity to participate in the decision-making. Before you permit your child to be enrolled in a special program or approve his IEP, be sure you have answers to questions like the following:

- What is your child able to do? What is he not able to do? How will the IEP help him learn to do these things?
- What services will your child receive? How exactly will they help him?
- Who will teach or work with your child, and who will be in charge?
- Where will this work be done? When?
- How will your child's progress be evaluated? How will you be involved?

Take the time to find out what your rights are. Two short but excellent documents are:

"94-142 and 504: Numbers That Add Up to Educational
Rights for Handicapped Children"
Children's Defense Fund
122 C Street, N.W.
Washington, D.C. 20001

"Special Education Checkup: What Federal Law Requires in Educating Your Child"
The National Committee for Citizens in Education
410 Wilde Lake Village Green
Columbia, Maryland 21044

The following organizations may be able to help you:

Association for Children and Adults With Learning Disabilities (ACLD)
4156 Library Road
Pittsburgh, Pennsylvania 15234

The Council for Exceptional Children
1920 Association Drive
Reston, Virginia 22091

Office of Special Education and Rehabilitation Services
U.S. Department of Education
Washington, D.C. 20202

Orton Society, Inc.
8415 Bellona Lane
Baltimore, Maryland 21204

And if you want to read more about children with learning
disabilities, we recommend the following:

Clarke, Louise. *Can't Read, Can't Write, Can't Talk Too Good Either: How to Overcome and Recognize Dyslexia in Your Child.* New York: Penguin, 1974.

McGuinness, Diane. *When Children Don't Learn.* New York: Basic Books, 1985.

Osman, Betty B. *Learning Disabilities: A Family Affair.* New York: Random House, 1979.

Osman, Betty with Blinder, Henriette. *No One to Play With.* New York: Random House, 1982.

"Taking the First Step," Association for Children With Learning Disabilities, 4156 Library Road, Pittsburgh, Pennsylvania 15234.

Communicating
With the Schools

Good schools are those in which parents and teachers work together to help children learn. When the school reflects the values of the home and the home supports the efforts of the school, children grow in an atmosphere of shared purpose and consistent expectations. There is no room for confusion about what is important. The child's total environment reinforces his efforts to achieve what he, his parents, and his teacher all accept as important goals.

Achievement of this unity of purpose requires effective communication between home and school. All schools attempt to communicate with parents to some degree; some schools do so better than others, as we shall see. Parents, too, have an obligation to keep informed about their own child's progress and about school programs and policies, and to communicate to school personnel any information about their child that may be helpful to those who work with him.

PARENTS' RIGHTS AND RESPONSIBILITIES

As a parent of a child in school, you have certain rights and responsibilities. You have the right to

- Know what your child is being taught. You have the right to see copies of any curriculum guides and to know if the teacher is following them.
- Know how the teacher conducts the class—how she teaches reading, how she groups children for instruction.
- Know how your child is doing—how he gets along with others, how he is progressing in his learning.
- Be told if your child experiences difficulty or seems unhappy.
- Be informed of school policies on such matters as attendance, illness, homework, discipline, and visiting the school.
- See all of your child's school records. (See the section "Pupil Records" below.)
- Visit your child's classroom provided you give the school advance notice.
- Appeal a decision of school authorities concerning suspension or placement in a special class.
- Request that your child be excused from reading books or engaging in school activities that you object to on religious, moral, or other reasonable grounds.
- Praise the teacher and criticize the teacher when appropriate, without fear of reprisal.
- Be spoken to courteously and plainly, without defensiveness or the use of jargon.

  Single parents also have rights.

- Noncustodial parents have the right, unless barred by a court order, to see all of their children's records. They also have the right, depending on the district of residence, to receive all routine school notices and communications, although they may have to pay for extra postage that the school may incur.

- Single parents have the right to expect the school to make reasonable accommodations to their work schedules, such as occasionally scheduling parent-teacher conferences in the early morning or in the evening.
- Single parents have the right to expect the school to refrain from criticizing their life-style, whether deliberately or thoughtlessly.

As a parent, you have the responsibility to

- Send your child to school rested, clean, fed, and ready to learn.
- Be aware of your child's work, progress, and problems.
- Inform the school if your child has an unusual problem at home.
- Read the material the school sends you—keep yourself informed about school matters.
- Volunteer your time, skills, or resources when they are needed and as you can do so.
- Treat school personnel courteously.

Good schools provide opportunities for the exercise of these rights and responsibilities. They conduct orientation programs for new parents. They hold Open Houses or Back-to-School Nights, at which parents can learn about the school program and meet their child's teacher. They schedule parent-teacher conferences at regular intervals. They call the home when the child is having trouble. They schedule early-morning or evening meetings with parents who work during the day. They include noncustodial parents on their mailing lists (unless a court decree forbids it,) and they make step-parents feel welcome. They support volunteer activity and encourage parents to express their views about educational policy. In general, they treat parents as partners in the education of their children.

KNOW YOUR CHILD'S TEACHER

In most states, your child will be with his teacher for the better part of his waking hours for over 180 days each year. That is a long time in his young life, and if things don't go well, it may be a long time in yours.

For these reasons, you should get to know the person who has such influence in your child's life. Plan to meet the teacher at the beginning of the year and on the other occasions that the school provides. Let the teacher know how interested you are in your child's progress. If you have time, drop by the school occasionally—pick your child up at lunch or at the end of the day—and exchange a friendly word or two with the teacher. If you cannot visit the school, write a note to express your appreciation when something nice happens. Call if you have a concern. If you have a problem, don't attack the teacher; describe the situation calmly and ask what the two of you can do together to improve things.

Remember, teachers are people, too, and they are often overworked and harried. Treat them as you would like to be treated, and they will care about your child all the more.

KNOW YOUR CHILD'S PRINCIPAL

Most experts agree that the principal sets the tone of the school. The principal's values, personality, and style of leadership all affect the atmosphere of the building in which your child is spending so much of his young life.

Most children in the elementary school spend little time with the principal. They will probably know the principal's name and what she or he looks like, but little more. Nor is there any reason for you as a parent to push your way into this busy person's life during the first few days of school. But gradually, as the weeks and months go by, you would do well to make the principal's acquaintance, to let the principal know how interested you are in your child's education, and to volunteer to be of help. (Parents can help in many ways. If you do not have time to sort books in the school library, you can write a short note to the superintendent praising something the principal and the teachers have done for your child.) In the normal course of events, the principal will be guiding your child's progress for several years. You should make yourself a partner in the enterprise.

PARENT-TEACHER CONFERENCES

The best way to communicate with the school about your child is to meet directly with the teacher. Face-to-face, you can raise questions and impart useful information about your child, and the teacher can report directly on your child's progress and tell you what you can do to help. Most schools schedule parent-teacher conferences for this purpose. However, if you feel there is a problem and no conference is planned, you should feel free to call the school and ask for one yourself.

How to Prepare for a Conference

In most cases, your time with the teacher will be limited, so it is well to prepare thoroughly in advance. Here are some ways to prepare:

- Talk to your child. Tell him that you are going to have a talk with his teacher. Ask him what you should look for in the classroom. See if there are any questions he wants you to ask.
- Make a list of the questions you want to ask the teacher. They may be general questions: "Is my child working up to ability?" or "How does my child get along with the other children?" Or they may be specific: "What math book is my child using?" or "May I see something my child has written recently?"
- Decide what you want to tell the teacher about your child. If there are unusual family problems that may be affecting your child's behavior, say so, without going into excessive detail. If your child seems bored or anxious, bring the matter up without accusing the teacher of being the cause.
- Do not be influenced by what you have heard about the teacher through gossip or rumor. Form your own impressions. All that matters is whether the teacher is good for your child.
- Find out exactly when and where the conference will be held. Determine how long it will be—if you only have ten minutes, you will want to plan carefully.
- Be prompt. Schools work on tight schedules, and you don't want to lose any of your time or to trespass on the time of others.

How to Participate in a Conference

Many parents are nervous about conferences with a teacher, especially when their children are very young. Remember, the teacher may be nervous, too. Teachers work with children all day, not with adults, and you may represent a threat. The tone you should strike is that of a relaxed, confident partner in the child's education. Be assured without being aggressive, pleasant without being overly deferential. Here are some things to do that may help:

- Begin the conference on a positive note. Tell the teacher how much your child liked doing the science experiment on batteries and bulbs, or how pleased you are with your child's reading. If you can't think of anything, thank the teacher for taking the time to see you.
- Listen carefully to what the teacher has to say. Take notes if you like—they will help you mull things over later.
- Don't be bashful about saying what you want to say. A good conference involves two-way communication.
- If the teacher gives you bad news about your child (for example, he behaves immaturely or he doesn't do his work), don't become angry or apologetic. Listen carefully and try to understand. Ask questions like "Could you give me an example" or "Does it happen often?" Find out what you can do to help. If you don't agree with the teacher, you can deal with that problem later, when there is more time.
- Keep the conference directed toward constructive outcomes. For either you or the teacher to lament that your child is lazy helps no one. Planning new learning approaches or motivational strategies may.
- End the conference on a positive note. Thank the teacher for her time and emphasize the constructive action you are going to take together.

How to Follow Up a Conference

If the conference has been effective, there may be much to think about and discuss later. Here are some steps you might take:

- Discuss the conference with your child. Emphasize the good things that were said. Be direct about any problems that came

up. Be clear about what constructive steps you and your child
will be taking to resolve them.

- Act quickly on any suggestions the teacher has made. If your
child's eyes should be tested, make the appointment right
away. If there are books you should get at the library, do so.
- Write a short note to the teacher thanking her for her time
and help. Your courtesy will help her feel good about your
child.
- Make sure that your child knows that you and the teacher are
working together in his interest. Your child should be secure
in the knowledge that the important adults in his life see
eye-to-eye on matters concerning him.

REPORT CARDS

Report cards are the traditional means by which the school
communicates in writing about how your child is doing. They
can be helpful in alerting you to a potential problem, and they
may give you and your child a satisfying sense of progress.
However, you should understand that no report card can fully
reflect your child's growth and that few written reports are as
productive as face-to-face communication with the teacher.

Schools vary widely in the kinds of report cards they send
home. Some provide letter grades and a few short comments;
some provide checklists of behavior; some provide written
comments only; some use no report cards at all. Figure 1 on p.
314 is a typical report from one suburban school system.

When you receive your child's report card, you should
discuss it with him. Ask him how he feels about it. Praise him
for what is good, and encourage him to do better in areas that
need improvement. Find out what you can do to help. And if
you are concerned, don't hesitate to call for an appointment

HOME REPORT OF ....**Grade Four**

Teacher ....**Date** ....

VG — Very good, S — Satisfactory, NI — Needs to Improve, NA — Not applicable at present

WORK HABITS AND SKILLS	VG	S	NI	NA	COMMENTS
Listens attentively					
Follows directions					
Works independently					
Uses time wisely					
Completes work in reasonable time					
Is organized					

PERSONAL AND SOCIAL DEVELOPMENT

	VG	S	NI	NA
Demonstrates a desire to learn				
Shows initiative				
Is responsible				
Is self-controlled				
Is considerate of others				
Accepts constructive criticism				
Is cooperative				

READING

	VG	S	NI	NA
Reads with understanding				
Applies word attack skills				
Reads with interest and enjoyment				
Reads orally with expression				

SPELLING

	VG	S	NI	NA
Learns assigned words				
Spells correctly in written work				

HANDWRITING

	VG	S	NI	NA
Forms letters correctly				
Writes neatly and legibly				

LANGUAGE ARTS

	VG	S	NI	NA
Organizes ideas				
Punctuates and capitalizes effectively				
Utilizes grammar and sentence structure				
Writes creatively				

MATHEMATICS

	VG	S	NI	NA
Knows basic number facts				
Understands basic concepts				
Demonstrates reasoning ability				
Computes with accuracy				

SOCIAL STUDIES

	VG	S	NI	NA
Understands concepts				
Participates in activities				
Utilizes research skills				
Interprets and applies facts				
Uses maps and globes				

SCIENCE

	VG	S	NI	NA
Understands concepts				
Shows interest				

To report to Wing...................In September.

with your child's teacher. Most teachers will be eager to cooperate with you on the child's behalf.

PUPIL RECORDS

All schools maintain records of their pupils. Almost always, schools record data concerning attendance, health, teacher and room assignments, the name and address of parents, and similar basic information. They may also record IQ and other test scores, disciplinary infractions, comments by teachers, or results of psychological testing or appraisal. The records are cumulative; they grow from year to year and may follow your child from school to school. Figure 2 on page 316 is a fairly typical pupil record form for a child in the intermediate years.

As a parent, including a noncustodial parent, you have the right to see all records pertaining to your child. The federal Family Educational Rights and Privacy Act of 1974, commonly called the Buckley Amendment, provides that parents have

the right to inspect and review any and all official records, files and data directly related to their children, including all material that is incorporated into each student's cumulative record folder and intended for school use or to be available to parties outside the school or school system, and specifically including but not necessarily limited to identifying data, academic work completed, level of achievement (grades, standardized achievement scores), attendance data, scores of standardized intelligence, aptitude and psychological tests, interest inventory results, health data, family background information, teacher or counselor ratings and observations and verified reports of serious recurrent behavior patterns.

Name: _____ _____ _____ School: _____
     Last   First   Middle   M F

Address _____ City _____ State _____ Zip _____ Telephone _____

Date of Birth _____ Evidence _____ Date of Entrance _____ From _____ Pre-School _____

Parents' Names: _____ _____ _____ _____ _____ _____
     Mother   Occupation   Bus Phone   Father   Occupation   Bus Phone

With whom does student live at above address _____ Mother _____ Father _____ Other _____ Other tel and address (if applicable) _____
    (Check appropriate people)   Specify

Names—Ages of Siblings _____

Transferred To _____ Date _____ Re—Entered From _____ Date _____

Referral Information

Grade	Year	Teacher	Absent	Present

If you want to see your child's records, you should call the teacher or principal to make your request and to set up an appointment. You may bring another person with you if you wish. If you think that any information in your child's file is misleading or false, you may ask that it be removed. If the school authorities refuse to do so, you have a right to a hearing before an impartial hearing officer. Once things are at this stage, you are probably in conflict with school officials and should seek competent advice.

Here are two organizations that may help:

Children's Defense Fund
122 C Street, N.W.
Washington, D.C. 20001
(202) 628-8787

National Committee for Citizens in Education
10840 Little Patuxent Parkway
Suite 301
Columbia, Maryland 21044
(301) 977-9300

HOMEWORK

As in other matters, elementary schools vary widely in the kind and amount of homework they assign. Some teachers give no homework at all. Some give it occasionally for a particular purpose or occasion. Some give it every day, for up to an hour or more each night. A recent national survey reported that in the intermediate grades children spend 4.9 hours a week on homework.

Teachers assign homework for a variety of purposes:

- To prepare for a class discussion or demonstration.

  Example   Read Chapter 14 in the social studies text; find and bring to class two magazine articles on the topic we are studying.

- To practice a skill learned in class.

  Example   Complete arithmetic problems 1–10 at the end of math Chapter 12; write a short paragraph using the new words we learned in class today.

- To encourage individual creativity or research.

  Example   Find and bring to class a poem on the theme we are studying; design and build a model of an Indian village (long-term homework project).

In addition, homework emphasizes the importance of the work done in school, helps to make a connection between home and school, develops self-discipline and organizational skills, and enables slower learners to catch up and more rapid learners to move ahead. It is a very important part of your child's education, and the time to establish steady, productive work habits is now. If you think you can wait until your son or daughter is a thirteen-year-old adolescent, forget it.

Parents can play an important role in their children's homework. Here are some ways that you can help:

- Provide a quiet, well-lit place. It doesn't need to be a corner of the bedroom or an oak-paneled study—the kitchen table will do just fine. But turn the television off and try to stay off the telephone.

- Establish a regular time. Some children prefer to come home from school, have a snack, and do their homework right away so that their evenings are free. Other children want to unwind when they first come home from school: for them, the period just before or after dinner usually serves well. Whatever period you establish, make working at this time a habit and do not deviate unless absolutely necessary.

- If you can't be at home when your child does his homework, establish a regular time anyway (and perhaps have him set an alarm clock), then discuss what he has done when you come home.
- Don't let your child dawdle. A thousand excuses to delay work can occur to all of us, and your child is no exception: "I have to sharpen the pencil"; "I need a drink of water"; "The dog wants to go out." One of our favorite teachers began his lecture on study skills with this maxim: "Begin at once." Heed his advice.
- Give your child a notebook or pad for writing down homework assignments. Ask him what the assignment is for the day and, if necessary, clarify directions.
- Ask your child if he needs help. If he does, work together with him. If he doesn't, stand back and give him room.
- If your child doesn't mind, check his work; ask questions and offer suggestions. But don't do his work—it is his, not yours.
- Be available to answer questions, but don't hover. Remember that your child is learning to be independent at the same time he is learning math.
- Talk about your child's homework project with the entire family and get others to contribute ideas.
- Don't fight with your child over homework. Make rules (such as no television until the homework is done) and stick to them, but avoid nagging and unnecessary confrontation. Remember that part of the purpose of homework is to develop responsibility and independence in your child— neither a tutor nor an enforcer be.
- Don't become impatient or irritated. If your child has continuing difficulty doing the work that the teacher assigns, talk to the teacher. But if for whatever reason your child can't or won't do the work, remember that he is as unhappy about it as you are.

DISCIPLINE

If your child attends a school whose values are reasonably consistent with your own and if your child is generally happy in school and making good progress, you probably need not be concerned about discipline in the elementary grades. Most serious school-related discipline problems occur in the junior and senior high schools. However, almost every year during the past two decades the public has identified discipline as the most serious problem facing American schools. And without question, poor disciplinary habits established at the elementary level are difficult to overcome later, when the stakes are higher.

Order is necessary for learning. Children cannot concentrate on their studies when their classmates are disruptive or when the atmosphere is pervaded by disrespect for the teacher and the work at hand. School personnel are responsible for maintaining the kind of safe, orderly environment that is conducive to learning.

On the other hand, a school that is preoccupied with discipline likewise does not promote learning. Young minds and imaginations do not stretch themselves freely when burdened by fear of criticism for the slightest of infractions. A desirable atmosphere, both in school and at home, is one in which all are expected to behave appropriately, and any departures from the norm are dealt with firmly but with support and love.

Achieving such an atmosphere is not just a matter of responding to infractions—it is what the school is all about. In schools where the values of the home and the community reinforce those of the school, where the staff obviously enjoys working with the children and with one another, where children are motivated to learn and respect adults and one another, discipline is not apt to be a problem. Unfortunately, not all schools share these happy characteristics. And even in the best schools, provision must be made for the occasional rambunctiousness of young human nature.

Accordingly, good schools, as the 1986 U.S. Department of Education study entitled *What Works* says, "contribute to their students' academic achievement by establishing, communicating, and enforcing fair and consistent discipline policies." Such policies make clear what behavior is acceptable and what is not, and they are completely enforced.

The following is one code of behavior developed by teachers, parents, and children in a suburban elementary school.

Pupils, Rights and Responsibilities—Elementary

Pupils have the right to a free, appropriate education.

Pupils have the responsibility to attend school regularly, to behave appropriately in school and on school grounds, and to do their schoolwork and their homework.

Pupils have the right to a clean, orderly school environment.

Pupils have the responsibility to come to school neat and clean and to treat the school grounds, classrooms, lunchrooms, and bathrooms with care.

Pupils have the right to work, listen, and learn without being annoyed by others.

Pupils have the responsibility to observe school rules and not to annoy others who wish to work, listen, and learn.

Pupils have the right to speak and be heard by others.

Pupils have the responsibility to listen to other pupils and to adults as appropriate.

Pupils have the right to be free from teasing and to make mistakes without fear of being laughed at.

Pupils have the responsibility to refrain from teasing others and to refrain from laughing at mistakes made by others.

Pupils have the right not to be abused verbally or physically by others.

Pupils have the responsibility not to abuse others verbally or physically.

Pupils have the right to be treated with respect by adults.

Pupils have the responsibility to treat adults with respect.

Pupils have the right to say no to a group they believe is wrong.

Pupils have the responsibility to refrain from trying to make others do something they do not wish to do.

Pupils have the right to have their possessions protected.

Pupils have the responsibility to respect the possessions of others.

You have the right to know what the rules of discipline in your child's school are. Ask the teacher or the principal about them, and don't be afraid to raise questions or make suggestions if the circumstances warrant it.

In the meantime, of course, you have a job to do at home. After all, children's behavior in school is as much a reflection of habits and attitudes they bring from home as of the way that teachers treat them. Acknowledging that disciplining children takes a great deal of effort, the National Education Association has published the following suggestions for parents:

- Let your children know you like them.
- Let your children know exactly what you expect of them—set limits.
- Encourage responsible decision-making.
- Set a good example.
- Encourage your children to respect proper authority.
- Have fun with your children.

Note that these suggestions approach the subject of discipline from a positive standpoint. In general, that is the best approach. However, if punishment is necessary, use it sparingly and make it fit the child and the offense. Avoid physical punishment; withholding a privilege is preferable because it can be focused on the misbehavior rather than on the child and because it breeds less resentment.

For the same reasons, most good schools refrain from the use of corporal punishment. Although such punishment is still permitted in many states in our country (it is forbidden throughout most of the Western world), good teachers and principals shun its use because they know that in the long run it is as likely to be counterproductive as to be helpful. (Punishment must be distinguished from the temporary use of physical force to prevent injury to people or property.) In any event, physical punishment should only be used as a last resort.

ILLNESS

Most children should attend school most days. However, all of us are prey to occasional colds or stomach upsets, not to mention more serious illness or injury. Here are some things to consider when your child is too ill to go to school:

- Care for your child appropriately, but don't let the day become a treat. You don't want to encourage frequent absence.
- Cooperate with the school's regulations. If you are required to send in a note the next day, do so. Don't let your busyness or inattention cause your child embarrassment.
- Find your child some lovely books to look at and to read. He may be too sick to go to school, but his mind and his imagination are still active. Don't consign him to a day of game shows and soap operas.

- If your child will be out for more than a day, call the teacher to find out what your child will be missing. A few days is a long time for a child, and you can help to make it easier when he returns.

If your child complains frequently of illness on school days—stomachaches, headaches, or dizziness are common—talk to him and try to get a sense of what is troubling him. Sometimes children have fears they can't communicate directly to their parents. Perhaps there is a bully on the bus or a best friend has proved unfaithful. Perhaps he thinks the teacher doesn't like him or that he can't do the work satisfactorily. Think about any tension in the home that may be affecting your child. If and when you figure things out, be understanding and supportive. Tell your child what you are going to do to help straighten things out. And if you can't determine the cause of the problem, see your teacher and, if necessary, your doctor.

MOVING TO A NEW SCHOOL

In our mobile society, many children move from one school to another during the elementary years, sometimes more than once. The loss of familiar people, places, and routines can be traumatic. If you help your child manage it well, you can ease the transition, possibly transforming the move into a positive, enriching experience. Here are some suggestions:

- Tell your child about the move well in advance. Children are highly sensitive to their parents' moods and behavior, and your child is almost certain to know that something is going on. Don't let his imagination make things far worse than the reality.

- Be positive about the move. Obviously, doing so is easier if you feel positive about it yourself. But even if you don't, remember that what may be less than joyous in your life need not be depressing in your child's life. Accentuate the positive!
- Find out as much as you can about the new school, and share the good points with your child. Write to the new school and ask for information about class size, library facilities (and librarians), special programs or features, school hours, and transportation arrangements. Most school districts have brochures for this purpose. If not, try the local Chamber of Commerce or Real Estate Board.
- If possible, visit the school with your child before you actually move. The visit will give him some idea of what the other children are like and what clothes they wear and will do much to reduce his apprehensions.
- If possible, time your move for the beginning of the school year. It is easier to start a new school before relationships among pupils and teacher in the class have been established. Also, there are apt to be other new children then, and your child will feel less alone.
- Arrange for your child's records to be transferred from his present school to his new one. (You may want to examine these records first; see the section "Pupil Records.")
- Meet your child's new teacher and principal as early as possible. You have a new partnership to establish.

How to Judge a Good Teacher

In schools as we know them, the quality of your child's education depends directly upon the quality of his teacher. No other variable, except possibly the nature of the children in the class, is as important.

As a parent, you have many opportunities to judge the quality of your child's teacher. You talk to your child about his experience in school, you see the work he brings home, you visit the classroom and talk with the teacher. You look for the signs of good teaching that are described in the earlier chapters of this book. In all these ways you begin to form an impression of this important person in your child's life—a person whose personal characteristics and teaching style shape the environment in which your child spends a large part of each working day.

WHAT TEACHING IS LIKE

Before thinking about what makes a good teacher, it may be well to consider what the conditions of teaching are like for most classroom teachers.

To begin with, teaching is hard work. It is true that there are long summer vacations and several breaks throughout the year. But dealing with a roomful of active children each day is emotionally demanding, exhausting work, involving not only keeping order, but motivating children, planning and conducting dozens of activities, keeping track of individual progress and problems, and creating a good feeling in the class as a whole. Most teachers are tired at the end of each day, and for good reason. Think about how you would feel if you had to run a birthday party all day, every day, for several dozen of your child's friends!

Another condition of teachers' lives is that they are constantly with groups of children. They must continuously expend the energy required to maintain discipline in the class. There is little time to be alone, to catch one's breath, and there is little opportunity to interact with other adults. For these reasons, many teachers speak of theirs as a lonely profession.

In many communities, teachers no longer enjoy the respect their predecessors did a generation or more ago. Years ago, the teacher was often one of the most educated and respected people in the community, the person who could read and write and impart to children the skills to enjoy a future brighter than their parents'. Today, many parents are better educated than their children's teachers, and respect is no longer automatic. (In some states, teachers must now take tests to demonstrate knowledge of their field—and not all teachers pass the tests.) Furthermore, the teacher may be subject to conflicting expectations from different parents. Some may want the teacher to adopt a more structured, disciplined approach; others may be concerned that the teacher is stifling their children's imagination and creativity.

When you're speaking to your child's teacher, you should keep these and similar considerations in mind. Your empathy will help you establish a relationship that permits effective communication.

WHAT MAKES A GOOD TEACHER

No one style of teaching is best for all children. Just as children vary in their temperament, maturity, abilities, and interests, so does the kind of teacher who suits the child best. Some children learn more from a teacher who is dynamic, exciting, energetic. Some respond better to a teacher who is calm, steady, patient. Some profit from a stern taskmaster, and some from a kindly, nurturing type. Some work better with an older teacher and some with a younger. Some work better with a female teacher, and some with a male.

To say that good teachers come in many forms is not to say, however, that all teachers are equally good. The teaching profession, like the rest of humankind, has its share of the bright and the dull, the inspired and the flat, the hard-working and the lazy. Most children and parents agree that a good teacher consistently displays the following qualities:

- *Respect* for children. The teacher likes most children and treats all well.
- *Enthusiasm* for her work. The teacher enjoys what she is doing.
- *Responsibility*—to the children and to the job. Activities are thoughtfully planned; homework is corrected and returned on time.
- *Caring* for individual children. The teacher knows who is struggling and whose spirits are down, and she takes steps to improve things.
- *Fairness* in dealing with the class and with individuals.
- *Friendliness* and overall cheerfulness.
- *Sense of humor* to make things sparkle and to help with the rough spots.
- *Patience* in dealing with children's difficulties.

- *Skill in communicating,* in understanding what children are thinking and in explaining things well.
- *Knowledge* of her subject and of what she is doing in the classroom.

Perfect 10's are rare in teaching, as in life. But if your child's teacher comes close, rejoice!

WHAT TO DO ABOUT A BAD TEACHER

Before your child finishes school, he will have many teachers. A few may stand out, the rare people who truly make a positive impression on your child. Most will be just fine, people from whom your child will learn the necessary skills and knowledge and perhaps a thing or two about human nature. And a few may be trouble, people who seem unable to provide a good program for your child or who may cause your child distress. What should you do if you think your child has such a teacher?

The first step is to talk with the teacher. Explain to her what you think the problem is, and listen to what she has to say. It is true that she may be defensive or resentful, but it is also possible that you may not have all the relevant information. (Remember, your chief source of information is your child, and his version of events, while honest, may not be entirely objective.)

Once you have established that there is indeed a serious problem, discuss with the teacher what can be done to resolve it. Perhaps your child needs to make an adjustment in his behavior, or perhaps the teacher needs to make an adjustment in hers.

Once you have decided on a course of action, allow time for things to change. Teachers often respond to such encounters once they know that a parent is concerned and monitoring the situation. However, if there is no improvement within a reasonable period of time, your next recourse is the principal.

You may approach the principal alone or with a small group of parents who share your concerns. (Avoid large groups or a lynch mob—you may provoke the system to defend itself and thus defeat your purpose.) Be specific about your complaints; avoid hearsay and stick to what you know to be true from your own child's experience. Most principals will want to help you solve the problem, particularly if you have talked to the teacher first.

The principal can't do some things, but she can do others. In most states, she can't fire a teacher, at least once the teacher has tenure. (In such states, teachers are appointed to tenure after a probationary period of about three to five years. After that, they may be discharged only for cause, and the legal proceedings are long, difficult, and expensive. Very few tenured teachers are discharged, and their cases tend to be extreme.) Nor can the principal, if your school has two classes on a given grade level, assign forty children to one class and ten to the other.

What she can do is confront the teacher with the problem and seek a way to resolve it. If the class is too large or too difficult, she may assign a teacher's aide. If supplies are inadequate, she may order more. She can visit the class more often or enlist the help of another teacher. She can require the teacher to submit lesson plans, to ensure that adequate planning is being done. If personal problems are interfering the teacher's effectiveness, the principal can suggest (or require) counseling. If the teacher is eligible to retire, she can suggest early retirement.

Much of what the principal does, once you leave her office, will not be visible to you. You should not therefore assume that nothing is being done. Much supervisory work should not be done in public, and most of it takes time. However, if the problem persists beyond a reasonable period, you should not hesitate to call or see the principal again. And if that fails, you should then contact the superintendent of schools.

How to Judge a Good School

Schools vary in methods, values, atmosphere, the mix of pupils, resources, size, age, and countless other ways. The authors have seen good schools in factory towns and inner cities and poor schools in affluent suburbs. (We have also seen poor schools in factory towns and inner cities and good schools in affluent suburbs.) How can conscientious parents choose a school that is right for their child? And if a choice is not possible, how can parents judge the quality of the school their child attends?

In the 1960s and 1970s, it was fashionable to maintain that schools made little difference in children's lives. Family and economic background were viewed as such powerful forces that schools could do little to help children rise above the circumstances in their home and neighborhood. Today, however, there is increasing evidence that good schools can make a difference. In such schools, children learn to read, write, compute, and think effectively no matter what their social, economic, racial, or ethnic background.

331

EFFECTIVE SCHOOLS RESEARCH

In recent years, various researchers have compared schools in which children attain a high level of achievement with lower-achieving schools with children of similar background, identifying the factors responsible for the effectiveness of the better schools. Among the most commonly mentioned are the following:

- Effective instructional leadership, usually from a strong principal. The principal sets the tone for the school. If she understands teaching and learning and knows what her goals are, she can influence others to follow.
- Consensus on goals among the principal, teachers, parents, and pupils. The energies of the entire school should be focused on the same objectives.
- High expectations of achievement. Children tend to work up to the level expected of them. Teachers who expect little, get little; teachers who expect much, given skill on their part and all-around effort, get much. Good schools expect children to do well, and they maintain a consistently positive attitude.
- A schoolwide, consistent emphasis on instruction, especially in the basic skills. Teachers work hard at getting children to learn, motivating them, trying different materials and techniques, finding a way for each child to succeed no matter what the difficulties. Teaching and learning are the school's chief priorities.
- Regular assessment of progress. Children are tested often to measure their achievement, and the results are used to guide the instructional plan. The principal and the teacher evaluate their own plan and efforts in light of children's achievement.
- A safe, orderly, purposeful climate. The children and adults show respect for one another and are safe from external disruption.

According to the U.S. Department of Education's 1986 handbook *What Works: Research About Teaching and Learning*,

> The most important characteristics of effective schools are strong instructional leadership, a safe and orderly climate, school-wide emphasis on basic skills, high teacher expectations for student achievement, and continuous assessment of pupil progress. . . . Schools that encourage academic achievement focus on the importance of scholastic success and on maintaining order and discipline.

OTHER INDICATORS OF QUALITY

The preceding factors apply to good schools in all situations. They are receiving increasing attention as the effective schools movement gains momentum. However, there are other traditional indicators of school quality that may make a difference.

Class Size

The research on class size is inconclusive. Studies tend to show that within the limits of fifteen to thirty children, class size makes little difference in achievement. On the other hand, the overwhelming testimony of teachers and parents is that, up to a point, the smaller the class the better. Clearly, the teacher can devote more time to each child if the class is smaller, and there may be advantages for children that are not reflected in the tests. In the intermediate years, the best class size is probably from fifteen to twenty-five children. Up to twenty-seven, you shouldn't worry; beyond that, you may want to lobby your school to reduce class sign or to assign additional help, such as a teacher's aide.

Teacher/Pupil Ratio

The teacher/pupil ratio describes the number of pupils in the school or school system for each teacher and other professional staff members. (In a school with 300 children, 15 regular teachers, 3 special teachers, a principal, and a librarian, the ratio would be 1/15.) In good schools, there is one professional staff member for every fifteen to twenty children. The number of adults can be increased by assigning teacher's aides or parent volunteers.

Special Teachers

Closely related to the pupil/teacher ratio is the number of special teachers in the school. Some schools have librarians, music teachers, art teachers, physical education teachers, remedial reading teachers, psychologists, and other special services personnel (see the chapter "School Resource People"). Whether or not such services are important depends upon the nature of the children who attend the school and upon your child's individual needs.

Special Programs

Some schools provide special programs for both handicapped and gifted children (see the chapters "The Gifted Child" and "The Child With Learning Problems"). Some maintain artists-in-residence, provide special music programs, or offer experimental instruction by computer. Some provide bilingual or

English as a second language instruction. The presence or absence of such programs can make a difference to your child's needs or talents. Look for them when choosing a school, or in your own school, find out what programs it offers in comparison with other schools in the surrounding area.

After-School Activities

Most children in the intermediate years are ready to go home at the end of the school day. However, in situations where both parents work or where children live in relative isolation from potential playmates, some schools offer after-school activities or child-care programs. (Sometimes these programs are conducted by school employees; sometimes they are run by the PTA or a parent cooperative.) Discover what your school offers to help meet your family's needs.

Budget

School budgets vary widely from one area of the country to another, depending upon the regional cost of living and the way school expenses are financed. Here are a few rules of thumb you can apply to determine whether your school is funded adequately:

- What is your school's expenditure per pupil? If it is below average for your region of the country, why? What is your child not receiving that other children are?
- What is your teacher/pupil ratio? Again, if it is below average for your region, why? What services do other children receive that your child does not?
- Do teachers come to your school district from other districts,

or do they leave to go elsewhere? How do salaries and fringe benefits compare?

- Do teachers have all the books and supplies they need, or must they cut back on what the children do?

WHAT TO LOOK FOR WHEN YOU VISIT A SCHOOL

The preceding comments should suggest some questions to ask at PTA or Board of Education meetings or to raise with appropriate school officials. However, you can learn much just by visiting the school and looking around. Here are questions that may help you:

- Is the building open to you? Do you get the sense that visitors are frequent and welcome? Or do locked doors and forbidding signs suggest otherwise?
- How do the secretaries treat you? Are you made to feel comfortable and welcome? Or are you eyed with indifference or suspicion?
- How do the children behave? Do they seem to know what they are doing, and are they going about it freely and easily? Or is the atmosphere too loose or too rigid?
- How do the teachers behave? Do they seem to enjoy what they are doing? At lunch or recess, do they interact with the children or do they stand apart and talk to one another?
- Is the building clean, well-lit, and in good repair?
- Are there separate facilities for music, art, and physical education? Are they used?
- Is children's work—artwork, poetry and other writing—displayed in the halls and classrooms? Does it look recent? Does it look as if someone cared?

- Are the children's bathrooms clean and accessible? Are they properly supplied?
- Is there a school library (and a librarian)? Is it well stocked? Are books attractively displayed? Are there children in the library? Are they working alone or in small groups and as a class? (If there are no children in the library when you visit, ask how and when children come there.)
- Are the classrooms busy and inviting, with materials and displays suggesting that much is going on? Is there a hum of busy activity?
- Do the classrooms contain textbooks and other instructional materials on many levels, to accommodate children's different levels of ability and interests?
- Are most books copyrighted within the past five years?

Every school building has a distinctive ethos, or climate, the product of the people who work there, the nature of the community, and the quality of the leadership. By spending some time in the school and checking against the above list, you will obtain a fairly good sense of what the school is like. If you are choosing a school, trust your instincts. Remember, in the final analysis, a good school is one that is good for your child.

School Resource
People

In the chapter "How to Judge a Good Teacher," we discussed classroom teachers, the most important people in your child's school life. In the chapter "How to Judge a Good School," we covered class size, teacher/pupil ratios, and school budgets. In this chapter, we will write about the other school employees whose presence or absence, kindness or indifference, skill or lack of it, may make an important difference to your child.

Not all schools have all the personnel described below. Elementary schools vary widely in size and financial resources, and children in different neighborhoods vary in their needs. Many schools have only classroom teachers, a principal, a secretary, a nurse, one or more custodians, and perhaps a librarian. But where there are other personnel, you should know who they are, what they do, and how you can call upon them to serve your child's interests.

THE PRINCIPAL

The principal is the key authority figure in the school. She decides on teacher and pupil assignments, evaluates the teachers, allocates the funds provided by the superintendent and the

Board of Education, develops the schedules and routines by which the school operates, and administers discipline when necessary. If she is good, she also leads her staff and parent body in formulating and carrying out an instructional plan for the entire school. Many experts agree that the principal sets the tone for the entire school. Without a good principal, schools are rarely successful.

ASSISTANT PRINCIPALS

In very large elementary schools there may be one or more assistant principals, who help the principal in carrying out her duties. The role of the assistant principal is often specialized, depending upon individual talents and the needs of the situation. For example, an assistant principal might be in charge of discipline, transportation, and the lunch program. Or she might spend the bulk of her time observing and evaluating teachers, and working with committees of teachers to improve the instructional program.

THE NURSE

Other than the classroom teacher, the school nurse is the person you may come to know best, particularly if your child has a physical or emotional problem. She may also be the person your child meets first, because one of her duties is to check the health of all children new to the school. After that, she maintains each child's health record, including immunizations and the results of vision, hearing, and medical examinations. She advises teachers on the necessary adjustments to make dictated by a child's health status. She brings safety conditions to the attention of the principal. She may teach a portion of the school's health program.

Most important, it is to her that your child will go when he is sick, injured, or upset. A good nurse must not only have good first-aid skills, she must be part psychologist, part detective, part mother. When there are no adults at home in the daytime, it is especially important that a sick, injured, or upset child have a skilled and caring nurse to turn to.

THE SCHOOL PHYSICIAN

Most school physicians, where they exist, are employed largely on a part-time basis. As a result, the functions they perform are limited. They may perform medical examinations when the child has not been examined privately. They provide information to the nurse as needed. They furnish advice about the school's health program. They assist teachers and others in reviewing the placement and program of children who may have handicapping conditions.

If your child is referred to the school physician, make it your business to find out why without delay.

THE SCHOOL SECRETARY

The school secretary does a great deal more than type the principal's letters and get the coffee. She answers the telephone, furnishes information and advice, greets visitors, finds lost lunches and rain boots, delivers a thousand messages each day, settles disputes between teachers, and generally keeps things glued together and operating. Next to the principal, she is most responsible for the tone of the school.

THE CUSTODIAN

The custodian, too, does more than just sweep the floors and take out the trash. First, he knows much about what goes on in the school—unlike the teachers and perhaps the principal, he is in most classrooms each day, and he is in a position to know the seamy underside of school life. Second, he is often an important male figure for boys otherwise surrounded by women. And finally, if he likes children, as many do, and has an amiable disposition, he can be of valuable help in carrying out school projects and activities.

THE LIBRARIAN

The school that has a good librarian is truly blessed. She is much more than the keeper of the books. Her greatest pleasure is in getting children to enjoy reading. She knows the books in her collection and is always ready to tell you about her favorites. She knows the children in the school—by name, by interest, by level of reading ability—and she helps them find books that stir their imagination and whet their appetite for more. She reads to the children. She consults with the teacher and brings books to class. She makes the school library a warm, inviting place. She is a joy in your child's life. Get to know her, and if you have time, help her out.

ART, MUSIC, AND PHYSICAL EDUCATION TEACHERS

Some schools have teachers with special training in art, music, or physical education. They teach the class once or more per week, while the regular teacher remains in the classroom to help out, prepares lessons, or takes a break. If the school is small, these teachers may be shared with one or more other schools. Such teachers can add expert knowledge to the program, and if your child has special talents or interests, they can become important figures to your child.

READING AND SPECIAL EDUCATION TEACHERS

Reading teachers are specially trained in helping children with learning disabilities to improve their reading skills. They typically work with an individual child or a small group of children, diagnosing individual problems and providing remedial help. The children leave the regular classroom and go to the reading teacher for that purpose. The reading teacher also works with regular classroom teachers, helping them plan and conduct their reading programs.

Special education teachers, like reading teachers, are specially trained to diagnose and deal with individual learning problems. However, their scope is somewhat broader, including writing, math, study skills, and other parts of the curriculum. They may work with a small class for a whole day (in a self-contained class), or they may deal with individual or small groups of children who come to their room at certain times (in a resource-room program). They are especially helpful with children who have learning disabilities (see the chapter "The Child With Learning Problems").

THE SPEECH TEACHER

Sometimes called a speech therapist or a speech clinician, the speech teacher works with individual or small groups of children on a wide range of speech and language problems, including stuttering, lisping, poor articulation, or language disorders. She also advises regular teachers on techniques to use with children in their classrooms who have speech or language problems. If your child is referred to a speech teacher, you should communicate with school authorities to find out about the exact nature of the problem.

THE SCHOOL PSYCHOLOGIST

The school psychologist gives tests to determine children's needs, abilities, and progress. She interprets test results to teachers and parents, and recommends appropriate instructional settings and techniques. She helps individual children with problems of school adjustment. If children are not doing well academically, she tries to determine why. She is not a psychiatrist, and she does not provide therapy. If your child is referred to a psychologist, approach her as a possible source of help, but make it your business to find out the reason for the referral. And remember that it is your right to be treated as a full partner in your own child's education.

THE SCHOOL SOCIAL WORKER

The school social worker provides a special link between school and home. She helps children and their families deal with situations that affect learning, such as problems of attendance, school adjustment, and peer relationships. She suggests helpful resources. She provides short-term counseling on school-related problems. She acts as an advocate for the child, helping the family to understand the school and the school to understand the family.

TEACHER'S AIDES

Teacher's aides may be hired to assist teachers in classrooms, to supervise lunch or recess, to work in the school library, or to help out in many other ways. They are usually people who like children and who have much to offer but who do not have the required license to teach. They can be very important to your child. Get to know the aides who deal with your child directly.

COORDINATORS

Some school districts have coordinators of subjects such as art, music, science, and reading. Normally these people are assigned to the central administrative offices and visit local schools periodically. They are responsible for planning the curriculum, supervising teachers, and providing instructional support in their subject areas. Your child is not likely to know them, but you may wish to know who they are in the event you have a question about curriculum that your principal cannot answer.

THE SUPERINTENDENT OF SCHOOLS

The superintendent of schools is the chief executive officer of the school district. On all matters pertaining to the routine operation of the schools, the buck stops with him. Chances are, however, that you will never have occasion to deal with him or her unless you become involved in a controversy of district-wide proportions, such as a school closing. The superintendent is nonetheless an important figure behind the scenes of your child's life, because he or she controls resources, appoints staff members, and sets the tone that affects the atmosphere of the schools under his or her control.

THE BOARD OF EDUCATION

Most school districts are governed by lay Boards of Education elected by the people. Boards have the final authority in school matters. They appoint the superintendent, establish policy, set budgets and tax rates, and oversee the overall long-term operation of the school district. They exert an important influence on the character and quality of the school district.

How to Improve Your School

The authors have spent their lives working with teachers and other school personnel. By and large, we like school people. As a group, they are more honest and more concerned about the welfare of others than the average person in many lines of work. And in general, they do a good job. For all its shortcomings, our system of public schools has indeed educated the masses and helped us create one people out of many.

At the same time, we have never seen a school that couldn't be improved. And the key to improvement is usually the involvement of an active, knowledgeable parent body. A wise school superintendent once said that "schools rarely rise above the expectations of the people who support them." If you want your child's school to be good, you and your friends and neighbors must get involved.

As an individual, you can read the school's material, get to know the school staff, join the PTA and work on its committees, volunteer to help in classrooms or the library, attend Board of Education meetings, ask questions, and make your opinions known. Some schools involve parents on curriculum committees (parents help decide *what* should be taught, teachers decide *how*) and on screening committees to interview new teachers or aides. Some schools have parent advisory committees that meet regularly with the principal to review all aspects of the school program or to monitor the progress of a new program (such as an extended-day kindergarten program or a new bilingual approach to instruction). Join such groups. The more informed and active you become, the more your influence will grow.

However knowledgeable you become, you can accomplish much more by working cooperatively with others. If you have a problem or concern that is not limited only to your child, express your views to other parents and find out if they feel the same. Then join together as a group—within the PTA, if the leaders will support you; as a separate group, if they do not—and approach the school authorities for help.

Perhaps the school has a teacher who is consistently ineffective or who is mean to children. Perhaps the principal is ineffectual or tired or doesn't like minority children. Perhaps the playground needs repair. Perhaps the school's reading scores are low, or the progress in art or music is unimaginative, or the library is underutilized, or there are no provisions for gifted children. Whatever the problem, organize yourself and others to address it. The following steps may help:

- Get your facts straight. Don't rely on hearsay; speak from first-hand experience. If your problem involves statistical information, such as test scores or budget accounts, do your homework. Nothing will weaken your case more than lack of knowledge.
- Define your solutions. It is not enough to complain; you must say what you want. If the class size is too large, do you want a teacher's aide or do you want to divide the class and hire another teacher?
- Get your group together. Make sure that everyone understands what the issues are and what solutions you are proposing. Never argue among yourselves in the presence of the school authorities.
- Approach the appropriate level of authority. If the problem is

one the teacher can correct (even if you think she won't), see the teacher first. If the teacher doesn't resolve the problem or if the problem is beyond the scope of her authority, see the principal. And if the problem is district-wide or if it requires resources that the principal does not command, see the superintendent or the Board of Education.

- Be polite but firm. You may wish to write a letter first or to discuss matters on the telephone, but the best way to resolve a problem is face-to-face. Let the school authorities know that you are counting on them to resolve the problem, that you mean business, that you are not going to go away.

- Persist. Don't be put off by jargon or evasiveness or the attitude that the issue is none of your business. It *is* your business if it involves your child. And don't be derailed by unnecessary delays. In fairness, some problems cannot be solved immediately, and not all that the school authorities do will be visible to you. But if you do not get satisfaction in a reasonable period of time, return and ask why.

- If necessary, raise the ante. Most school problems can be resolved cooperatively if parents and school people show a little skill and patience and a willingness to try. But in particularly difficult situations, confrontation may be necessary. Get the support of some teachers. Write to the local newspaper. Organize a large group at the next meeting of the Board of Education. Talk about a boycott.

In the authors' experience, most situations need never get that far. Reasonable people on both sides can achieve much without letting things get out of hand. If the school authorities are willing to be accommodating, don't push too hard, even if you don't get everything you want. The object is to improve the school, not to win a battle. And remember: In the end, your child will return to the school that these people control.

The National PTA publishes the handbook *Looking in on*

Your School, a Workbook for Improving Public Education. Write to:
    The National PTA
    700 North Rush Street
    Chicago, Illinois 60611-2571

The National Committee for Citizens in Education (NCCE) publishes several useful pamphlets, including "Effective Schools: How to Evaluate Them, How to Get Them," "Finding Out How People Feel About Local Schools," "Parents Organizing to Improve Schools," and "Your School: How Well Is It Working?" Add $1.00 handling charge for each order, and write to:

    NCCE
    410 Wilde Lake Village Green
    Columbia, Maryland 21044

Some of the Authors' Favorite Books

By the time your child has reached the intermediate years, reading to himself should be a pleasurable activity. The librarians at school and the public library and his teacher should help him select books that will be fun to read. Long after he is able to read by himself, you should continue to read aloud to him. Sharing a book is a pleasure for parent and child in the intermediate years, as well as in the primary. Many educators believe that reading aloud to your child should continue for as long as you both are comfortable. A shared activity, it is an entirely different experience from reading silently to oneself. Before the advent of radio and television, reading aloud was a common family activity, many families sharing the great classics in this way.

As your child grows older and feels comfortable reading aloud himself, he might enjoy reading some of his favorites to a younger sibling.

Some picture books you read aloud to your child in his primary years are so lovely and timeless that in the intermediate years he may continue to enjoy hearing and looking at them. Others offer beautiful artwork that can be appreciated even if there is no text. Many of the picture books listed are classics, some are fairy tales, some are beautifully illustrated American

Indian or Asian folk tales. Also included are a few nonfiction and poetry picture books.

The longer books, sometimes called *chapter books*, provide an opportunity for you to have a sustained reading experience with your child. Some may take a few weeks to complete, and some even longer.

The following list, limited by necessity, describes some of the authors' favorite books for reading aloud. Many of the authors have written other books that are also literary treasures. We have included the phrase *and more* if the title character appears in other books by the same author. Should you exhaust this list, your school or public librarian will be happy to supply you with additional titles.

This list may also be used as a reading list of books for your child to read to himself. Many families discover that after having a book read aloud, some children wish to read it to themselves.

The following books were mentioned in the K-2 Bibliography. Children in Grades 3 to 5 will continue to enjoy them.

SHORT BOOKS

Andersen, Hans Christian. *The Ugly Duckling.* Retold and illustrated by Lorinda Bryan Cauley. New York: Harcourt Brace Jovanovich, Voyager, 1979.

The traditional tale of the ugly duckling who turns into a beautiful swan. Told beautifully, with lovely illustrations.

Brown, Marcia. *Cinderella.* New York: Scribners, 1954.

Magical pastel illustrations go hand in hand with the old story told well.

Burton, Virginia Lee. *Life Story.* Boston: Houghton Mifflin, 1962.

A marvelous account of the changing earth in geologic terms from the beginning of time till today. An unusual book, with marvelous illustrations.

Clark, Mary Lou. *Dinosaurs.* Chicago: Children's Press, 1981. Dinosaurs, what came before and after them, why they disappeared, and how we know about them.

De Brunhoff, Jean. *The Story of Babar* (and more). New York: Random House, 1937. After an adventure in the city, Babar and Celeste are crowned King and Queen of the elephants.

Garrison, Christian. *The Dream Eater.* Illustrated by Diane Goode. Scarsdale, N.Y.: Bradbury Press, 1978. As beautiful as an Oriental scroll, this book is a wonderful tale of the baku—a dream eater who likes nightmares best.

Goble, Paul. *Buffalo Woman.* Scarsdale, N.Y.: Bradbury Press, 1984. An old Native American legend that tells the love story between a young brave and a beautiful young woman who is really a female buffalo. Fantastic color illustrations.

Goble, Paul. *The Gift of the Sacred Dog.* Scarsdale, N.Y.: Bradbury Press, 1984. This is a lovely tale celebrating the native American's love for the horse. Splendid illustrations.

Goble, Paul. *The Girl Who Loved Wild Horses.* Scarsdale, N.Y.: Bradbury Press, 1978. A native American girl's love for horses leads her to go live with them. Illustrated with beautiful paintings.

Grimm. *The Fisherman and His Wife.* Translated by Randall Jarrell; illustrated by Margot Zemach. New York: Farrar, Straus and Giroux, 1980.

Beautiful illustrations enhance this wonderful translation of the story about a fisherman who has a wife who is *never* satisfied and always wants more.

Ike, Jane Hori, and **Baruch, Zimmerman.** *A Japanese Fairy Tale.* Illustrated by Jane Hori Ike. New York: Warne, 1982.
Beautiful watercolor illustrations. Lovely tale of the love between a beautiful woman and her ugly husband.

Miles, Miska. *Annie and the Old One.* Illustrated by Peter Parnall. Boston: Little, Brown/Atlantic Monthly Press, 1971.
Poignant tale of relationship between a young native American girl and her grandmother.

Simon, Seymour. *The Smallest Dinosaurs.* Illustrated by Anthony Rao. New York: Crown, 1982.
Descriptions and illustrations of seven small dinosaurs believed to be the ancestors of today's birds.

Steig, William. *The Amazing Bone.* New York: Penguin, Puffin Books, 1977.
Suspenseful tale of a magical and powerful bone.

Steig, William. *Sylvester and the Magic Pebble.* New York: Simon and Schuster, Windmill Books, 1969.
Sylvester the donkey finds a wonderful magic pebble that gets him into terrible trouble.

Yagawa, Sumiko, *The Crane Wife.* Translated by Katherine Paterson. Illustrated by Sue Kichi Akaba. New York: William Morrow, 1981.
One of Japan's most beloved folktales with magnificent traditional illustrations.

Zolotow, Charlotte. *My Grandson Lew.* Illustrated by William Pène du Bois. New York: Harper & Row, Trophy, 1985.

Lewis and his mother share the wonderful memories they both have of his grandfather and the love he brought to them.

LONGER BOOKS

Atwater, Richard, and Florence Atwater. *Mr. Popper's Penguins.* Illustrated by Robert Lawson. New York: Dell, 1978.
Hilarious story of a house painter who adds twelve penguins to his household.

Baum, L. Frank. *The Wonderful Wizard of Oz.* New York: Penguin, Puffin Books, 1983.
The story of Dorothy and her comrades on their way to the Emerald City is as captivating as ever.

Blume, Judy. *Freckle Juice.* Illustrated by Sonia O. Lisker. New York, Dell, 1978.
A hilarious story about a boy who wants to have freckles.

Bond, Michael. *A Bear Called Paddington* (and more). Illustrated by Peggy Fortnum. Boston: Houghton Mifflin, 1960.
Paddington, a bear from Darkest Peru, comes to live with the Brown family and causes delightful havoc.

Cleary, Beverly. *Henry Huggins* (and more). Illustrated by Louis Darling. New York: Dell, Yearling Books, 1979.
Henry meets a stray dog in the drugstore, names him Ribsy, and brings him home. Together they start their adventures.

Cleary, Beverly. *Ramona the Pest* (and more). Illustrated by Louis Darling. New York: Dell, Yearling Books, 1982.

Spunky Ramona, Henry Huggins's little sister, enters kindergarten.

Dahl, Roald. *Charlie and the Chocolate Factory.* New York: Bantam-Skylark, 1981.
About Charlie and his friends, and Mr. Willy Wonka's Chocolate Factory. Filled with suspense and humor.

Dahl, Roald. *James and the Giant Peach.* Illustrated by Nancy Ekholm Burkert. New York: Bantam-Skylark, 1981.
James, an orphan who is treated cruelly, escapes into a giant peach that is growing in his backyard, where he meets a cast of intriguing characters.

Estes, Eleanor. *The Hundred Dresses.* Illustrated by Louis Slobodkin. New York: Harcourt, Brace & World, 1968.
Wanda lives on the wrong side of town and wears the same faded blue dress to school every day. When her classmates tease her, she tells them that she has a hundred dresses in her closet at home.

Estes, Eleanor. *The Moffats* (and more). Illustrated by Louis Slobodkin. New York: Harcourt, Brace & World, 1968.
The four Moffat children and their mother don't have much money but they do have good times together.

Fitzhugh, Louise. *Harriet the Spy.* New York: Dell, 1984.
An only child and a little bit lonely, Harriet keeps a notebook of what she observes about her parents, classmates, and neighbors.

Grahame, Kenneth. *The Wind in the Willows.* Illustrated by John Burningham. New York: Penguin, Puffin Books, 1984.
Wonderful humor and sensitivity live on in this classic tale of the joy of simple life in the forest.

Greene, Constance. *A Girl Called Al* (and more). Illustrated by Byron Barton. New York: Dell, Yearling Books, 1977.
Al is a little bit fat, is the child of divorced parents, and claims to be a nonconformist. The warm and funny story of a friendship between two girls who live in an apartment house.

Lawson, Robert. *Ben and Me.* New York: Dell, Yearling Books, 1973.
Wonderfully entertaining biography of Benjamin Franklin written by his good friend Amos the mouse, who claims to be largely responsible for Franklin's inventions and discoveries. Appealing drawings.

Lindgren, Astrid. *Pippi Longstocking* (and more). Translated by Florence Lamborn; illustrated by Louis S. Glanzman. New York: Penguin, Puffin Books, 1977.
The fantastic adventures of independent, idiosyncratic redheaded Pippi.

MacLachlan, Patricia. *Sarah, Plain and Tall.* New York: Harper & Row, 1985.
Caleb's mother died a day after he was born and his papa places an ad in the newspaper for a new wife. Sarah answers the ad and comes in the spring with her cat, Seal.

McCloskey, Robert. *Homer Price.* New York: Penguin, Puffin Books, 1976.
Zany episodes in the life of a small-town American boy.

Milne, A. A. *Winnie-the-Pooh* (and more). Illustrated by Ernest H. Shepard. New York: Dell, Yearling Books, 1970.
Classic story of Christopher Robin and his wonderful friends.

Sobol, Donald J. *Encyclopedia Brown, Boy Detective* (and more). New York: Bantam, 1978.

Adventures of a famous boy detective who gives the reader an opportunity to solve mysteries.

Taylor, Sydney. *All-of-a-kind Family* (and more). Illustrated by Beth and Joe Krush. New York: Dell, 1966.
Life with a Jewish family in New York at the turn of the century. Warmly told.

Travers, P. L. *Mary Poppins* (and more). Illustrated by Mary Shepard. New York: Harcourt Brace Jovanovich, 1981.
Delightful nonsense about a remarkable nursemaid who blew in with the east wind.

Warner, Gertrude Chandler. *The Boxcar Children.* Niles, Ill.: Albert Whitman, Pilot, 1977.
Four orphans determined to care for themselves find a home in a boxcar.

White, E. B. *Charlotte's Web.* Illustrated by Garth Williams. New York: Harper & Row, Trophy, 1952.
The powerful relationship between two barnyard animals: Wilbur, a pig, and Charlotte, a spider.

White, E. B. *Stuart Little.* Illustrated by Garth Williams. New York: Harper & Row, Trophy, 1945.
The charming adventures of an engaging mouse. A classic.

White, E. B. *The Trumpet of the Swan.* Illustrated by Edward Frascino. New York: Harper & Row, Trophy, 1973.
Louis, who is a mute trumpeter swan, is given a trumpet by his father.

Wilder, Laura Ingalls. *Little House on the Prairie* (and more). Illustrated by Garth Williams. New York: Harper & Row, Trophy, 1973.
Story of a pioneer family in the nineteenth century.

OTHER BOOKS FOR GRADES 3–5

Armstrong, William H. *Sounder.* Illustrated by James Barkley. New York: Harper & Row, Trophy, 1972.
Touching, sensitive tale of a turn-of-the-century Southern black family.

Babbitt, Natalie. *Tuck Everlasting.* New York: Farrar, Straus & Giroux, 1975.
A beautifully written story about ten-year-old Winnie, who comes across a family that knows the secret of immortality.

Bauer, Marion D. *On My Honor.* New York: Houghton Mifflin, Clarion, 1986.
Joel is distraught when Tony, his best friend, drowns in the river in which they have been forbidden to swim. Terrified, Joel cannot face either set of parents with the truth.

Blume, Judy. *Are You There God? It's Me, Margaret.* Scarsdale, N.Y.: Bradbury, 1970.
Very popular story about a girl's early adolescence.

Blume, Judy. *Tales of a Fourth-Grade Nothing.* New York: Dell, 1986.
Fourth-grade Peter copes with his pesty younger brother and his entertaining activities.

Bulla, Clyde Robert. *Shoeshine Girl.* Illustrated by Leigh Grant. New York: Crowell Junior Books, 1975.
Spoiled Sarah works as a shoeshine girl during the summer and learns a great deal about independence, responsibility, and friendship.

Bunting, Eve. *Someone Is Hiding on Alcatraz Island.* Boston: Houghton Mifflin, Clarion, 1984.

After offending the Outlaws, a tough street gang, Danny escapes to abandoned Alcatraz Prison and finds himself in a dangerous trap.

Cleary, Beverly. *Dear Mr. Henshaw.* Illustrated by Paul O. Zelinsky. New York: Dell, Yearling Books, 1984.
Sixth-grader Leigh Botts, whose parents are divorced, has a correspondence with his favorite author, Boyd Henshaw.

Cleary, Beverly. *Ramona Forever* (and more). Illustrated by Alan Tiegreen. New York: William Morrow, 1984.
Ramona is in third grade and things have changed for her. Her father is looking for a new teaching job and she is worried that she may have to move.

DeClements, Barthe. *Nothing's Fair in Fifth Grade.* New York: Viking, 1981.
After many difficulties, overweight Elsie Edwards, new to the fifth grade, is finally accepted by her classmates.

DeClements, Barthe. *Sixth Grade Can Really Kill You.* New York: Viking, 1985.
A realistic and sensitive story about Helen, a sixth-grader with a serious reading disability.

Fitzgerald, John D. *The Great Brain* (and more). Illustrated by Mercer Mayer. New York: Dial, 1967.
A small-town boy at the turn of the century, ten-year-old Tom masterminds marvelous schemes.

Haviland, Virginia. *Favorite Fairytales Told Around the World.* Illustrated by S. D. Schindler. Boston: Little, Brown, 1985.
A collection of timeless international fairytales told by a wonderful storyteller. Beautiful black and white illustrations.

Hildick, E. W. *The Case of the Vanishing Ventriloquist* (and more). Illustrated by Kathy Parkinson. New York: Macmillan, 1985.

Mari, a visitor from Japan, joins with Jack McGurk and his (detective) Organization in a new, exciting adventure.

Hurwitz, Johanna. *Aldo Ice Cream* (and more). Illustrated by John Wallner. New York: William Morrow, 1981.

Nine-year-old Aldo spends much of his summer helping and getting to know some of the town's senior citizens, while he tries to save enough money to buy an ice-cream freezer for his sister's birthday.

Hurwitz, Johanna. *Baseball Fever.* Illustrated by Ray Cruz. New York: William Morrow, 1981.

A humorous and touching account of ten-year-old Ezra, who tries to convince his intellectual father that his love for the New York Mets will not destroy his mind.

Juster, Norton. *The Phantom Tollbooth.* Illustrated by Jules Feiffer. New York: Random House, 1961.

A wonderful fantasy about Milo's adventures beyond the phantom tollbooth in such places as Dictionopolis and The Doldrums.

Krumbold, Joseph. *Onion John.* Illustrated by Symeon Shimin. New York: Harper, Trophy, 1959.

The unusual story of the friendship between Andy and Onion John, who lives in a house made of stones and bathtubs and does his grocery shopping at the Serenity Dump.

Lewis, Marjorie. *Wrongway Applebaum.* New York: Coward, McCann and Geoghegan, 1984.

Applebaum has a difficult time playing baseball, but discovers his own particular talent at the end of the season.

Lindbergh, Anne. *The Worry Week.* Illustrated by Kathryn Hewitt. New York: Harcourt Brace Jovanovich, 1985.
Three sisters elude their parents, and spend a memorable week on a secluded Maine island.

Locker, Thomas. *The Mare on the Hill.* New York: Dial, 1985.
Beautiful paintings and gentle prose tell the story of two children and a pregnant mare.

Locker, Thomas. *Where the River Begins.* New York: Dial, 1984.
Splendid landscape paintings help to tell the tale of a grandfather, his two grandsons and their journey to find where the river begins.

Lowry, Lois. *Anastasia on Her Own* (and more). New York: Dell, Yearling Books, 1985.
While her mother is out of town, Anastasia discovers (along with her father) that running a household is more complicated than she thought.

Norton, Mary. *The Borrowers* (and more). Illustrated by Beth and Joe Krush. New York: Harcourt Brace Jovanovich, Voyager, 1986.
The Borrowers live in a miniature fantasy world, borrowing what they need to survive.

Nozaki, Akihiro. *Anno's Hat Tricks* (and more). Illustrated by Mitsumasa Anno. New York: Putnam, Philomel, 1985.
Attractive pictures and a straightforward text introduce children to problem-solving, logic, and imaginative thinking.

Paulsen, Gary. *Dogsong.* New York: Bradbury, 1985.
A fourteen-year-old Eskimo boy travels 1400 miles by dog sled across the tundra, mountains, and ice fields in search of himself and his heritage.

O'Brien, Robert C. *Mrs. Frisby and the Rats of Nimh.* Illustrated by Zena Bernstein. New York: Atheneum, 1971.
Rats who become superintelligent as a result of a laboratory experiment come to the aid of a widowed mouse and her sickly son.

Van Allsburg, Chris. *The Stranger.* Boston: Houghton Mifflin, 1986.
Farmer Bailey's visitor, a stranger who is recuperating after an accident, has a magical effect on the changing seasons. Magnificent full-color artwork.

Van Allsburg, Chris. *The Polar Express.* Boston: Houghton Mifflin, 1985.
A little boy takes a fantastic trip to the North Pole on the Polar Express. Mysterious large illustrations.

Wisler, G. Clifton. *Buffalo Moon.* New York: E. P. Dutton, Lodestar, 1984.
Full of the adventure of the Old West, a story about a courageous boy from a Texas ranch who lives with the Comanche Indians for six months.

POETRY

Kennedy, X. J., and Dorothy M. Kennedy, compilers. *Knock at a Star: A Child's Introduction to Poetry.* Illustrated by Karen Ann Weinhaus. Boston: Little, Brown, 1982.
A wonderful collection of poems, many of them rare in anthologies. Particularly good for reading aloud.

Prelutsky, Jack. *The New Kid on the Block.* Illustrated by James Stevenson. New York: Greenwillow, 1984.
Rollicking verse for children.

Prelutsky, Jack. compiler. *The Random House Book of Poetry for Children.* Illustrated by Arnold Lobel. New York: Random House, 1983.
Lovely anthology of poems, with delightful illustrations, particularly appealing to children.

Silverstein, Shel. *A Light in the Attic.* New York: Harper & Row, 1981.
Delightful collection of poems and drawings by Silverstein.

Silverstein, Shel. *Where the Sidewalk Ends.* New York: Harper & Row, 1974.
Another spectacular collection.

Untermeyer, Louis. editor. *Rainbow in the Sky: Golden Anniversary Edition.* Illustrated by Reginald Birch. New York: Harcourt Brace Jovanovich, 1985.
Classic collection of five hundred poems including works by traditional American and British poets.

Additional Reading About Children and Education

Alvino, James, and **editors of** *Gifted Children Monthly.*
Parents' Guide to Raising a Gifted Child. Boston: Little, Brown,
1985.
Practical advice and techniques for families by experts in the
field of education for the gifted.

Calkins, Lucy. *Lessons From a Child.* Portsmouth, N.H.: Heine-
mann, 1983.
A sensitive observation of young children learning to write
about the things that mean the most to them.

Chall, Jeanne. *Learning to Read: The Great Debate.* New York:
McGraw-Hill, 1967.
A classic compendium of research on the teaching of
reading by a sane and wise teacher.

Clarke, Louise. *Can't Read, Can't Write, Can't Talk Too Good
Either: How to Recognize and Overcome Dyslexia in Your Child.*
New York: Penguin, 1974.
A modern-day classic—the touching story of the personal
struggle of a mother to understand her son's learning
disability and find him the help he needs.

Coles, Robert. *The Moral Life of Children.* Boston: Atlantic
Monthly Press, 1986.
A searching exploration of children's moral awareness and

reactions to life at home, at school, and in the street by a well-known and beloved child psychiatrist.

Commission on Reading. *Becoming a Nation of Readers.* Washington, D.C.: The National Institute of Education, 1985.
The foremost contemporary statement of desirable practices in the teaching of reading.

Copeland, Richard W. *How Children Learn Mathematics: Teaching Implications of Piaget's Research.* New York: Macmillan, 1984.
With its foundation in Piaget's research, an intelligent explanation of the way children learn mathematics.

Elkind, David. *The Hurried Child: Growing Up Too Fast Too Soon.* Reading, Mass.: Addison-Wesley, 1981.
A child psychologist suggests that today's children are experiencing stress because they are being hurried through childhood by the schools, the media, their parents, and society in general.

Elkind, David. *A Sympathetic Understanding of the Child: Birth to Sixteen.* Boston: Allyn & Bacon, 1974.
A clear and intelligent guide to the personal, social, and mental development of the child by a respected child psychologist.

Flesch, Rudolf. *Why Johnny Can't Read and What You Can Do About It.* New York: Harper & Row, 1966.
Written in 1955, the original attack on the look-say method of teaching reading, with a plea for an emphasis on phonics.

Flesch, Rudolf. *Why Johnny Still Can't Read—A New Look at the Scandal of Our Schools.* New York: Harper & Row, 1981.
A continued argument for reading programs that emphasize phonics.

Frith, Terry. *Secrets Parents Should Know About Public Schools.* New York: Simon and Schuster, 1985.
A school administrator provides hints that can help parents make the public school system work for their children.

Goodlad, John. *A Place Called School: Prospects for the Future.* New York: McGraw-Hill, 1984.
Result of an eight-year research project on the current state of schooling in the United States. A valuable insight into current educational practices in American public schools.

Grollman, Earl A., and **Gerri L. Sweder.** *The Working Parent Dilemma.* Boston: Beacon Press, 1986.
Advice about major issues and problems facing working parents. Includes specific suggestions about working with the schools.

Gross, Beatrice, and **Ronald Gross,** eds. *The Great School Debate: Which Way for American Education?* New York: Simon and Schuster, 1985.
Excellent anthology of the current reform movement. Includes excerpts from important reports and studies, as well as essays by leading American educators and scholars of child development.

Leach, Penelope. *Your Growing Child: From Babyhood Through Adolescence.* New York: Knopf, 1986.
An encyclopedia of important and helpful information for parents by a sensitive and realistic child psychologist.

Moore, Linda Perigo. *Does This Mean My Kid's a Genius? How to Identify, Educate, Motivate and Live With the Gifted Child.* New York: Plume, 1982.
A practical and intelligent guide about life at home and at school for parents who think they have a gifted child.

National Commission on Excellence in Education. *A Nation at Risk: The Full Account,* May 1983.
Prestigious panel appointed by the U.S. Secretary of Education reports on the weakness of American schools and makes suggestions for improvement.

Osman, Betty. *Learning Disabilities: A Family Affair.* New York: Random House, 1979.
A common sense approach to the problems faced by learning-disabled children and their families. Written by an educational specialist who has had extensive experience with learning-disabled children.

Osman, Betty, in association with **Henriette Blinder.** *No One to Play With: The Social Side of Learning Disabilities.* New York: Random House, 1982.
Advice about the "living disabilities" of the learning-disabled by a specialist in the field.

Papert, Seymour. *Mindstorms: Children, Computers and Powerful Ideas.* New York: Basic Books, 1982.
A classic on computers and children by the developer of LOGO, a computer language for young children.

Pulanski, Mary Ann. *Understanding Piaget: An Introduction to Children's Cognitive Development.* New York: Harper & Row, 1980.
A lucid presentation of Piaget's theories about cognitive development.

Rioux, William. *You Can Improve Your Children's School: Practical Answers to Questions Parents Ask Most About Their Public Schools.* New York: Simon and Schuster, 1980.
More than 200 answers to the questions parents have about their children's schools. Includes questions and answers

about school records, textbooks, and school board decisions.

Schimmel, David, and **Louis Fischer.** *The Rights of Parents in the Education of Their Children.* Columbia, Md.: National Committee for Citizens in Education, 1977.
A clear presentation of parents' legal rights concerning the education of their children.

Smith, Sally L. *No Easy Answers: The Learning Disabled Child at Home and School.* New York: Bantam, 1981.
Helpful book on the nature of learning-disabled children and how to help them by the founder and director of the Learning Disabilities Program at the American University in Washington, D.C.

U.S. Department of Education. *First Lessons: A Report on Elementary Education in America.* Washington, D.C.: 1986.
A detailed report about the condition and direction of American elementary education, including observations and recommendations about its future.

U.S. Department of Education. *What Works: Research About Teaching and Learning.* Washington, D.C.: 1986.
A brief summary of research findings about a multitude of educational issues, including phonics, reading to children, independent reading, discipline, and storytelling.

Index